WOMEN
IN MODERN
AMERICA:
A BRIEF HISTORY

Second Edition

WOMEN
IN MODERN
AMERICA:
A BRIEF HISTORY

Second Edition

Lois W. Banner
University of Southern California

HARCOURT BRACE JOVANOVICH, PUBLISHERS
San Diego   New York   Chicago   Austin
London   Sydney   Toronto

PREFACE

Until the mid-1960s, the history of women was neglected by historians. A few general works were written from time to time, but most authors assumed that the women's suffrage movement was all there was to it. Increasing concern with social history on the part of historians and the advent of a new feminist movement coincided to stimulate studies about women. The result has been to create a field of historical investigation that seeks to rescue both major figures and the ordinary woman from obscurity and provide a corrective to the traditional histories from which women are absent.

This book examines the history of women in America from 1890 to the present. Three periods, each characterized by distinctive qualities, seem to stand out. The first, from 1890 to 1920, was one of energy and innovation; many of the traditional discriminations against women came to an end, and an impressive number of feminist and women's reform groups were organized. The second period, from 1920 to 1960, was one of greater complacency about women's problems; the nation struggled with depression and war, and feminist groups declined in size and vitality. The third period, from 1960 to the present, witnessed the emergence of a feminism more radical than any of its predecessors.

In my study of this era, I have had three aims: to explore the reasons why feminism rose and fell and rose again; to examine the history of various groups of women, including the working class, blacks, immigrants, farm women, and the middle class, each of which responded to the pressures and opportunities of the times in a different way; and, finally, to focus on the dramatic and continuing struggle waged by determined, innovative women to achieve their rights.

I have attempted to examine and correlate the complex factors that have affected women's lives. Common strains run through every period. One has been the influence of a society undergoing rapid changes—the progress of industrialization and the move to the cities; changing attitudes toward sex and marriage; the growing power of the mass media as cultural conditioners; the expansion of the economy and of certain occupations within it, such as secretarial work; two world wars that opened up new jobs for women; a depression and a war that made the family seem a haven of stability and security; and technological advancements that offered women more leisure time. A second factor influencing women in America throughout these years has been the deep and abiding image of woman as the "good" wife, mother, homemaker, and repository of human virtue on the one hand (the "virgin Mary" image of Christian belief) and as the "evil" temptress (the Pandora of classical mythology and the Eve of Judeo–Christian belief) on the other—two stereotypes that have dominated thinking about women throughout the history of western culture and that continue to exist today. A third factor has been the overriding discrimination against women in every area of their lives, whether they have been seeking education, jobs, justice under the law, or simply the freedom to lead their lives as they see fit.

This history of women is also a history of *feminism*, a term that is difficult to define precisely. Generally, "feminism" has meant the advocacy of the rights of women. But the view of what constitutes those rights has changed since the mid-nineteenth century, and most especially since the term "feminism," first coined in France, was introduced in this country in about 1910. Subsequently, "feminism" came to replace the standard nineteenth-century American term "woman's rights." To solve the problem of definition, different terms are used to distinguish the various kinds of feminism. I use the term *feminist* broadly to apply to those men and women who have consciously worked to end discriminations against women and to gain gender equality. *Radical feminist* refers to those who envision a fundamental reordering of society and/or gender relationships as necessary to achieve equality. For those feminists whose position is uncompromisingly hostile to patterns or institutions of discrimination, I use the term *militant*. *Social feminist* (a term first coined by historian William O'Neill) applies to activists for whom working for social reforms (generally involving women) takes priority over such strictly women's causes as suffrage or the Equal Rights Amendment. Finally, *domestic feminists* are those who argue that a fundamental solution to women's problems lies in raising the status of homemaking and ending the common deprecation of domesticity and motherhood within American culture.

To help the reader who wishes to pursue any particular aspect of this history more fully, I have provided a critical bibliography at the end of each chapter.

I am grateful for the assistance I received in preparing this volume. I am particularly grateful for the careful critical reading given by Susan M. Hartmann, University of Missouri-St. Louis, and Kathryn Kish Sklar, University of California, Los Angeles. I would also like to acknowledge the editorial assistance of Drake Bush, Mary George, and Harriet Meltzer, and the production assistance of Lynn Edwards, Michael Farmer, and Avery Hallowell, all of Harcourt Brace Jovanovich.

Lois W. Banner

CONTENTS

Chapter 1 The Emergence of the Modern American Woman: The 1890s

Women's Status in 1890 1
  Legal Codes 1
  Educational Opportunities 3
  Occupations 6
  Medicine and Sexuality 14
  A "Strange New Note" 17
  Women's Organizations 18
  Public Image—The "Gibson Girl" 21
Roots of Change 22
  Dress Reform 24
  Expansion of the Women's Labor Force 28
  New Inroads 31
    Women in College 31
    Women in Medicine and Law 34
    Women in Journalism 36
    Conservative Arguments Produce Progressive Results 37
  Men—A Help and a Hindrance 39
  Technology and Housekeeping 40
  Women's Separate Culture 41

Notes 44
Bibliography 45

Chapter 2 The American Woman from 1900 to the First World War: A Profile

The Main Prospect—Marriage and Motherhood 51
  The Middle-Class Wife 52
  The Rural Wife 57
  The Working-Class Woman 61
    Asian Immigration 64
    Black Women 65
    Working Conditions 67
    Strikes and Unions 69
    Married Life 78
The Other Way—Prostitution 80
  The Practitioners 81
The New Sensuality 83
  The World of the Waitress 85

Notes 87
Bibliography 88

**Chapter 3 Women as Organizers and Innovators: Suffrage,
Reform, and Feminism, 1890–1920**

Suffragism on the Wane 93
Feminism and Progressivism: A Case of Give and Take 99
  The Organizations: Growth and Changing Goals 100
  The Settlement Houses 105
  A Measure of Success 107
The Radicals 108
  A Ferment of New Ideas 108
  A New Breed of Scholars 111
  Feminist Action Groups: A Faint Voice 112
Shaky Grounds for Argument 115
  Women's Frailty and Special Legislation 115
  Housekeepers in Government—and Out 116
  Suffrage as a Cure-All 117
  Sex Versus Soul 120
Two Generations 123
Suffrage Achieved 125
  A United Front 125
  Tactics and Techniques 127
  The Aftermath of Victory 129

Notes 132
Bibliography 135

Chapter 4 The 1920s: Freedom or Disillusionment?

Women's Organizations in Transition 139
Antifeminist Undercurrents and Feminist Conservatism 148
"Flaming Youth"—New Liberties, Old Attitudes 153
Women at Work: Progress and Setbacks 161
  Professional Women 161
  Working-Class Working Women 165
The New Heroines 169

Notes 177
Bibliography 179

Chapter 5   Women in Depression and War: 1930–1945

Feminism and Women's Organizations   183
Eleanor Roosevelt: Exemplar of Her Era   185
The Women's Network and New Deal Programs   192
Changes for the Working Woman: Unemployment, New Union
    Strength   198
The Securities of Marriage in an Insecure Age   205
Fashions and Movies: Old and New Images   211
Black Women and Popular Culture   217
Women as Part of the War Effort   218

Notes   224
Bibliography   226

Chapter 6   Feminism Comes of Age: 1945–1984

A General Consensus on Woman's Role   230
  Women Under Attack   230
  Expert Opinion: Freud and Functionalism   234
  The Evidence from Popular Culture   235
  The Back-to-the-Home Movement   236
  Sex and Childrearing   240
  Feminism in the 1950s   240
  The Reemergence of Domestic Feminism   241
Evidence to the Contrary   243
  New Economic, Demographic, and Medical Factors   243
  The New Trends—Revolutionary or Not?   244
The Shift to Militancy   246
  A New Reform Climate   246
  New Faces and the Formation of NOW   251
The Feminist Position in the 1960s   256
  Marriage and the Family   258
An Assessment of Feminist Achievements and Potentials   261

Notes   272
Bibliography   274

Appendix   278
Photo Credits   282
Index   283

1

The Emergence Of The Modern American Woman: The 1890s

"AT THE OPENING of the twentieth century," wrote suffragist Ida Husted Harper, women's status "had been completely transformed in most respects."[1] Her judgment was only partially correct. Much had been gained for most women by the 1890s, but much remained to be achieved. The 1890s were years of transition, during which the advances women had made in the preceding decades began to add up to significant progress, and women's organizations entered a period of rapid growth. But discrimination still existed in every area of women's experience.

WOMEN'S STATUS IN 1890

Legal Codes

The legal codes pertaining to women had not undergone a transformation, but states had come a long way in amending discriminatory laws. By 1890, many states had modified the common law doctrine of *femme couverte,* under which wives had been chattels of their husbands, with no direct legal control over their own earnings, children, or property, unless a premarital agreement had been negotiated and their property placed in trust.* New laws in many states gave wives control over their inherited property and their earnings, although in 14 of the 46 states then in existence earnings still belonged to husbands. In 37 states, married women were still denied any rights over their children, although the general legal practice in the case of divorce was to award children to mothers, in line with the cultural conviction that women by nature were best able to carry out the child-rearing function.

In every state, laws still discriminated against women. The most important of these were the voting laws. In some states, women could vote in local school-board and municipal elections, but in only four states—Wyoming, Utah, Colorado, and Idaho—could women vote in

---

*Under the normal trust, the husband had control over his wife's income but not over her property, which was under the guardianship of trustees, usually male relatives or associates of the woman's father. Such prohibitions on property ownership and income did not apply to single women, who were classified as *femme sole* under the common law.

The suffragist executive committee, including foreign delegates, that arranged the first International Council in 1888.

In the front row are Susan B. Anthony (second from left) *and Elizabeth Cady Stanton* (fourth from left).

general state and federal elections. In *Minor v. Happersett* in 1874, the Supreme Court ruled unanimously that voting was not coextensive with citizenship (as feminists argued) and that the states could withhold the vote from women. In some states, women could not enter into business partnerships without the consent of their husbands; in most states, husbands had the right to determine where the family would live.

Such discriminatory laws vary from state to state. It has taken a century of feminist agitation to abolish them; some are still on the books. As late as 1930, for example, one-fourth of the states did not allow wives to make contracts, and married women's property rights

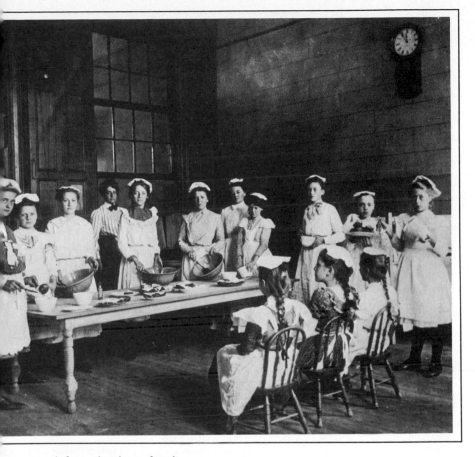

*A domestic science class in a
public school in the early 1900s.*

over real estate were not equal to their husbands' in 17 states. As legal
beings, women had made progress by the 1890s, but full equality
under the law was still not theirs.

Educational Opportunities

In education, women had made more promising gains. At the beginning of the nineteenth century, it was difficult for women to secure

any education. No colleges accepted them. In many areas of the country, public grammar schools as well as private academies restricted their pupils to boys or allowed girls to attend only in the summer when sons were needed to work on family farms and classrooms were vacant. It was considered sufficient that girls learn to read and write—skills they could acquire from their mothers or at local "dame" schools established for that purpose. The educated woman was looked on with derision and suspicion for stepping outside the domestic sphere.

By the end of the century, however, elementary and secondary education was generally available to women. In fact, because boys more often than girls dropped out of high school to seek gainful employment, more girls than boys were graduating from high school by 1890. Higher education, too, was open to women by then. Before the Civil War, enterprising men and women had founded private academies for women and a number of states had established teacher-training institutes, known as "normal schools," which attracted mostly women students. A few colleges, too, had opened their doors to women during the antebellum period—notably Oberlin in 1837 and Antioch in 1853. In the years after the Civil War, numerous colleges for women were established, particularly in the Northeast, where the elite male colleges were especially opposed to coeducation. The women's colleges included Vassar (1861), Wellesley (1870), Smith (1871), and Bryn Mawr (1885). In 1888, Mount Holyoke Seminary, founded in 1837 as a high school, gained collegiate status. In these same years, many state institutions, particularly in the Midwest and the West, ended their restrictions against women, and new private colleges dedicated to the principle of coeducation appeared. By 1900, 80 percent of the colleges, universities, and professional schools in the nation admitted women.

This significant educational gain was crucial to the expansion of women's roles in the 1890s and 1900s. Not only were women now able to enter such esteemed professions as law and medicine, but their new-found education also provided them with the self-confidence and critical perception that would later lead them to question their position in American society. Most college-trained women became elementary-school teachers, and most professional schools admitted only a small number of women. Still the fact that women were going to school—

Vassar College advertises for students in The American Agriculturist *April 1877.*

Lillian Russell, idol of theater audiences around the turn of the century.

that they were gaining knowledge and confidence in themselves—was fundamental to the growth of the woman's movement in the late nineteenth and early twentieth centuries.

Occupations

The employment situation for women was more ambiguous. True, more women had jobs: in 1870, about 15 percent of all women over 16 years of age were regularly employed away from home for wages; by 1900, the statistic had risen to 20 percent.* Women were being

---

*Some historians now argue that such statistics underrepresent women's actual participation in the work force. First, these figures do not include the numbers of women working at home. Second, women's work experience is discontinuous and episodic, whereas census and survey figures record only the numbers of women working at the point in time the survey is taken. Thus, the lifetime work experience of women remains unknown.

*Women harvesting hops on an
upstate New York farm in the
1880s.*

taught new employment skills, including typing and stenography, and
they were beginning to dominate such professions as nursing and
teaching. Women had even forced their way into the professions of
ministry, law, and medicine over the course of the century. In the
theater, prima donnas like Lillian Russell and Lily Langtry com-
manded huge salaries and avid newspaper publicity. In 1840, Harriet
Martineau, prominent English feminist and author, contended that
only seven occupations in the United States were open to women:
teaching, needlework, keeping boarders, setting type, working as
servants, or laboring in bookbinding and cotton factories. But in fact
women were unrepresented in only nine of the 369 occupations listed
in the census of 1890.

*Women trimming currency at
the Treasury Department in
Washington D.C., under the
supervision of male foremen,
1907.*

From the census of 1910, we can glean what kinds of work women
did. Immediately apparent from this data is that over 50 percent of all
working women were employed as farm workers or as domestic servants: 18 percent in the former occupation and 37 percent in the latter.
Nearly 30 percent of all working women were employed in manufacturing; 8 percent, in professions (mostly as teachers and nurses); 5
percent, in clerical occupations; and about 4 percent, in trade (mostly
as saleswomen). A small number of women were classified in transportation and in public service, primarily as telephone and telegraph
operators.

Yet there was still significant discrimination against working women.
In almost every profession and occupation, skills were divided into

*Woman employed in a shoe
factory,* circa 1905.

men's and women's jobs. This phenomenon was partly a product of
women's propensity to seek employment related to their traditional
work in the home. In the field of manufacturing, which employed a
sizable minority of working women by 1900, most women worked in
clothesmaking, textile, and millinery factories, in commercial food
production, and in the cigar, tobacco, and shoemaking industries, for
which women had previously done piecework in their homes.

In all these industries, women performed the less prestigious and
lower-paid tasks. For example, in the ladies' garment industry, which
became one of the largest employers of factory women by the early
twentieth century, men were the cutters and pressers (positions of
higher authority and pay) and women were the sewers and finishers.

*An elementary-school classroom
in Valley Falls, Kansas, in the
early 1900s.*

This situation resulted partly from the fact that most factory women
were young and unmarried and therefore transient members of the
work force. In general, however, women had little chance for advancement. They were the assemblers, not the skilled operatives. At best,
a long-term female employee might be promoted to the position of
forewoman over a group of female workers. But even in this position,
she could expect to be paid less than male foremen, just as women

*Lady "typewriters" spend their
15–30 minute lunch break on
the steps of Trinity Church,
New York City.*

workers across the board were paid less than male workers, even when their jobs were similar.

This division between men's work and women's work was also characteristic of the professions. The few women who became doctors and lawyers typically undertook tasks related to conventional feminine roles. Most women lawyers found their place in quasi-office work, collecting claims or preparing probate papers. Most women doctors were gynecologists or pediatricians. One woman doctor in general practice, who found attracting patients almost impossible, recounted a tale she thought characteristic: Gratified finally to be sought out by a mother with a sick child, she discovered that the choice was motivated by the presumption that the rates of a "lady" doctor would be less than those of a "real" doctor.[2]

The overwhelming majority of women who entered the professions became teachers and nurses, still following the woman's traditional family role of teacher to the young and nurse to the ailing. And as women moved into these occupations in large numbers, men either

A typical office scene, when men still dominated the clerical labor force.

left these fields to pursue other careers or moved up to the elite positions in the professions. By 1910, 77 percent of all teachers were women. Like women factory workers, women teachers were predominantly young and single, and many school systems prohibited them from continuing to teach once they married. They clustered in elementary-school positions, while men dominated university teaching and administrative positions in elementary and secondary schools. A similar pattern was apparent in nursing and in librarianship—professions that women have also dominated throughout the twentieth century. So common has this development become that, to denote it, sociologists have coined the term *feminization.* It refers to the process whereby,

As the field of clerical work   *lunchroom in the Metropolitan*
expanded, increasing numbers   *Life Insurance Company in New*
of women were hired, as this   *York City reflects.*

as women become a majority within a profession, a small number of men assume the leadership roles and most men desert it. This desertion inevitably lowers the status of the profession.

This pattern is evident even in clerical labor, which more than any other occupation has come to characterize women's work in the twentieth century. This field first opened to women when typewriter manufacturers discovered that attractive women demonstrators sold more machines than male demonstrators had. Then, as clerical work underwent a rapid expansion during this period of general business growth, it became apparent that women could be paid less than men. Once women became typists and stenographers, men left the clerical field, which they had previously dominated. Some moved up to sales and managerial positions, where they earned higher salaries and more prestige, while others sought work in nonfeminine occupations. But office work, despite its obvious advantages over factory labor of higher pay and a shorter work day, had its embarrassments. For several decades, typists were known as "typewriters," and the confusion between this appellation and the name of the machine they used occasioned considerable merriment at their expense in offices and in popular journalism alike.

Medicine and Sexuality

The 1890s were also a time of advancement in the medical treatment of women and in the medical and popular views of female sexuality. From 1850 to 1900, the life expectancy for women rose from 40 to 51 years. This increase was partly due to considerable improvements in medical care. Improved sanitation and new vaccines for diseases like yellow fever headed the list of such advances, but developments in gynecological surgery made curable such chronic and debilitating female disorders as a prolapsed, or displaced, uterus—a condition common among women who have borne a number of children. The introduction of antiseptic techniques in delivering babies greatly lessened the danger of puerperal fever, an infection of childbirth that had killed thousands of women and newborns for centuries. Moreover, by the late nineteenth century, doctors were less prone to diagnose female illnesses, including neurosis, as uterine disorders and to treat them by blistering and bleeding the vagina. The "hysterical" or neurotic woman who was unmarried might still be advised to marry to cure her difficulty, and the surgical excision of the uterus, a procedure first attempted in 1881, was called a "hysterectomy," but the ancient belief that a woman was controlled by her reproductive organs was on the way out.

Women were beginning to be viewed more as human beings and less as fragile creatures prone to periodic illnesses and nervous disorders. After years of debate, reformist doctors and feminists who advocated simplicity of dress for women and attention to diet and exercise were gaining authority. For two decades, educators, doctors, and the general public had debated whether a woman's constitution could withstand the rigors of a college education. The argument intensified after Dr. Edward H. Clarke, in his influential *Sex in Education* (1873), proposed that the strain of learning would make a woman sterile. But by 1900, this debate had become academic, as statistics proved that college women maintained levels of scholarly ability and physical health equal to those of male students. Moreover, ministers no longer preached sermons, as they had earlier in the century, in which they identified the supposed weakness of women as part of the "curse" of Eve, whom God had more severely punished than Adam because she had first taken the apple from the serpent in the Garden of Eden. It was not uncommon among women, however, for menstruation to be called "the curse."[3]

In addition, menstruation and childbirth were beginning to be considered natural functions, rather than illnesses during which women went to bed. And some progressive doctors like Edward Bliss Foote, author of numerous popular editions from the 1880s to the 1900s of *Plain Home Talk on Love, Marriage, and Parentage,* openly challenged the Victorian notion that sexual intercourse was unhealthy and often forced on women by men who could not control their sex drives. Indeed, Foote even counseled in the 1904 edition that it was physiologically damaging for women to engage in intercourse if they did not enjoy it.

Yet many individuals were not open about sexual matters. Few Americans regarded masturbation as anything more than immoral and eventually bound to result in bodily ailments and insanity. Sex was often still a taboo subject between parents and children. Journalist Rheta Childe Dorr remembered that when a girl turned 14, scores of new rules were introduced, "and when you asked for an explanation, you met only embarrassed silence."[4] For many girls, the onset of menstruation was a shock because, given Victorian prudery, they had not been told about it. Children then, as later, often learned about sex from their classmates. The bride who married knowing nothing about sex was not uncommon. Such was the experience of novelist Frances Parkinson Keyes, who was married in 1904. In her middle-class circle, the mother of the bride was supposed to have "a little talk" with her daughter shortly before the wedding ceremony. But, explained Keyes, mothers were generally so embarrassed at this encounter that they said nothing enlightening. Besides, continued Keyes, "many mothers felt very strongly that prenuptial revelations about the marriage relationship would sully a young girl's innocence and make her less desirable to the 'right man.'"[5]

Nor had attitudes about childbirth everywhere changed. In the 1890s, Elizabeth Peabody, daughter of the wealthy Peabody family of Boston, was shocked when a schoolmate directly referred to one of her mother's yearly pregnancies.[6] Frances Parkinson Keyes remained in bed for weeks before and after the birth of her first child, and she was stunned to discover that one of the maids, for whom there had been no hiatus in household labor, had given birth secretly and on her own to an illegitimate child shortly after Keyes' own carefully attended pregnancy and childbirth. The middle class could afford to support the idea of the fragile female; for the working class, it was a different matter.

In the latter part of the nineteenth century, restrictions regarding sex became even more severe as most states moved to outlaw the sale of contraceptives and the dissemination of birth-control information. "Social purity" was a major objective of many late nineteenth-century Victorians and even of many reform-minded individuals. At their best, social-purity advocates—a heterogeneous group that included organizations like the Woman's Christian Temperance Union (WCTU) and the Young Women's Christian Association (YWCA)—worked to eliminate prostitution and to simplify women's dress. Ultimately, social purists were an important force in encouraging the American public to openly discuss social problems like prostitution and venereal disease. However, even many reformers held the view that birth control was a means, not of liberating women, but of freeing men to pursue their supposedly greater sexual urges outside the marital bond.

In 1873, opposition to birth control gained particular emphasis when Congress passed the so-called *Comstock Law*, named after its chief proponent—the single-minded, antivice crusader, Anthony Comstock. This law banned the dissemination of pornography, abortion devices, and "any drug, medicine, article, or thing designed, adapted, or intended for preventing contraception." Most states thereafter passed their own laws modeled after the Comstock statute. Birth control was, by implication, cataloged with pornography as immoral, and there were overtones within the laws of the old belief that birth control, like masturbation, sapped bodily energy and produced physical decay.

Abortion, too, was prohibited by state laws during the post-Civil War years. Under common law, abortion had been permitted until the sixth month of pregnancy—the normal time of "quickening," or the first felt movements of the fetus in the womb. On one hand, prohibition was justified: abortionists, often poorly trained, used crude medical techniques. Also, once nineteenth-century scientists had discovered that the egg was fertilized by the sperm soon after intercourse, anti-abortion doctors became uneasy about defining life as beginning at six months. But prohibitionists were also engaged in a drive to control and professionalize medical practice in the United States, and abortion prohibitions would help drive out of business the alternatively trained physicians outside the medical establishment who had flourished in the early nineteenth-century climate of medical ignorance.

Moreover, anti-abortionist men were concerned about evidence that showed rising rates of abortion among white, middle-class women. By 1870, in fact, as many as one in every five pregnancies among such women was being medically terminated. Conservative and nativist, the anti-abortion doctors began to advance the kinds of "race suicide" arguments that Theodore Roosevelt would later popularize. Women of the middle class, they argued, were destroying the nation's fabric by reducing the number of their offspring in comparison to that of immigrants and workers. Even more, they were threatening the structure of the traditional family by taking such extreme measures to control one of its essential functions.

A "Strange New Note"

Despite the prohibition on birth control and abortion, family size continued to decrease in the late nineteenth century, as it had ever since 1800. In 1804, the birth rate stood at about 7 children per family; in 1880, at 4.24; and in 1900, at 3.56. Some historians consider this "demographic transition" to be the single most important factor in the history of modern women. It freed women from constant pregnancy and childbirth and allowed them some flexibility in life choices. And indications are that women themselves supported reproductive control; the high rates of abortion would indicate that this was so. What nineteenth-century woman's rights advocates called "voluntary motherhood" seemed to be widely popular. Whether couples employed continence, coitus interruptus, douching, or condoms (and historians disagree over what method was used), women were beginning to assert major control over an important part of their lives.

Writing about the frontier Illinois of her youth, Mary Austin dated women's decision to practice birth control there from about 1870. "The pioneer stress was over," she wrote, and with it had ended "the day of large families, families of from a dozen to fifteen." According to Austin, "A strange new note had come into the thinking of the grand-daughters of the women who had borne their dozen or so cheerfully and with the conviction of the will of God strong in them."[7] And this "strange new note," as Austin described it, grew out of the yearning of these women for leisure, culture, and some world outside the home.

Women's Organizations

Women were beginning to view themselves differently, and it led them increasingly to organize—not only to gain the vote, but also to achieve a variety of professional, cultural, and reform goals. Women were active in the major farmer and labor organizations of the day: the Knights of Labor, the Farmers' Alliances, and the Populist Party. As many as one-fourth of the members of the Southern Alliance were women, and Populist Party women were especially active as public speakers in the 1890s. Mary Elizabeth Lease, renowned as the orator who told farmers "to raise less corn and more hell," was replicated by many others who crisscrossed the Midwest and the South.

The emergence of women doctors, lawyers, and college graduates resulted in the formation of the first professional women's associations, while other women flocked into local women's clubs seeking education, cultural uplift, a better understanding of the nature of women, and a chance to involve themselves in civic concerns that went beyond the home. In 1873, the Woman's Christian Temperance Union was formed, and in 1890, the national General Federation of Women's Clubs was organized. In that same year, the two branches of the women's suffrage movement, which had split in great acrimony in 1869, were reunited in the National American Woman Suffrage Association (NAWSA). Among the women's groups that appeared during the 1880s and 1890s were the Young Women's Christian Association (YWCA), the Daughters of the American Revolution (DAR), the Association of Collegiate Alumnae (later to become the American Association of University Women), the Congress of Mothers (later to become the National Parent–Teachers Association), and the National Council of Women.

"A Clarion Call for World Prohibition"—the WCTU presents the Great Temperance Petition to the state legislature in Albany, New York.

Even the Protestant churches experienced women's organizational initiative. Early in the century, women's auxiliaries to their missionary boards had been the main form of women's organization. In addition, these groups had served as important precursors to women's antebellum temperance and abolitionist societies and women's service organizations during the Civil War. After 1865, denominational women's missionary boards came to dominate the entire religious missionary movement. Especially in the South, where traditionalism and evangelicalism remained strong throughout the nineteenth century, women's organizations had a religious base. According to historian

The temperance campaigns of the WCTU alienated powerful liquor interests from the suffrage movement.

Anne Scott, the public life of every southern woman leader in this period began in a church society.[8] The largest of these societies was the Methodist Board of Foreign Missions—a group whose members contributed to women's clubs and suffrage organizations but also were responsible for the initiation of the social settlement movement in the South.

In 1893, women captured public attention by participating in the Chicago Columbian Exposition, the world's fair of the century. A special woman's building at the fair housed a year-long display of arts

*A meeting of the Daughters of
the American Revolution, 1898.*

and handicrafts by women and provided a forum for continual speeches
by prominent women and conferences of women's organizations. The
participation of women in the fair was a brilliant publicity stroke. Early
in the nineteenth century, it had been considered a disgrace for a
woman's name to appear in print. Now, as one observer noted, women
were constantly "in the glare of publicity."[9]

Public Image—The "Gibson Girl"

The "New Woman" she was termed—by feminists, who lauded her,
and by the press, which both praised and derided her. For the most
part, she worked only until she married, although she might be one
of those women who, even in the 1890s, chose a career instead of

marriage. She could be easily identified by her new style of dress. Instead of yards of trailing petticoats and beribboned gowns, which women had laboriously embroidered by hand, the "New Woman" wore a tailored suit or a dark skirt and a simple blouse, or "shirtwaist," modeled after men's attire. Her skirts might not have risen above her ankles, but if she were particularly daring, she might loosen her corset—that torture instrument of Victorian dress that gave women 18-inch waistlines but also caused fainting spells and sometimes even permanently damaged internal organs.

The "New Woman" of the 1890s was in many ways typified by the popular "Gibson Girl" of the period. The creation of artist Charles Dana Gibson in a series of drawings in *Life* magazine in the 1890s, this healthy and athletic maiden, simply dressed, became a national favorite. Prints of Gibson drawings appeared on the walls of countless American homes. The Gibson girl was not designed to be a sex object, as were the "vamp" of the 1920s and the "siren" of the 1950s. Although she might be permitted some décolletage for evening, her regular attire was chaste and maidenly. Often, she wore a shirtwaist blouse and a simple skirt. She was not, however, pictured in employment outside the home. Gibson's pictures centered on the traditional themes of love, courtship, and marriage, but the "Gibson girl" was also depicted playing tennis and golf, bicycling, and even driving an automobile. She was the American virgin-woman, but around her was a refreshing aura of health, sensuality, and rebellion.

ROOTS OF CHANGE

Why were women, who in the 1820s had no legal, professional, or educational standing, seemingly on the road to achieving equality with men by the 1890s? Most often, change was brought about by the interaction of two factors—new social, economic, and cultural forces on one hand, and the efforts of individuals on the other. In case after case, feminists and reformers agitated for change, and their arguments gained force as altered conditions in an industrializing nation made new life styles and relationships for women imperative.

The Gibson girl: a hint of rebellion.

The Gibson girl playing golf and
overwhelming men, in a
drawing entitled "Advice to
Caddies."

Dress Reform

In the 1840s, health reformers and liberal educators had begun to rail
against the middle-class woman's mode of dress, particularly the corset. Few Americans had listened to them. In those years, feminists
Susan B. Anthony and Elizabeth Cady Stanton, among others, had
adopted a modified version of Victorian dress—the so-called "bloomer

A 1900 corset, made of steel and bone, that pushed the bust up, the stomach in, and the bottom out.

costume," a long-sleeved, mid-calf dress worn over a pair of baggy trousers—but soon had to give it up due to public ridicule. By the 1890s, however, attitudes were changing. One reporter at the Columbian Exposition was amazed to find that audiences responded enthusiastically to fashion shows at the woman's building that featured simple styles and shortened skirts. Standing in the audience, she heard many women express "their great desire to be free from the bondage of skirts—women, too, who would, one would suppose, rather die in long skirts than let the world know they had legs."[10]

By the 1890s, women, with their new freedoms, were bolder than they had been before. Besides, women no longer had such a vested interest in adhering to Victorian fashions. Once, to the upwardly mobile, middle-class woman, they had bespoken status: With her wasp waist and her well-defined bosom and hips, she bore little resemblance to farmers' or laborers' wives, whose often shapeless figures and simple clothes mirrored a life of hard work. By late in the century, however, simplicity in dress had become associated, not with the poor or with radicals like Stanton and Anthony, but with exciting role models—the actress, the working woman, the college woman, the sportswoman.

Women began to appreciate the ease and comfort of simple, light clothing as they began to participate in sports. In the early years of the nineteenth century, genteel women exercised as little as possible due to their supposed physical delicacy. But as ice-skating became popular in the 1850s and croquet in the 1860s, it seemed foolish to bar women from these simple activities, especially since many doctors were contending that American women did not get enough exercise. Bicycling first appeared in the 1880s and soon became a national craze. Everyone who could afford a bicycle rode one, for pleasure and as a means of transportation. To pedal their machines, women had to wear simpler and shorter garments. In the 1890s, tennis and golf became popular. Moreover, dancers like Ruth St. Denis and Isadora Duncan, with their free-flowing movements and classical dress, were adding a new excitement to classical ballet, creating the foundations for modern dance and also demonstrating to women a new freedom in movement and dress.

New styles did not appear overnight. Skirts remained generally long until the First World War. Novelist Edna Ferber recalled that in the 1890s neighbors in her home town of Appleton, Wisconsin, were shocked when her mother, who ran the family store, began to wear shirtwaist blouses and skirts that did not reach the ground.[11] Crinolines, bustles, and tightly laced corsets were slowly abandoned, but most women continued to wear some form of corset until the 1920s. There was, however, a willingness to consider more rational styles of dress. But who could resist the tide of change when even the *Ladies' Home Journal*, the venerable organ of middle-class female opinion, in 1893 endorsed the right of women to choose their own clothes on the basis of comfort? Thus, dress reform came into being because of the preachings of doctors and health reformers, because of the rise of sports, because women at work and at school had to have simpler

*WCTU leader Frances Willard
receiving her first cycling
lesson.*

*Photographs taken by Alice
Austen in 1896 for Maria
Ward's book* Bicycling for   Ladies, *showing* (left)
dismounting and (right)
wheeling.

clothes, and because women and men slowly found the notion of the
emancipated woman appealing.

Expansion of the Women's Labor Force

In employment, changing demographic and industrial patterns were
probably more important than feminist arguments or individual actions
in opening up new jobs for women. Even before the Civil War, migra-

tion patterns had created sex imbalances in many areas of the country; particularly in older settlement areas, women outnumbered men. Work had to be found for these women; there simply were not enough husbands, fathers, or brothers available to support them. Moreover, the average age of first marriage for women in the nineteenth century was about 22. Thus, for a number of years between maturity and marriage, many women were able to contribute to family support or to save money for their own marriages.

Within the burgeoning American economy, there was a demand for this supply of workers. Owners of the earliest factories in the nation—the textile mills in Lowell and Waltham, Massachusetts—turned to young women as a logical labor source in the 1810s. Later in the century, even after immigration had created a larger labor pool, industrialists continued to employ women, particularly after domestic piecework moved into factory production, because women could be paid less than men. Similarly, the rapid growth of public-school systems created the need for more teachers, while local communities found persuasive the common judgments that women were particularly suited to elementary-school teaching and that, as in manufacturing, they would accept lower salaries than those paid to men.

Moreover, the Civil War—as have most modern wars—acted as a social force to extend women's employment. With men on the battlefield, more women were needed in the fields of teaching and manufacturing, and some new job areas, including the federal civil service, were beginning to open up to women. By the early twentieth century, industrial necessity plus the available pool of women opened up clerical work to them.

For the most part, the expansion of women's employment outside the elite professions occurred without feminist pressure. Some historians view the movement from home to factory as a step toward self-realization on the part of individual women and thus a feminist act. But to what extent the attitudes of a young woman who worked for a few years as an unskilled laborer and then married were changed is debatable. With regard to teaching, however, feminists were partly responsible for women's expansion into the field. Indeed, a number of prominent nineteenth-century women leaders—including suffragist Susan B. Anthony, temperance leader Frances Willard, and educator Catharine Beecher—began their careers as schoolteachers.

New Inroads

Women in College   Women's entry into higher education was to a large extent the result of the actions of individual women and men. Eastern women's colleges like Vassar and Smith were founded partly because the major private male institutions—Yale, Harvard, and Princeton,

Black women workers weighing wire coils and recording weights, 1919.

Cotton mill workers,
circa *1900.*

among others—refused to admit women. In 1889, Barnard College
was opened as a coordinate branch of Columbia University after 15
years of pressure by women seeking admission and by prominent civic
and women's groups. Radcliffe College began under similar circumstances as an annex to Harvard.

*Sophomores at a Vassar College
commencement carry the
traditional "Daisy Chain,"
which marks the seniors' seats.*

Some Western colleges were caught in the overexpansion of institutions of higher education during this period and had to admit women
to fill the ranks of their student bodies to remain solvent, particularly
because the Civil War often decimated the numbers of available male
undergraduates. But state colleges in the Midwest and West became
coeducational in many instances also because women pressured
authorities to admit them. The example of the University of Indiana
and Sarah Parke Morrison is characteristic. An 1857 graduate of Mount
Holyoke Seminary, Morrison was determined to integrate the public
college of her home state. In her favor was the fact that her father, a
trustee of the university, was sympathetic to her cause. The administration and the faculty, however, were against her. Even the undergraduates, who did not want women competing in their classes or
fraternizing in their clubs, opposed her admission. It took her nine
years to achieve her goal.

According to Thomas D. Clark, historian of the University of Indiana, Morrison was equal to the task. She "remembered Lucy Stone and Susan B. Anthony and asserted her rights."[12] Indeed, her victory seemed doubly assured when, two years after her admission in 1866, 12 other women were admitted to the university. But Victorian prejudices did not die easily. As were many women pioneers in education, Morrison was subjected to petty annoyances throughout her college career. Commencement, for example, was a difficult experience, for she feared, with good reason, that the audience would subject her to "curious" and "hostile" stares as she walked across the stage to receive her diploma and that her ankles might be exposed to "immodest views."

Sarah Morrison is a minor figure in American history. Yet her determination to advance the cause of women was an important ingredient in the mixture of forces that brought coeducation to state colleges in the Midwest and West. States that had more recently passed through a frontier stage, it is true, seemed more willing to integrate their colleges than did state legislatures and college administrations in the older states of the Union. But it is incorrect to conclude from this evidence that a democratic "frontier" spirit alone brought about coeducation in the West. Outspoken women—and male allies—were present to put pressure on faculties, administrations, and state legislatures.

Women in Medicine and Law   Individual women were responsible for gaining admission to the elite professions, often against tremendous odds. The medical profession is a typical example. Harriot Hunt, a self-trained doctor with a private practice in Boston, was repeatedly refused admission to Harvard Medical School because of her sex and never received a medical degree. Elizabeth Blackwell, the first licensed woman doctor in the United States, was turned down by medical schools throughout the nation and was admitted in 1848 to the Geneva Medical College in Geneva, New York (now part of Hobart College) only because the male students thought it would be "amusing" to have a woman there. Despite the difficulties she encountered, Blackwell graduated at the head of her class—although, like Sarah Morrison, she feared the graduation ceremony and refused to appear on the stage to receive her diploma. Although Blackwell boarded with a family in Geneva, the townspeople avoided her because they thought that only a woman of loose morals would attend medical college. This was

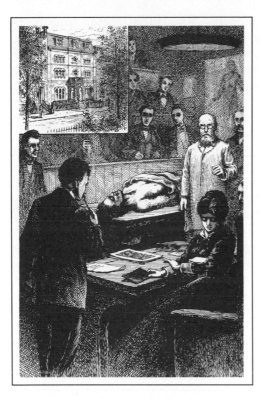

Elizabeth Blackwell as a student in the medical-school operating room. (inset) *The Women's Hospital and Infirmary, New York City.*

a charge not infrequently leveled against women in professional training as well as against working women in general.

Once women were admitted to professional schools, not only were higher standards demanded of them, but they were also subjected in and out of class to hostile jokes and embarrassing off-color stories. Mary Putnam-Jacobi, one of the first medical-school graduates after Blackwell, even reported that women students in several major Eastern hospitals were able to observe operations only after forcing their way through cordons of male students determined to keep them out of operating rooms.[13] County and state medical associations, too, were loathe to certify women doctors: Only after a 24-year battle did the Massachusetts Medical Society admit women to its membership in 1879.

Women found it even more difficult to become lawyers than to become doctors. Since English common law prohibited women from being called to the bar, the law had to be changed in each state before application could even be made to state licensing boards. And although practicing medicine could be seen as an extension of woman's nurturing role, practicing law intruded on man's public sphere. Arabella Mansfield, the nation's first woman lawyer, gained her training by studying with her brother and was licensed by the Iowa bar in 1869 with no difficulty. Other women, however, had more difficult experiences. Like many law schools, particularly in the Northeast, the Columbian College of Law (now George Washington University) in 1869 and 1887 refused to admit women on the grounds that coeducational classes would be an "injurious diversion of the attention of the students" and that "women had not the mentality to study law."[14] In California, the law schools and the state bar admitted women only after a long and expensive legal contest produced a judicial ruling in their favor. In Illinois and Wisconsin, aspiring women lawyers had to secure special legislation to overturn adverse rulings of state bar associations and courts. As late as 1910, there were only 1,500 women lawyers in the nation, compared to almost 9,000 women doctors.

Women in Journalism   The profession of journalism offers perhaps the most impressive example of women's intrepid persistence in the face of professional hostility. Since mid-century, women had been employed on newspapers as gossip columnists, as editors of women's pages, and sometimes as roving correspondents. But only rarely had a woman been hired as a regular reporter on general news stories. It took a succession of determined women to overcome this barrier. Elizabeth Seaman, who worked for the New York *World*, was the most famous of them. Like most women journalists of her time, Seaman assumed a pseudonym, and hers, Nellie Bly, came from the title of a popular Stephen Foster song. Her persistence in hounding editors brought her initial assignments, and the stories she wrote and submitted were so extraordinary that editors could not reject them. Flamboyant exposés of corruption and exploitation were her specialty. She feigned insanity and spent some time in a state asylum to study conditions there; she made paper boxes in a factory to see how workers were treated; she had herself arrested to investigate conditions in the city jail; and she posed as a high-class prostitute to expose the city's roués. In 1889, Bly accomplished her most famous exploit: She traveled

New York World *reporter Nellie Bly.*

around the world in 72 days to prove that a woman could complete the trip in less than the 80 days it had taken the fictional Phileas Fogg.

Conservative Arguments Produce Progressive Results   It is incorrect to assume that the vigorous action that Nellie Bly and other women professionals took on their own behalf necessarily implied that they were militant feminists. Women pioneers in the professions and in education were often conservative in orientation, and their moderate rhetoric served to create a sympathetic climate for them. The most common argument for professional medical and legal training for women, for example, was not that women had the right to it, but that women patients and clients had the right to consult professionals of the same sex in order to protect their womanly modesty. How could any woman, the argument went, submit to a gynecological examination by a male doctor and preserve her sense of honor? When conservatives contended that only a woman of dubious virtue would want to know about cases of rape, adultery, and prostitution that were matters of daily adjudication in the courts, supporters of women lawyers argued that many of the defendants in these cases were women and had the right to female counsel. No woman, whether she was involved in a divorce suit or a rape case, could be expected to discuss the details of her situation openly with a male lawyer.

Many of the arguments advanced in favor of women's education were similarly moderate in tone. Among other educators, Henry Durant, who founded Wellesley College, felt that women ought to be educated to take a role in shaping society. But L. Clark Seelye, the first president of Smith College, reported that "it is to preserve her [the young woman's] womanliness that this College has been founded; it is to give her the best opportunities for mental culture, and at the same time, the most favorable conditions for developing those innate capacities which have ever been the glory and charm of true womanhood."[15]

The most compelling conservative argument for the education of women, however, was one advanced early in the century by, among others, Catharine Beecher, sister of author Harriet Beecher Stowe and founder of one of the first secondary schools for women in the nation. Beecher wanted to educate women, in the first instance, for their own intellectual profit. But she was even more concerned that education render them the intellectual equals of their husbands, better mothers for their children, and experts in proper nutrition and hygiene. Aside from the profession of teaching, she did not envision a future in which remunerative employment would be standard for women. As were many women leaders in the nineteenth and twentieth centuries, Beecher was concerned primarily with improving the position of women in the home both by upgrading the status of housekeeping and by teaching women more effective domestic techniques. In this quest, Beecher

and others of her generation were the forerunners of the domestic
science movement of the 1910s and the home economics movement
of the 1920s. In terms of the debate over women's roles, these women
might be classified as "domestic feminists"; in terms of women's education, their arguments spoke powerfully to a nation in which the
institution of the family was considered crucial to social stability.

Even though the higher education of women was often viewed as
a way of extending women's traditional roles, in practice such education often produced different results. Particularly among the women's
colleges of the Northeast, the belief that women students had to equal
or excel male students elsewhere and that college-educated women
had a special mission to society and to women was quickly generated.
M. Carey Thomas, president of Bryn Mawr—in many ways the most
feminist of the Eastern women's colleges—captured its spirit when
she wrote in 1901 that the college was "the nursing mother of women
yet unborn," that its graduates would chart new paths in the professions, that they would emerge as social innovators, and that they
would establish marriages based on equality and shared roles rather
than on the traditional division of duties.[16]

Men—A Help and a Hindrance

Men were not always antagonistic to the potential competition of
women. The head of the Bucks County Medical Association led the
fight in Pennsylvania for the certification of women doctors; another
male doctor donated the funds to build the Women's Medical College
in Philadelphia because he wanted his sister, who had supported him
through school, to have the medical education she had deferred on
his behalf. The original endowments for several private women's colleges in the Northeast, such as Vassar and Bryn Mawr, were provided
by wealthy men. In both medicine and law, many early women careerists, like Mary Putnam-Jacobi, were married to men in the same field
who wholeheartedly supported their wives' endeavors. Indeed, a study
of 31 of the approximately 200 women lawyers in the nation in 1896
revealed that a number of them originally became interested in the
law after they married lawyers and worked as clerks in their husbands'
offices.[17]

Many men also agitated for the opening of elementary and secondary education to women. Fathers as well as mothers wanted their

daughters to be educated. Men, too, took an active part in modifying the common law statutes regarding married women. Given the volatile nature of the American economy in the nineteenth century, fathers of means could not help but be concerned over the legal and economic security of their daughters. After all, the financial ruin of a son-in-law might also include the money his wife had brought to the marriage.

Men's aid was not so disinterested in other instances. Women were permitted to become foreign missionaries because many non-Western cultures did not allow any contact between male missionaries and native women. Eminent anthropologist Franz Boas encouraged Barnard students to enter anthropology because he needed reports on native women's rites that only women were permitted to observe.

But it was not easy for nineteenth-century men to allow wives and daughters independence. Anna Howard Shaw—minister, physician, and president of the National American Woman Suffrage Association (NAWSA) from 1904 to 1911—was afraid to tell her family, who had homesteaded in Michigan, of her invitation to preach her first sermon because "to them it would mean nothing short of personal disgrace."[18] Rheta Childe Dorr's husband wanted her to become a novelist in the tradition of George Eliot, who reflected on public events from a distance, but he could not tolerate her ambition to be a journalist in the center of public controversy. Novelist Mary Austin thought it was the tyrannical attitudes of Victorian men that produced most feminists. According to Austin, when women meeting at suffrage conferences discussed what made them suffragists they invariably credited the way they and their mothers had been treated in their families. "'Well, it was seeing what my mother had to go through that started me'; or 'It was being sacrificed to the boys in the family that set me going'; or 'My father was one of the old-fashioned kind.'" Austin remembered how "women of high intelligence and education went white and black telling how, in their own families, the mere whim of the dominant male member had been allowed to assume the whole weight of moral significance."[19]

Technology and Housekeeping

Whether due to male support or hostility, women's organizations grew phenomenally in the late nineteenth century. Some recent historians of women have argued that this growth resulted from the advent of labor-saving appliances, which gave housewives the leisure time for volunteer activities. This thesis, however, is only partially correct. The advent of canned goods, the sewing machine, and new kitchen appliances had lessened the burdens of housekeeping by the 1890s. But as Helen and Robert Lynd reported in *Middletown*, their study of Muncie, Indiana, many women in the 1890s were still baking their own bread and canning their own fruits and preserves—partly to economize, partly out of habit, and partly because society expected that an able wife should demonstrate extensive housekeeping abilities.[20] Even wealthy Maude Nathan of New York City felt so guilty about leaving her home to do volunteer philanthropic work that to assuage her conscience and the objections of the family, she did all the marketing for the family, closely supervised the servants, and planned and directed the making of sheets and towels as well as her own clothes. Once a year, she herself canned a year's supply of pickles, preserves, and corned beef for the household.[21]

By late century, most women were using sewing machines, but they still made their own and their children's clothes. Indeed, the only mechanical aids in most homes in 1890 were the sewing machine, the egg beater, and the nonelectric carpet sweeper. But the crucial time-savers for the housewife were the vacuum cleaner, the refrigerator, the washing machine, and other electrical equipment. Although a fully electric kitchen was displayed at the Columbian Exposition in 1893, electrical equipment was not readily available until the 1920s.

Women's Separate Culture

Women's increased education and leisure time sparked an organizational explosion among women in the late nineteenth century. Moreover, their activism was a logical outgrowth of a central theme of nineteenth-century women's lives—their intense involvement with other women. At the core of nineteenth-century gender-role definitions was the belief that men and women had different natures and therefore should occupy different societal spheres. The public world of affairs belonged to men; the private sphere of the home to women. Undergirding such ideas was the culture's devotion to the nuclear family and the fear (related to the tensions generated by a rapidly-modernizing world) that if women moved out of the private sphere and into the public one, the traditional family might be destroyed.

In a culture with rigid gender-role differentiations and prohibitions on heterosexuality, intense friendships among women flourished. Frances Willard, the temperance leader, wrote: "The loves of women for each other grow more numerous each day. . . . That so little should be said about them surprises me, for they are everywhere."[22] Something approaching a separate culture of women came into being, and it was strikingly evident in the relationships between individual women that contemporaries called "Boston marriages," in the passionate letters women routinely wrote to one another a century ago, and in the female bonding surrounding marriage, childbirth, and death. Out of such gender solidarity proceeded women's organizational initiatives. On occasion, anger against men prompted women's movement from friendship networks to social organizations. The Woman's Christian Temperance Union (WCTU), for example—by far the largest nineteenth-century women's organization—emerged from women's rage against men's drinking and the consequent violence and disorder families experienced. But the politicizing of the community of women was more often in harmony with the sentiments of the age—an age that was not entirely conscious of the passionate friendships it furthered among women but that included in the definition of women's special identity the belief that good women were innately morally superior to men.

This belief in the moral superiority of women provided intellectual support for the underlying concept of women's separate sphere as well as justification for women leaving the private world of home and family for the public one of reform and association. For when feminists argued that morally superior women should be allowed to reshape society, it was difficult for conservatives, despite their desire to restrain women's morality to the home, to disagree. And as we will see, the argument for women's moral superiority became a leitmotif of women's organizational activity in the early twentieth century, both furthering and restraining the ultimate effectiveness of women's appeals for social reform and sexual equality.

Housekeeping was still hard work and the woman's responsibility.

NOTES

[1] Elizabeth Cady Stanton *et al.*, *History of Woman Suffrage*, 6 vols. (New York: Fowler & Wells, 1881–1922), Vol. 5: Ida Husted Harper, p. xvii.

[2] Mabel S. Ulrich, "A Doctor's Diary, 1904–1932," *Scribner's* (June 1933). Reprinted in *Ms.*, I (July 1972): 11–14.

[3] Margaret Mead, *Blackberry Winter: My Earlier Years* (New York: William Morrow, 1972), p. 76.

[4] Rheta Childe Dorr, *A Woman of Fifty* (New York: Funk & Wagnalls, 1924), p. 50.

[5] Frances Parkinson Keyes, *All Flags Flying: Reminiscences of Frances Parkinson Keyes* (New York: McGraw-Hill Book Co., 1972), p. 5.

[6] Marian Lawrence Peabody, *To Be Young Was Very Heaven* (Boston: Houghton Mifflin, 1967), p. 169.

[7] Mary Austin, *Earth Horizon: Autobiography* (New York: Literary Guild of America, 1932), p. 31.

[8] Anne Firor Scott, *The Southern Lady: From Pedestal to Politics, 1830–1930* (Chicago: University of Chicago Press, 1970), p. 141.

[9] Lydia Commander, *The American Idea* (1907; reprint ed., New York: Arno Press, 1972), p. 144.

[10] *Arena*, IX (1893): 305.

[11] Edna Ferber, *A Peculiar Treasure* (Garden City, NY: Doubleday, 1938), p. 33.

[12] Thomas D. Clark, *Indiana University, Midwestern Pioneer*, I (Bloomington: University of Indiana Press, 1970): 125.

[13] Mary Putnam-Jacobi, "Women in Medicine," in Annie Nathan Meyer (ed.), *Woman's Work in America* (New York: Henry Holt, 1891), pp. 139–205.

[14] Karen Meyer Willcox, "Women Lawyers in the United States, 1870–1900," unpublished senior honors thesis (New Brunswick, NJ: Douglass College, 1973), p. 28.

[15] L. Clark Seelye, *The Early History of Smith College, 1871–1910* (Boston: Houghton Mifflin, 1923), p. 29.

[16] M. Carey Thomas, notes for the opening address at Bryn Mawr College, 1901, quoted in Barbara M. Cross (ed.), *The Educated Woman in America: Selected Writings of Catharine Beecher, Margaret Fuller, and M. Carey Thomas* (New York: Columbia Teachers College Press, 1965), p. 41.

[17] Willcox, "Women Lawyers," p. 28.

[18] Anna Howard Shaw, *Story of a Pioneer* (New York: Harper & Row, 1915), p. 60.

[19] Austin, *Earth Horizon*, p. 128.

[20] Helen Merrell Lynd and Robert S. Lynd, *Middletown: A Study in Contemporary American Culture* (New York: Harcourt Brace Jovanovich, Inc., 1929), pp. 156–68.

[21] Robert Smuts, *Women and Work in America*, 2nd ed. (New York: Schocken Books, 1971), pp. 13–14.

[22] Frances Willard, *Glimpses of Fifty Years: The Autobiography of an American Woman* (Chicago: Woman's Temperance Publication Association, 1889), pp. 641–42.

BIBLIOGRAPHY

The details of women's changing status in the late nineteenth century, especially in the area of legal rights, have not yet been systematically explored. On the law, some useful information is contained in Albie Sachs and Joan Hoff Wilson, *Sexism and the Law: Male Beliefs and Legal Bias in Britain and the United States* (New York: The Free Press, 1974). The changing role of women in education and the professions, on the other hand, has recently drawn the attention of a number of scholars. On general educational change, Thomas Woody, *A History of Women's Education in the United States*, 2 vols. (New York: Science Press, 1929), although outmoded, is still the definitive work. On primary and secondary education, Redding Sugg, *Motherteacher: The Feminization of American Education* (Charlottesville: University Press of Virginia, 1978), provides some information. More work is available on the entry of women into higher education. In particular, see Roberta Frankfort, *Collegiate Women: Domesticity and Career in Turn of the Century America* (New York: New York University Press, 1977); Ellen Condliffe Lagemann, *A Generation of Women* (Cambridge, MA: Harvard University Press, 1979); and Elaine Kendall, *"Peculiar Institutions": An Informal History of the Seven Sister Colleges* (New York: G.P. Putnam's Sons, 1975), on the establishment of the elite eastern women's colleges known as the "seven sisters." In *Frontier Women: The Trans-Mississippi West, 1840–1880* (New York: Hill & Wang, 1979), Julie Roy Jeffrey provides information on western coeducation as well as on the life of western women. For an interesting study of women at Cornell University, the first major eastern institution to admit women, in 1872, see Charlotte Williams Conable, *Women at Cornell: The Myth of Equal Education* (Ithaca, NY: Cornell University Press, 1977).

On the entry of women into the professions, Barbara Harris, *Beyond Her Sphere: Women and the Professions in American History* (Westport, CT: Greenwood Press, 1978), contains some information, although the work is primarily a general history of American women. Numerous studies of the position of women in specific occupations and professions have recently appeared. Among these are Margery W. Davies, *Woman's Place Is at the Typewriter: Office Work and Office Workers, 1870–1930* (Philadelphia: Temple University Press, 1982); L. Dee Garrison, *Apostles of Culture: The Public Librarian and American Society, 1876–1920* (New York: The Free Press, 1979); Marion Marzolf, *Up From the Footnote: A History of Women Journalists* (New York: Hastings House, 1977); Barbara Melosh, *"The Physician's Hand": Nurses and Nursing in the Twentieth Century* (Philadelphia: Temple University Press, 1982); Margaret W. Rossiter, *Women Scientists in America* (Baltimore: Johns Hopkins University Press, 1983); Mary Roth Walsh, *Doctors Wanted—No Women Need Apply: Sexual Barriers in the Medical Profession, 1835–1975* (New Haven: Yale University Press, 1977).

On women in the creative arts, see Christine Ammen, *Unsung: A History of Women in American Music* (Westport, CT: Greenwood Press, 1980); Eleanor Munro, *Originals: American Women Artists* (New York: Simon & Schuster, 1979); and Claire Richter Sherman and Adele M. Holcomb (eds.), *Woman as Interpreters of the Visual Arts, 1820–1979* (Westport, CT: Greenwood Press, 1981). For interesting studies of women and the development of modern dance, see Elizabeth Kendall, *Where She Danced: American Dancing, 1880–1930* (New York: Alfred A. Knopf, 1979), and Suzanne Shelton, *Divine Dancer: A Biography of Ruth St. Denis* (Garden City, NY: Doubleday, 1981).

Women's participation in the work force more generally has also aroused recent attention. In particular, see Milton Cantor and Bruce Laurie (eds.), *Class, Sex, and the Woman Worker* (Westport, CT: Greenwood Press, 1977); Susan Easterbrook Kennedy, *If All We Did Was to Weep at Home: A History of White Working-Class Women in America* (Bloomington: Indiana University Press, 1979); Alice Kessler-Harris, *Out to Work: A History of Wage-Earning Women in the United States* (New York: Oxford University Press, 1982); and Barbara Mayer Wertheimer, *We Were There: The Story of Working Women in America* (New York: Pantheon Books, 1977).

A large literature is developing on female sexuality and medical treatment in the nineteenth century. Much of this literature is summarized in Carl N. Degler, *At Odds: Women and the Family in America From the Revolution to the Present* (New York: Oxford University Press, 1980), although his conclusions have occasioned debate. See also John S. Haller, Jr., and Robin M. Haller, *The Physician and Sexuality in Victorian America* (Urbana: University of Illinois Press, 1974). For a rousing attack on nineteenth-century medical treatment, see G.J. Barker-Benfield, *The Horrors of the Half-Known Life: Male Attitudes Toward Women and Sexuality in Nineteenth-Century America* (New York: Harper & Row, 1976); Ann Douglas Wood, " 'The Fashionable Diseases': Women's Complaints and Their Treatment in Nineteenth-Century America," in Mary S. Hartman and

Lois W. Banner (eds.), *Clio's Consciousness Raised: New Perspectives on the History of Women* (New York: Harper & Row, 1974), pp. 1–22; and Regina Morantz's rejoinder to Wood and Barker-Benfield in the same volume. Childbirth and midwifery are covered in Judy Barrett Litoff, *American Midwives: 1860 to the Present* (Westport, CT: Greenwood Press, 1978), and Richard W. Wertz and Dorothy C. Wertz, *Lying-In: A History of Childbirth in America* (New York: The Free Press, 1977).

On abortion, see James C. Mohr, *Abortion in America: The Origins and Evolution of National Policy* (New York: Oxford University Press, 1978). On birth control, see Linda Gordon, *Woman's Body, Woman's Right: A Social History of Birth Control in America* (New York: Grossman, 1976), and James Reed, *From Private Vice to Public Virtue: The Birth Control Movement and American Society Since 1830* (New York: Basic Books, 1978). The most recent study of the antivice reformers of Victorian America is David J. Pivar, *Purity Crusade: Sexual Morality and Social Control, 1868–1900* (Westport, CT: Greenwood Press, 1973). In *Female Complaints: Lydia Pinkham and the Business of Women's Medicine* (New York: W.W. Norton, 1981), Sarah J. Stage has written a fascinating study both of a successful businesswoman and of women's health.

On changes in domestic technology, both in this period and later, see Robert Smuts, *Women and Work in America*, 2nd ed. (New York: Schocken Books, 1971), and Susan Strasser, *Never Done: A History of American Housework* (New York: Pantheon Books, 1982). On the dress-reform movement, the relationship between female fashions and social change, and the influence of actresses on women's self-perception, see Lois W. Banner, *American Beauty* (New York: Alfred A. Knopf, 1983). For demographic analysis, Robert V. Wells, "Women's Lives Transformed: Demographic and Family Patterns in America, 1600–1970," in Carol Ruth Berkin and Mary Beth Norton (eds.), *Women of America: A History* (Boston: Houghton Mifflin, 1979), pp. 17–33, is useful. Anne Firor Scott, *The Southern Lady: From Pedestal to Politics* (Chicago: University of Chicago Press, 1970), is a good introduction to the subject of southern women, as is Janet James (ed.), *Women in American Religion* (Philadelphia: University of Pennsylvania Press, 1980), to the subject of women and religion. For an interesting narrative of women in the 1893 Columbian Exposition, see Jeanne Madeline Weimann, *The Fair Women* (Chicago: Academy, 1981).

The most important exploration of the "separate culture of women" argument is Carroll Smith-Rosenberg, "The Female World of Love and Ritual: Relations Between Women in Nineteenth-Century America," *Signs: Journal of Women in Culture and Society*, 1 (Autumn 1975): 1–25. Blanche Wiesen Cook has explored its lesbian overtones in "Female Support Networks and Political Activism: Lillian Wald, Crystal Eastman, Emma Goldman," *Chrysalis*, 1 (1977): 43–61. Both of these articles are reprinted in Nancy F. Cott and Elizabeth

Pleck (eds.) *A Heritage of Her Own: Toward A New Social History of American Women* (New York: Simon & Schuster, 1979).

For every period of the history of American women, numerous biographies and autobiographies are available. Useful for the late nineteenth and early twentieth centuries are Mary Austin, *Earth Horizon: Autobiography* (New York: Literary Guild, 1932); Lois W. Banner, *Elizabeth Cady Stanton: A Radical for Woman's Rights* (Boston: Little, Brown, 1979); Elizabeth Blackwell, *Pioneer Work in Opening Up the Medical Profession to Women* (London and New York: Longmans, Green, 1895); Edna Ferber, *A Peculiar Treasure* (Garden City, NY: Doubleday, 1938); Helen Thomas Flexner, *A Quaker Girlhood* (New Haven: Yale University Press, 1940); Maude Nathan, *Once Upon a Time and Today* (New York: G.P. Putnam's Sons, 1933); Kathryn Kish Sklar, *Catharine Beecher: A Study in American Domesticity* (New Haven: Yale University Press, 1973); Jean Strouse, *Alice James: A Biography* (Boston: Houghton Mifflin, 1980); Elizabeth Cady Stanton, *Eighty Years and More (1815–1897): Reminiscences of Elizabeth Cady Stanton* (New York: European Publishing, 1898); and the revealing autobiographies of Agnes de Mille, *Where the Wings Grow* (Garden City, NY: Doubleday, 1978); Rheta Childe Dorr, *A Woman of Fifty* (New York: Funk & Wagnalls, 1924); and Frances Parkinson Keyes, *All Flags Flying: Reminiscences of Frances Parkinson Keyes* (New York: McGraw-Hill Book Co., 1972).

Several acclaimed contemporary novels, also useful in understanding women's lives throughout this period, include Willa Cather, *My Antonia* (1918); Kate Chopin, *The Awakening* (1890); Theodore Dreiser, *Sister Carrie* (1900); Charlotte Perkins Gilman, *The Yellow Wallpaper* (1892); and Edith Wharton, *The House of Mirth* (1905).

Several analyses of the history of women in the twentieth century have informed my narrative. They include William H. Chafe, *Women and Equality: Changing Patterns in American Culture* (New York: Oxford University Press, 1977); Peter Gabriel Filene, *Him/Her/Self: Sex Roles in Modern America* (New York: Harcourt Brace Jovanovich, Inc., 1974); Sheila M. Rothman, *Woman's Proper Place: A History of Changing Ideals and Practices, 1870 to the Present* (New York: Basic Books, 1978); and especially William Chafe, *The American Woman: Her Changing Social, Economic, and Political Roles, 1920–1970* (New York: Oxford University Press, 1972). In addition, a number of useful compilations of primary source documents and secondary articles have been published in recent years, including Rosalyn Baxandall, Linda Gordon, and Susan Reverby (eds.), *America's Working Women: A Documentary History—1600 to the Present* (New York: Random House, 1976); Carol Ruth Berkin and Mary Beth Norton (eds.), *Women of America: A History* (Boston: Houghton Mifflin, 1979); W. Elliott Brownlee and Mary M. Brownlee (eds.), *Women in the American Economy: A Documentary History, 1675 to 1929* (New Haven: Yale University Press, 1976); Nancy F. Cott and Elizabeth Pleck (eds.), *A Heritage of Her Own: Toward a New Social History of American Women* (New York: Simon & Schuster, 1979); Jean F. Friedman and William G. Shade (eds.), *Our American Sisters: Women in American Life and Thought*, 3d ed. (Boston: Allyn & Bacon, 1980); Mary S. Hartman and Lois W. Banner (eds.), *Clio's Consciousness Raised: New Perspectives on the History of Women* (New York: Harper & Row, 1974); and Linda K. Kerber and Jane DeHart Mathews (eds.), *Women's America: Refocusing the Past* (New York: Oxford University Press, 1982).

Indispensable to any research on women's history is Edward T. James, Janet Wilson James, and Paul S. Boyer (eds.), *Notable American Women, 1607–1950*, 3 vols. (Cambridge, MA: Harvard University Press, 1970), a collection of brief biographies; and Barbara Sicherman and Carol Hurd Green (eds.), *Notable American Women: The Modern Period* (Cambridge, MA: Harvard University Press, 1980), the continuation of the James's work. Valuable also are Barbara Haber, *Women in America: A Guide to Books, 1963–1975, with an Appendix on Books Published, 1976–1979* (Urbana: University of Illinois Press, 1981); Andrea Hinding, Ames Sheldon Bowers, and Clarke A. Chambers, *Women's History Sources: A Guide to Archives and Manuscript Collections in the United States* (New York: R.R. Bowker, 1979); and Albert Krichmar, *The Woman's Rights Movement in the United States, 1848–1970* (Metuchen, NJ: The Scarecrow Press, 1972), a bibliography of works on the woman's rights movement.

In recent years, the dynamic interest in the history of women has sparked an interest in the history of male roles and behavior. For an introduction to this subject, see Joe L. Dubbert, *A Man's Place: Masculinity in Transition* (Englewood Cliffs, NJ: Prentice-Hall, 1979), and Elizabeth H. Pleck and Joseph H. Pleck (eds.), *The American Man* (Englewood Cliffs, NJ: Prentice-Hall, 1981).

2

THE AMERICAN WOMAN FROM 1900 TO THE FIRST WORLD WAR: A PROFILE

I N THE YEARS before the First World War (1914–1918), the lives of women of every class, ethnic group, and region were governed by the simple statistic that the overwhelming majority would marry and become housewives and mothers. Throughout the twentieth century, approximately 90 percent of all American women have married at some time during their lives. Most women who worked prior to marriage left their jobs to look after their homes and families. Of all married women in the nation in 1900, only 5 percent were gainfully employed outside the home. By 1910, this statistic had increased to 11 percent.

THE MAIN PROSPECT—
MARRIAGE AND MOTHERHOOD

Marriage was a life goal for women, and adolescence was a time of preparation for it. Many women were undoubtedly content with the expectation and fulfillment of their role. The image of the happy housewife that dominated the popular media from early women's magazines to the television serials of the 1980s has always been based on a real type. And for the unmarried working woman who spent endless hours as a seamstress or laundress, becoming a housewife and mother offered release from a life of drudgery.

Yet the married woman's role was not always happily occupied. Sociologists of the family argue that the appearance of the modern state resulted in a decline in the functions that the family performed. Education became the responsibility of the school; health care, the responsibility of the doctor; and the production of the family income shifted from the family-centered farm to the office or the factory. New information about sexuality, the new legal and educational status of women, and the influence of the women's movement and its critique of the Victorian patriarchal family operated to increase women's—and men's—expectations of personal satisfaction in marriage. Also, the increased life expectancy of both men and women meant that marriage partners could anticipate spending a much longer lifetime together. In earlier times, death had provided a release from marital discontent. Now divorce, with its attendant anxieties, was on the rise: By 1905, one out of 12 marriages was ending in divorce.

The Middle-Class Wife

These forces particularly affected middle-class women. Victorian strictures had been difficult for them, but at least nineteenth-century America had clearly defined their role. They were to marry, to have children, to obey their husbands. But by the 1900s, many middle-class women had been to school, and some had worked before marrying. They now had before them the example of women who devoted their lives to their careers. By the second decade of the twentieth century, studies were showing that close to one-half of the alumnae of women's colleges were unmarried and that many of these women were supporting themselves in professional occupations. By then, the spinster was no longer looked on with derision; unmarried women in reform movements and in the professions were proving that alternatives to marriage were not only possible, but exciting. In the nineteenth century, suffragists and career women had been effectively caricatured as ugly, shrewish, and, worst of all, "strong-minded." But many women, like Jane Addams and Florence Kelley, leaders in social welfare in the early twentieth century, were lauded by the press and applauded by a humanitarian society, and professional women living in cities were called "bachelor girls"—a term reflecting glamour and an attractive independence.

Yet the entire middle class was experiencing a vast and perplexing expansion and regrouping during these years. The managerial needs of a complex industrial society were creating not only new business tycoons but also scores of new middle-level plant executives, insurance underwriters, and traveling salesmen—a group that Arthur Miller brilliantly apotheosized into the classic American male in his 1947 play *Death of a Salesman*. In 1910, these middle-level workers numbered almost 5 million. Between 1870 and 1910, their number had increased eight times. Often upwardly mobile, they were anxious to establish a claim to gentility. Typically, they adopted the "white collar" on their shirts as the symbol of emancipation from manual labor and as the badge of their claim to genteel status. Yet many still preserved rural and lower-class roots. "They were faddish and volatile," writes one analyst. "They sought sensation; they supported yellow journalism."[1]

At the very least, such forces were leading a sizable number of well-to-do women to demand more from their marriages than the older standards would allow. Like women throughout history, some of them

Women in Black River Falls,
Wisconsin, get together for tea,
gossip, and sewing.

turned their drives inward on their families and became the shrews
and matriarchs who have long been stock characters of fiction. The
wealthy and pampered Mrs. Hurstwood in novelist Theodore Dreiser's *Sister Carrie*, who waits for her husband's first peccadillo so that
she might destroy him, could exist in any age. Other women displayed
symptoms of neurosis, and physicians consistently reported that most
of the patients they treated for nervous disorders were women.[2] In
many ways, the wife's lot had improved by the early twentieth century,
but with new freedoms came new frustrations. Women were no longer
told to submit to their husbands as a matter of course: By 1909, the
word *obey* was no longer included in civil marriage vows, and many
churches had dropped it from their marriage ceremonies. Observers
commented that *companionship* was the new standard in marriage.[3]

But companionship was difficult to achieve in a culture that expected
men to be materially successful no matter what the cost. In pursuit of
success, according to many accounts, men were rarely at home. "The
habit and fury of work," wrote one critic, "is a masculine disease in
this country." Left to their own devices, many wives were drawn to

shopping as sublimation: Among them, according to one observer, bargain hunting had become a "mania."[4] Or they turned to social climbing. And according to sociologists Helen and Robert Lynd, "The coinage in this social market is much more subtle than that with which their husbands deal."[5] Middle-class women, not their husbands, resorted to the divorce courts with increasing frequency. According to one conservative critic, fashionable young matrons were drinking, smoking, using make-up, playing bridge for money, and demanding an "absolute independence of any power in heaven or in earth."[6] As a general summary of middle-class behavior in the 1900s, such judgments were overstated, but they nevertheless identified an important trend in fashion and life style.

The discontent and confusion of many middle-class women—their difficulty in coping with increased leisure, the breakdown of old standards, and the rise of a new code of freedom for women that could easily be used to justify self-indulgence—were particularly evident in the way they treated their servants (and in the decades before the First World War, status considerations plus the still-demanding nature of housework dictated that every family of means have a servant). The 1900s and the 1910s produced an outpouring of writings on the so-called servant problem—the shortage of women willing to work as maids and cooks. This literature made clear that female employers, and not just working conditions, were driving servants away. It was not simply that servants were expected to work long hours and were paid poorly; they were also subject to the whims and status anxieties of their mistresses. One analyst of domestic service concluded that middle-class women did not want intelligent, responsible servants; rather, they wanted employees to whom they could feel superior and whose lives they could control.[7] So empty were the lives of many of these well-to-do women, wrote one observer in exasperation, that the "3 D's" occupied their time—"dress, disease, and domestics."[8]

Some women were able to find fulfillment by joining voluntary associations. Many obviously found contentment in home and family: One could argue that as the older functions of the family eroded, women found new ones to take their place. As families grew smaller, for example, children became increasingly important, and the concerned mother took great care with her children's upbringing and education. The growth of publishing and the development of the

*A middle-class family and
servants—the Drummonds on
the back porch of their home on
West 22nd Street in New York
City,* circa 1910.

domestic-science movement produced no end of books advising wives
on home management, and their ultimate message reinforced wom-
en's traditional roles. Magazines like the *Ladies' Home Journal* (first
published in 1889) glorified the home and motherhood. Women joined
a host of new organizations devoted to the study of childrearing, and
by 1912, these groups were coordinated into the Federation for Child
Study. In 1914, Congress responded to these trends by declaring the
second Sunday in May the nation's official "Mother's Day." With some

justification, Barbara Ehrenreich and Dierdre English argue that, in fact, the ideal role for women in the early twentieth century was neither the career woman nor the reformer but the homemaker.[9]

The majority of women probably adhered to traditional views about woman's nature. Novelist Frances Parkinson Keyes expressed this view when she wrote that marriage and motherhood were a woman's destiny. Speaking eloquently from the experiences of her own life, Keyes wrote that love was a woman's "whole existence." In the sex act, according to Keyes, the woman "surrendered" to the man, and the birth of a child produced a sense of "blinding glory." Finally, Keyes extolled the emotional experience of nursing, which she viewed as one of the two closest relationships, in addition to marriage, a human being could have.[10]

Despite her belief in the centrality of marriage and motherhood to a woman's life, Keyes herself was both a wife and a careerist, although she took up writing in large part because her husband's salary as governor and later senator of Vermont was insufficient to support their family. Other women, too, were able to combine marriage and a career—among them, the significant number of women lawyers and doctors married to men in the same profession. For many women, however, it was not easy. Margaret Sanger, leader of the birth-control movement, suffered a nervous breakdown because she felt stagnant in a seemingly happy marriage. She had to leave her husband and children and embark on her own career before she completely recovered. Charlotte Perkins Gilman, the most important feminist writer of the decades preceding the First World War, had a similar experience. (Later in life, both Sanger and Gilman remarried.) Carrie Chapman Catt, president of the National American Women Suffrage Association, felt it necessary to draw up a contract with her fiancé before marriage stipulating that she would be guaranteed freedom from the responsibilities of marriage for three months each year to fulfill her duties as president of the NAWSA.

In the early decades of the twentieth century, women who tried to combine marriage and a career faced obvious problems. Senator Keyes opposed his wife's career because he thought it degraded his position as head of the household. It took an exceptional man to tolerate a working wife in an era that regarded such an arrangement as a clear sign of a lack of masculinity and an inability to provide. One woman doctor married to a colleague cataloged further difficulties. Intellec-

*Maintaining the farm: a family
enterprise.*

tually, her husband accepted her career; emotionally, he wanted her
to stay home. As she saw it, his attitudes about women were set by
his mother when he was a child. He wanted his wife to measure up
to the memory of his mother's dependence and dedication to home
and husband. In subtle but effective ways, he undermined her career.
Yet, she concluded, "it can't be so easy being the husband of a 'modern' woman. She is everything his mother wasn't—and nothing she
was."[11]

The Rural Wife

Discontentedness with marriage was perhaps less evident among
women who lived in rural communities, and as late as 1914, the majority of American women still did. By 1900, in most Western farmlands,

The Walters, Lubert County,
Georgia, 1896.

the frontier era—in which women had shared equally with men the burdens of heavy field labor and family defense—had ended. In 1910, one observer did find that families in the far West of Montana and Colorado were still living in isolation in log cabins held together with mud, but these frontier conditions were no longer characteristic of the farmlands in the Midwest.[12] Yet there, as in New England, women still bore heavy responsibilities in terms of maintaining the farm, which was typically a family enterprise. In addition to housekeeping chores, the farm wife cared for the family's vegetable plot and for its supply of livestock for family use. During harvest time, she cooked around the clock for her family and the farm hands. Among the majority of farm families who were not wealthy, daughters typically worked as

A rural family in East Custer County, Nebraska, 1888.

teachers or as domestic servants in other households to supplement the family income. In the South, the prolonged post-Civil War agricultural depression forced white women as well as black women to join husbands and fathers in the fields, while many daughters of the less well-to-do found employment in the still-rural cotton textile mills.

On the surface, the life of the rural woman appears busy and uneventful. Enmeshed in the traditionalist attitudes of rural culture, herself the mainstay of a conservative Protestant ministry, and geographically isolated from urban sophistication, her adjustment to her role seems foreordained. Yet surveys of farm wives were filled with complaints of hard work, isolation, and lack of entertainment. And farm life, no less than city life, could be volatile. The fluctuation in

*Suffragists work on a farm as
part of the war effort, 1917.*

income that was characteristic of farming introduced an elementary
uncertainty, as did the steady movement of the farm population to
the city (and sometimes back again). There were also conflicts between
the generations within farm families, particularly after daughters and
sons began attending public elementary and high schools. Divorce
rates were consistently higher in the West than in the East, although
in part this reflected the less stringent divorce laws in many Western
states. Furthermore, by the 1890s, small towns dotted the rural land-
scape, and the isolated farm was an increasing rarity. Women on farms
and in small towns dominated the Woman's Christian Temperance
Union, and they were not absent from the ranks of suffragists.

Yet not all farm women were married. The sizable percentages of
working women that the censuses of this period classified as farm

workers were largely single women who hired themselves out, like men, to pick crops and do farm chores. Most members of this group were black women in the South. The census of 1900 also counted 300,000 women—predominantly native-born whites—who were farmers, planters, and overseers. Most of these women were probably widows working land they had inherited, but some single women did own and farm land they themselves had acquired. Single women, for example, could acquire the free land offered by the 1865 Homestead Act, and about 12 percent of the entries for land claims in Colorado and Wyoming were filed by women.

The Working-Class Woman

Middle-class women faced a problem characteristic of modernizing societies—how to reconcile freedom with responsibility, how to combine in some satisfactory way the traditional role of wife and mother with the new possibilities of freer sexual expression and of professional commitment. The difficulties for working-class women were no less profound. For them, subsistence was the first problem. Peasant immigrants, who had fled economic upheaval and political tyranny in Europe, began to flood American shores in the 1880s. Without funds or experience and thrust on an industrial, urban society, they and their families became prey to industry's demand for cheap labor. They jammed cheap tenement flats in decaying city districts and crowded company towns in the New England mills and the Pennsylvania mining fields.

Among the working class, primarily unmarried daughters, widows, and spinsters worked for remuneration outside the home. For immigrant women, these percentages were high. In 1900, approximately 25 percent of all unmarried immigrant women worked, compared with 15 percent of all native-born women. And immigrant women entering the work force encountered a status hierarchy that reflected their own rural past as well as the nativism rampant during the period. White native-born women monopolized clerical work, sales work, and semi-skilled factory labor. Immigrant women of Slavic background found employment in unskilled factory labor and in domestic work. But Jewish women entered the garment industry in significant numbers, and they were even employed in skilled positions—largely because they had often performed such work in the Eastern European

Immigrants arriving in the United States, circa 1910.

towns from which they had fled anti-Semitic persecution. Italian women, too, were often exempt from such categorizations because their work patterns were influenced by a patriarchal Italian society in which a woman's virtue was guarded constantly by fathers, brothers, and husbands. Italian women, for example, were rarely employed as domestic servants, because in these positions they might have to work with males to whom they were not related.

Yet ethnicity was not the only factor that determined the degree to which immigrant women participated in the work force. The type of industry in operation where they settled and its location in relation to their communities was also important. Women in cities with a variety of light industries, like New York and Philadelphia, were more likely to work in factories than women in heavy-industry towns, like Buffalo and Cincinnati, or in single-industry towns, like Homestead, Pennsylvania, devoted exclusively to steel production. In Pittsburgh, however, Italian women entered a variety of industrial occupations, because the proximity of these industries to Italian neighborhoods allowed male family members to escort their women to work and the large numbers of Italians employed in Pittsburgh industries provided reinforcement for expected behavior. And in textile mill towns like Lawrence, Massachusetts, entire families, including women and children, were employed in the mills.

Most immigrant women who worked outside the home, like their native peers, were young and unmarried. Yet it is incorrect to assume that immigrant married women, no matter how patriarchal their culture, did not provide substantial financial contributions to the family economy. Italian and Polish wives and daughters, for example, often had experienced significant periods of independent living in their native countries while husbands and fathers went back and forth to the United States as part of the sizable seasonal migration to secure temporary, better-paying jobs in the United States. Nor were they unaccustomed to working in their lands of origin. In Buffalo, New York, Italian married women picked crops in the summers in nearby farm areas, where their agricultural labor was similar to what they had done on Italian farms. Married Jewish women in New York City pushed vending carts or tended family stores, as they had in the Eastern European *shtetl*.

When married immigrant women did not work outside the home, they found remunerative employment within it. They ironed and laundered for middle-class women—immense tasks in an age with no electric washing machines or wash-and-wear fabrics. Or they took in piecework from garment and other factories. And they housed boarders, accommodating the large numbers of single men among European migrants, expecially Slavic immigrants. In Homestead, Pennsylvania, for example, where women could not find employment, more than 40 percent of the families housed at least one paying boarder.

Most of this work went unrecorded by census takers, since women from patriarchal cultures often did not want to reveal work that might demean their husband's sense of masculinity. Still work was an important part of their lives, and they made a major contribution to the support of their families.

*An immigrant woman and her
children do piecework at home.*

Asian Immigration   Chinese and Japanese immigrants also migrated
to the United States in the late nineteenth century. Settling primarily
on the West Coast, the Chinese immigration was composed almost
entirely of single men who worked in the mines and on the transcon-
tinental railroad or who founded laundries (women's work that native
men scorned). Often these men provided support for families on the
verge of starvation in the overpopulated and economically depressed
Chinese province of Canton from which most of these immigrants
came. Chinese women involved in the immigration were generally
prostitutes, who were kidnapped or purchased from their families by
business associates to ensure that Chinese men would not become
involved with native women and would remain loyal to their families
of origin.

West Coast nativism against the Chinese was virulent; and in 1882,
Congress prohibited any further Chinese immigration, thereby continuing the predominantly male character of Chinese communities for
many decades. The Japanese, whose migration in the 1890s was sparked

A cotton field in Georgia.

by Chinese exclusion, met similar nativist sentiment. In 1907, President Theodore Roosevelt concluded a "Gentlemen's Agreement" whereby the Japanese would restrict their own immigration. Paradoxically, this treaty's major effect was to bring numbers of Japanese women to this country to join their isolated fellow countrymen. In contrast to the Chinese, the Japanese had reconstituted a stable family structure by the 1920s, although the numbers of each group within the population were not large until the 1950s.

Black Women Among American women, black women have born the double burden of gender and race discrimination. In 1900, 43 percent of all black women were employed outside the home, compared with 15 percent of white native women and 25 percent of all immigrant women. One-fourth of all black married women were in the work force, compared with less than 4 percent of all white wives. Almost all black women were employed as farm workers or domestics. Sales and clerical work, in addition to factory labor, were almost completely denied them.

In the years before the First World War, American racism reached the heights of virulence. Schools and public facilities in the North and the South were segregated. In the South, where the vast majority of blacks lived, lynchings and riots were regularly unleashed against black males and communities. Black women were commonly stereotyped as "mammies" (maternal, dimwitted, loyal domestics) or as oversexed, willing sexual partners. In southern black schools, female students were taught to dress and to behave as formally as possible when off campus to discourage the attentions of white men. Some states forbade black women to use the titles "Miss" or "Mrs." or to try on clothing before purchasing it. The penalty for committing rape against a black woman was generally less stringent than when a white woman was the victim. Separate washrooms were provided for white women and men in public places, but black women and men often had to share the same facilities.

Faced with such difficulties, black women were not nourished on the myth of female fragility. They commonly expected to assume as much responsibility for family support as husbands and fathers. Often, black women could secure work more easily as domestics than their husbands could as laborers. Surveying conditions for blacks nationwide, muckraker Ray Stannard Baker concluded that "a Negro woman of the lower class rarely expects her husband to support her."[13] Such strength also underlay the success of those black women who entered the professions. In medicine and law, the percentages were actually higher for black women than for white women. In 1910, about 3 percent of all black lawyers were women (1/2 percent for whites) and 13 percent of all black doctors were women (6 percent for whites). At the same time, black women's professional advancement may have represented a useful adaptation to economic realities. Upwardly mobile black women could not enter clerical work and therefore had to secure professional training. Most would become schoolteachers; many were more highly educated than their husbands.

The pressures of discrimination, poverty, and increasing urbanization placed great stress on the traditional black family structure, leaving many women as heads of households. Yet such family patterns did not necessarily represent disorganization or result from male desertion. Death rates among black men were higher than among black women, and many black women were widows. And the northward migration of blacks contained a disproportionate number of women, for whom there were simply not enough men to marry.

The black nuclear family, recent research makes clear, remained intact during slavery and Reconstruction. But even then, important patterns of support through extended kinship relationships were beginning to emerge. By relying on relatives informally grouped together into extended families—a pattern not uncharacteristic of people who live in poverty—black women and the black family were able to cope with the problems of survival in an often hostile world.

Working Conditions   In all occupations, conditions were difficult for women workers. Without strong unions to represent the workers' interests, wages were low and employers were able to violate state safety and sanitary laws with impunity. Domestic workers complained about the loneliness of their occupation and the irrationality of their employers. Waitresses often worked under unsanitary conditions and depended on tips for a living. Even department-store clerks—who occupied positions of higher status—often had no vacations, no rest breaks, and no chairs on which to sit (store owners wanted saleswomen to appear busy even when the store was empty).

Similar exploitative conditions characterized factory labor for women— as well as for men. This is well-illustrated in the ladies' garment industry—a large employer of factory women in the early twentieth century. Centered in the cities, the industry was organized around a system that included both factory and home labor. Major firms often sent finishing work to individual subcontractors, who set up small workshops in tenement apartments where rents were low and where they could hire laborers—particularly women who lived nearby—for a pittance. It was a cheap method of production, but the "sweatshops," as these workrooms came to be known, became a national scandal due to their unsafe and unsanitary conditions.

Women who worked in garment factories could expect to labor at least 10 hours a day and half a day on Saturday, to be paid little, and to be required to buy their own equipment. Finally, they would be relegated to less prestigious and lower-paid tasks than those the male factory workers performed. Women garment workers suffered other

Long hours and low wages were the lot of working-class women, from waitresses in New Hampshire (above) to the garment pieceworker on New York City's lower East Side (below).

indignities as well. At the Triangle Shirtwaist Company in New York City—eventually to become notorious in 1911 as the scene of a major industrial fire—doors were locked so that employees could not abscond with company merchandise and a guard at the one open door searched each woman's pocketbook as she left the factory. Given these working conditions, it is not surprising that pilferage became a form of protest.

Under such circumstances, why did working-class women work? Most Americans at the time believed that they did so to accumulate a dowry and to buy clothes and other frivolities. Some native daughters of Anglo-Saxon parentage may have worked for this reason. Yet, studies by private foundations and government agencies proved that the "pin-money theory" was a myth. Daughters of the working class worked because they had to, because their fathers and brothers did not earn sufficient money to support their families. The large number of working women who lived with their families did so, not to save money to spend on themselves, as pin-money theorists argued, but because there was insufficient housing in American cities for unmarried working women; because it was considered a disgrace in many immigrant cultures for an unmarried daughter to live alone; and finally and most important, because many working women were not paid enough money to afford private apartments or boarding houses. A 1910 Women's Trade Union League survey of Chicago department-store saleswomen showed that as many as 30 percent of these workers earned little more than a subsistence wage.

Strikes and Unions   Why, then, did working women not rebel against their lot? They often did. Leaders of the labor movement included women as well as men—heroines like nonagenarian Mary "Mother" Jones, who devoted her long life to organizing laborers among the most oppressive industries in the nation (coal, Western mining, and the Southern cotton mills), and Elizabeth Gurley Flynn, whose fiery oratory brought her to public prominence at the age of 17. Women also participated in local strikes and labor organizations. Layoffs or wage cuts could arouse the anger of women workers as well as men. In 1898, women glovemakers in Chicago went on strike when new assembly-line techniques were introduced. They had tolerated piece-work wages, tyrannical male foremen, and having to buy their own equipment, but an increase in the monotony of their work and a probable decline in wages were more than they could bear. In 1905 in Troy,

A sweatshop in New York City,
circa *1900.*

New York, 8,000 women laundry workers went on strike as a result of
the introduction of fines for talking and lateness, irregular work
assignments, and a new machine—all of which substantially cut wages.

Between 1909 and 1913, such episodes became regular, particularly
in the garment industry. In 1909, 20,000 shirtwaist workers in New
York City and Philadephia took to the streets in the century's most
famous women's strike. In 1910 in New York City, 60,000 workers in
the cloak and suit business struck; 10 percent of these workers were
women. That same year, strike activity spread to garment workers in
Chicago, Cleveland, and Milwaukee. In 1911, as a protest against conditions that produced the Triangle fire, 80,000 workers marched up
Fifth Avenue for four hours. And in 1912, the determination of striking

*Working conditions show little
improvement as women make
Army uniforms in 1917.*

women textile workers in Lawrence, Massachusetts, was central to the
success of one of the decade's most violent confrontations between
industry and labor.

The evidence of these strikes demonstrates that it is incorrect to
assume that working women in the early twentieth century did not
have the capacity for labor militancy or for organization. The International Ladies' Garment Workers Union (ILGWU), founded as an
AFL (American Federation of Labor) affiliate in 1900, vastly increased
its membership as a result of these strikes and was the third largest
AFL affiliate by 1913. Some observers at the time were convinced that
women made better strikers than men—either because they possessed
a "characteristic feminine tenacity," as one analyst put it, or because,

Mary "Mother" Jones, labor
organizer, 1916.

without husbands and children dependent on them, women workers
felt freer in their response.[14]

Yet it was extremely difficult for strikes to succeed. To break up such
protests, employers had the power to use the courts, the organs of
public opinion, and the police, who did not hesitate to use brutality
against women strikers. In part, the 1909 shirtwaist worker's strike
succeeded because a number of well-to-do philanthropists joined the
picket lines and provided bail money. Their participation brought public sympathy to the strikers and forced the owners to settle. But even
in this strike, not all the workers were successful. Women at the Triangle Shirtwaist Company who had been among the organizers of the
strike gained no concessions from their employers. Instead, many of
them were killed in the devastating fire at the Triangle Company building in 1911.

Moreover, despite the growth of the ILGWU, to unionize women
workers was difficult. In 1900, about 3 percent of all factory women
were unionized; in 1913, after the garment strikes, the statistic stood
at only 6 percent. Employers often hired women from various immigrant backgrounds, and the resulting suspicion and language barriers
among the workers made organization difficult. The female labor force
was unstable. Many women did seasonal work and were laid off during slack periods. Young women, who made up the majority of the

Shirtwaist workers on strike.

female work force, looked on work as a temporary occupation before marriage. Trained to be dependent, many women workers hesitated to assert their individuality by joining a union and challenging parental authority.

And the workplace itself could be intimidating, reinforcing the sense of powerlessness inculcated by families and the environing culture. Many male supervisors were aggressive, continually reprimanding the workers under them in line with the general prejudice that unskilled laborers were invariably lazy and inefficient. To ensure productivity, women were not permitted to sit down in many factories. Moreover,

*The bodies of workers killed in
the 1911 Triangle Shirtwaist
Company fire.*

sexual harrassment was not uncommon. Faced with such difficulties, it was easier for young women to repress complaints against the rigors of their jobs and to focus on the rites of courtship and the opportunities to socialize with their friends in the workroom. Still adolescents in many cases, women workers declared off-limits divisive topics like unions and politics.

Finally, women failed to unionize because existing labor unions were hesitant to organize them. The Knights of Labor, which flourished in the 1880s, had welcomed women as members, had supported their strikes, and had actively recruited among them. But violence and economic depression destroyed the Knights of Labor in the 1890s, and the American Federation of Labor (AFL), founded in 1886, came to dominate organized labor. The AFL was then composed almost exclusively of skilled craftsmen. Intent on bettering their own position in an industrial world where the owners of industry had the support of the police and the courts, these workers had little interest in taking on the problems of the unskilled trades in which women clustered. (Blacks and most immigrant males were also excluded from the craft-

*Shutters buckled and fire escapes
collapsed in the Triangle fire.*

organized AFL.) Nor did AFL members desire the job competition of women (always a cheap supply of labor). The AFL constitution officially outlawed sex discrimination among member unions, and most unions nominally complied. But because women and men performed different tasks in many industries, union leaders simply excluded women's work when defining the crafts included in their union, even when this work might be considered skilled labor. One official of the International Association of Machinists told a labor investigator that "there are few real machinists. A machinist is born and not made. One must have a feeling for machines, and women haven't got that."[15] Such beliefs about women dominated many skilled crafts. Even in those few AFL unions like the ILGWU, where women members predominated, the officers (except the secretary, who was frequently a woman) were invariably men.

There were other reasons for the exclusion of women. For a man, the union was also a club, a refuge from the family, a place where he could socialize and escape from the difficulties of everyday life. Unions generally met in saloons, traditional bastions of male camaraderie. Moreover, many wives of working men were probably opposed to allowing other women to fraternize with their husbands. Even many women workers viewed unions as "male" institutions.

The sex discrimination of the AFL was not so true of the more radical unions. Like the Knights of Labor before them, the Industrial Workers of the World (IWW) did not exclude women from positions of leadership or membership. Initially focusing on unskilled, mass production industries in the West and the South, they filled their picket lines with the nonworking wives of copper and coal miners, who battled the police with brooms and buckets. When the IWW moved East, its members concentrated on the textile mills, which employed entire families. The IWW was the central force behind the 1912 strike in Lawrence, Massachusetts.

Similarly, the militant activism of socialist women was central to the garment strikes of 1910. Led within the party by a strong Woman's National Committee, socialist women's neighborhood locals gave them community access to the garment workers, many of whom were young Jewish women whose Eastern European backgrounds reflected a tradition of radicalism. Still both the IWW and the socialists emphasized class struggle above feminist concerns, while male members exhibited gender chauvinism. Such attitudes were particularly true of the IWW, which never outgrew the male culture of western mining in which it had first taken root.

The sexism of male unions—in addition to middle-class reformism and cultural imperatives toward sisterhood—resulted in the cross-class alliance of women to improve conditions for all working women. Two major organizations of the Progressive era grew from this alliance. The first, the Consumers' League, was formed in 1890 to improve working conditions for department-stores saleswomen through consumer boycotts. The second, the Women's Trade Union League (WTUL), was founded in 1903 at a convention of the AFL. Its goal was to educate and organize both middle-class and working-class women to support the cause of women's labor. The WTUL consistently remained an amalgam of the workers and the well-to-do. Among its early state and national presidents, for example, were Alice Henrotin, a former president of the General Federation of Women's Clubs; Margaret Dreier Robins, a wealthy New York philanthropist; and Mary Anderson, a

Rose Schneiderman, initially a capmaker, became a leader in the International Ladies' Garment Workers Union and the Women's Trade Union League.

daughter of Swedish immigrants, who began her career working in a shoe factory and later became director of the Women's Bureau in the Department of Labor between 1919 and 1944. In addition to other efforts, the WTUL led the garment strikes in 1910 and was involved in the 1912 Lawrence strike, despite an AFL directive not to participate.

Yet even with some funding from the AFL, the WTUL was always short of money, and its success was limited. Middle-class members in local chapters often were too eager to stress cultural uplift rather than union organization. Although its constitution stipulated that a majority of its board should be working-class women and middle-class members were called "allies," workers often felt patronized by the genteel style of the allies and compromised by their notion of a vague union of classes in which the workers' own struggle against class exploitation was too easily overlooked. The strong socialist contingent in the WTUL felt particularly embittered. By 1913, these growing aggravations, plus the WTUL's difficulty in organizing women outside the garment trades, led the League to abandon union campaigns in favor of agitating for legislative solutions to women's difficulties. Still, for ten years, it successfully brought women of varying economic and social status together. The WTUL has been one of the few women's organizations in the twentieth century in which women have been able to cross class barriers in support of a common cause.

Married Life   In any case, the paramount goal of young working women was not improved working conditions, but marriage. Films, plays, and novels hammered the theme home. The message of popular culture supported both the traditional goals of parents anxious to make good matches for their daughters and the rebelliousness of those daughters for whom marriage seemed the only way of ending their status as perpetual dependents, supplementing their elders' income.

Yet marriage among the working class produced its own stresses. Particular conditions varied among different cultures, regions, income levels, and age groups. Still, some general conclusions can be drawn.

Life was not easy for working-class families. With the exceptions of artisans and skilled laborers, the incomes of most working-class men were so small that their wives and daughters had to work to supplement them. Men left the responsibility for contraception to their wives, who were expected to be sexually available at their husbands' behest. But information about birth control was not easy to come by. One commentator noted that many mothers tried to prolong the nursing of their infants in the mistaken belief that lactating women could not conceive.[16]

According to many sociologists, the patriarchal family remained the model in the working class longer than it did in the middle class. One observer at the time wrote that "the conventions of the working class are more rigid than any other class. They are the last to be affected by changing psychology or institutions."[17] The concept of companionship in marriage differentiated middle-class values from working-class values. Given the economic pressures on the working class, the patriarchal ideal often served as a justification for the harsh treatment of wives by husbands and of children by parents. Under these circumstances, many marriages became strained, with husbands and wives living, according to one observer, with "little affection" and "little spiritual comradeship."[18] Husbands generally gave wages to wives to distribute, so that working-class women gained power within their families. But then husbands and wives characteristically retreated to their own territories—the men to newspapers, saloons, or sporting events; the women to homes or children. For the working class, divorce was difficult; it was expensive, it required a lawyer and, among Catholics, it

A visiting nurse calls on a family in a city slum, circa *1890.*

was a disgrace. This is not to imply, however, that discontented couples always remained together. Cases of desertion were numerous among the working class, and by the 1920s, the divorce rate had begun to equal and even surpass that of the middle class. Poverty, ignorance, the shock of American culture and urban living, and traditional views about the nature of male–female relationships made marriage as difficult, if not more difficult, among the working class as among the well-to-do.

Yet, like women of the middle class, working-class women often found respite from their marriages by joining organizations. Immigrant groups founded churches and ethnic societies, which nurtured traditional values and helped offset insecurity and isolation. Local chapters of the American Federation of Labor (AFL) formed women's auxiliaries, where wives could make friends and gain some under-standing of their husbands' work. And for some, there was relief from constant child-bearing; studies showed that knowledge and use of contraceptives grew among working-class women as income rose and length of residence in the United States increased.

But what they all had was hope—hope for the future of their chil-dren. That was the promise of American life. It was a viable hope, for their daughters as well as their sons. The young woman factory worker might become a secretary or a nurse, with the promise of greater status and a higher salary; she might even marry a businessman or a doctor. For society in general, such possibilities—and, more important, the belief in them—acted as a powerful safety valve. That women took advantage of these opportunities is shown by statistical studies. In 1900, almost all women who worked were domestics, farm laborers, or unskilled factory workers. By 1910, however, stenography and typ-ing employed 7 percent of all women workers. By 1920, this statistic had risen to 16 percent; by 1930, to almost 19 percent. By 1940, clerical work was the largest single field of women's employment. The tran-sition from domestic to factory to office work was rarely made in the same generation. But for the immigrant mother whose sons became lawyers and doctors and whose daughters became secretaries, nurses, and the wives of lawyers and doctors, the American promise was fulfilled.

THE OTHER WAY—PROSTITUTION

Not all American women in the early twentieth century assumed the socially approved roles of wife and mother or of volunteer worker or paid employee. Some turned to prostitution.

It is difficult to determine the number of prostitutes in the United States in the 1900s. Because the occupation was illegal, few women would willingly reveal their participation. In any event, prostitution seems to have been on the increase in the late nineteenth century—a result of the explosive growth of cities during that period. Public offi-cials were aware of the existence of prostitution, but with a character-istic Victorian attitude, they looked on it as a "necessary evil" to protect the virtue of pure women. In most cities, the police had driven pros-titution—at least as practiced in brothels—into so-called "red-light districts," away from the middle class who might be offended by it.

Thus gathered together, prostitutes provided revenue to city officials and policemen, who threatened them with arrest unless regular payments were made. Among the red-light districts, which also functioned as havens for criminals, the French Quarter in New Orleans and the Barbary Coast in San Francisco were best known, but their replicas existed in cities large and small. Even Muncie, Indiana—a city with a population of about 11,000 in the 1890s—had 20–25 brothels, with four to eight women per house.

In the nineteenth century, municipal officials in many cities tried to introduce the system of licensing used in Europe, under which prostitutes were licensed by the state and required to have periodic examinations for venereal disease. In every instance, however, coalitions of feminists and social-purity reformers prevented them. After 1900, cities and states appointed vice commissions to study prostitution and make recommendations for ending it. As a result of their reports, red-light districts had disappeared by the 1920s. But clever madams reopened their houses under the guise of dance studios and massage parlors and also invented "call-girl systems," keeping lists of women whom they could telephone to arrange meetings with clients at convenient locations. Prostitution seems to have declined in the 1920s, but the reasons may have stemmed more from the freer morality of that era than from the work of the vice commissions.

The Practitioners

Many prostitutes worked in brothels, where madams—often innovative and resourceful businesswomen—assumed the responsibility for their solicitation and protection. Others were connected with male pimps, then called "cadets," to whom they gave their earnings. The 1916 New York City Kneeland investigation suggested that the pimp–prostitute relationship there had grown out of friendships among boys and girls in street gangs and that these pimps solicited for their women. Many prostitutes worked on their own, making assignations in dance halls and saloons or on the streets and then using hotels that catered to prostitutes and clients. Prostitution was always a possible occupation for women who could find no other work or who wished to supplement their wages. There was, as reporter Frances Donovan described it, a certain amount of "semi-prostitution" among working women.[19]

Prostitution—innate depravity,
or just another kind of work?

Why did women become prostitutes? The widespread belief at the time was that prostitutes were forced into a "life of vice" by male procurers employed by national and international syndicates. For a time around 1910, concern about the "white-slave trade" reached the level of a national hysteria, pervaded by rumors that men with hypodermic needles traveled crowded streetcars and haunted amusement parks seeking likely victims to drug and abduct. This paranoia was given currency by some well-documented cases of women who actually were drugged and awakened in brothels. There were men who hung around dance halls, trying to strike up an acquaintance that might turn into a seduction. Among some immigrant groups—Italians and Orthodox Jews were examples—a fall from virtue, if discovered, could result in ostracism from the family. But with the exception of Chinese prostitution in the West, there was little evidence that any large syndicates lurked behind the recruitment of prostitutes.

Most surveys of prostitution played down the white-slave theory and looked elsewhere for an explanation of why women became prostitutes. The most common factor appeared to be economic need. Women most often became prostitutes because they could not find employment or because they could earn much more money as a prostitute than as a seamstress or even a salesclerk. "Poverty causes prostitution," concluded the writers of the Illinois Vice Commission Report in 1916, and other vice commissions agreed.[20] In addition, most studies singled out domestic work as the most common previous occupation of prostitutes.

Yet the argument that poverty caused prostitution—however satisfying to a society still ambivalent about female sexuality—provided only a partial explanation. Perceptive observers could not fail to note that many prostitutes disclosed that they had entered the occupation due to a "personal inclination." As early as 1858, in the first detailed investigation of prostitution in the United States, Dr. William Sanger of New York City found that approximately 25 percent of his sample of 2,000 women said that they had become prostitutes simply because they had wanted to. Despite Sanger's medical training, he could not accept this explanation. To this Victorian, "personal inclination" indicated "an innate depravity, a want of true womanly feeling, which is actually incredible." He reasoned that liquor or drugs must have produced the sexual arousal these women reported.[21] It did not occur to Sanger that they might have come from a world where sexuality was openly expressed and prostitution was simply another kind of work.

THE NEW SENSUALITY

By the 1890s, a new civilization was emerging in America—one that was more secular, more scientific, more modern. Concomitantly, the growth of the pleasure ethic was eroding older values of self-control

*"Crib girls"—prostitutes at a
drinking "bee" at White Chapel
in the mining town of Dawson,
Alaska, at the turn of the
century.*

and self-abnegation. Commercial entrepreneurs exploited this trend.
Department-store owners constructed ever more lavish buildings that
housed increasingly larger stocks of consumption items. Beauty parlors with elaborate systems for curling hair and massaging skin
appeared. New forms of entertainment celebrated sybaritism and did
not veil sensuality. There were dance halls, the ubiquitous amusement
parks, like Coney Island, at the end of trolley lines, and by the early
twentieth century, the movies. Sensational daily newspapers (so-called
"yellow journals"), which focused on celebrities, scandal, and violence, were successfully launched by such publishers as Joseph Pulitzer
and William Randolph Hearst. New music and dances, like ragtime
and the two-step, became widely popular.

By and large, these institutions of pleasure were designed for young,
urban, working-class men and women—an expanding group of consumers who were eager to establish their autonomy and who had

limited space at home for courtship. To many working-class women who aspired to higher status, it was clear that virtue was a valued possession of middle-class women, and they enforced on themselves and their daughters strict middle-class standards of behavior. Other working-class women took an opposite direction. Work brought them into contact with young men, while responsibility gave them the nerve to scorn parental restraints. They expected to go to dance halls and amusement parks and to meet men. For some, sex was the next step. Investigators for the Massachusetts Vice Commission reported in 1914 that in every Massachusetts city, sizable numbers of young women loitered around cafes and dance halls, waiting to be picked up by men. "To the total stranger," the investigators reported, "they talk willingly about themselves, their desire to 'see life,' to 'get out of this dead hole,' to go to Boston or to New York." Many of these women, the investigators found, were willing to have sexual relations with them. Assuredly, this was sexual license, but it was not prostitution, as the Massachusetts investigators were quick to point out. For most of these women were incensed by the offer of direct payment for an assignation. They drew a line between their own definitions of virtue and vice: Payment meant prostitution, and they were not prostitutes.[22]

These women represented the new and freer morality that was emerging in the United States in the 1900s. In fact, the concern about prostitution and the 1910 hysteria over white slavery was at base a misplaced reaction on the part of middle-class molders of public opinion to a widespread cultural phenomenon they dimly recognized. The new morality appeared first among young, working-class women and, by 1912, was evident among their middle-class peers. In that year, the so-called "dance craze" appeared. All over America, it seemed, respectable citizens suddenly thronged dance halls and cabarets to dance the bunny hug, the turkey trot, and the tango—dances previously confined to working-class places of amusement. The new vogue of sensual dances signaled the emergence of a new sensuality among women—as important a strain of liberation as the new movements into the work force, or education, or the professions.

The World of the Waitress

For several months in 1920, reporter Frances Donovan donned a uniform to study the occupation of the waitress. A number of such studies of working women were conducted in the early twentieth century:

Many educated young women eager to advance themselves and the cause of women found it challenging to enter the working-class world and record their experiences. Few, however, investigated their subjects with as much candor, or were so challenged by their findings, as was Donovan.

At first Donovan was shocked as she plumbed the world of the waitress. Here, sexuality was always present. In their spare time, her new acquaintances boasted of their affairs and openly discussed their abortions. Her sheltered upbringing had not prepared her for this or for the women's constant use of obscenities and profanities. She could not reconcile herself to their penchant for retelling off-color jokes heard from patrons or pointing out men who supposedly were sexual perverts.

But slowly Donovan came to respect these women. She began to believe that their way of life represented a negative appraisal of middle-class culture. Their behavior went far beyond a simple openness about sexual relations. They had lived, Donovan judged, in a way that no middle-class woman, bound to convention, could. Many of them had married and had left their husbands, and that fact, plus their economic independence, lay at the heart of the matter. They were free from the dominance of men. "With economic independence, the waitress has achieved a man's independence in her relations with men; she doesn't have to get married, and she doesn't have to stay married very long. . . .She is a free soul," wrote Donovan.[23]

Undoubtedly, Donovan romanticized the life of the waitress—a life of long hours, hard work, and subservient status. Like many feminists she allowed her suspicion of men to color her interpretation. Yet there was more than a grain of truth in what she had to say. Were not these waitresses more honest about life and work than their middle-class peers? "To go out into the world and grab from it the right to live in spite of the competition of youth is vastly more interesting than to make weekly pilgrimages to the beauty parlor in the vain attempt to get rid of the symbols of old age that bear witness to the fact that you have never lived. . . .Here," Donovan concluded, "we have the feminist movement and ideals embodied in a class."[24]

To a certain extent, Donovan was correct: Without sexual liberation, women could never be free. But was sexual liberation enough? And did women not have other responsibilities—to themselves, to their families, to society? Should marriage and the nuclear family so easily be assumed to be oppressive? And if women left the home, as Donovan's waitresses did, who would raise their children? (Curiously, any mention of children is absent from Donovan's narrative.) These were some of the basic questions facing American women of all classes in the early years of this century, and the increased freedom of expression and action that the new century brought only served to make it more difficult for women to work out the answers in their own lives.

NOTES

1 Albert F. MacClean, Jr., *American Vaudeville as Ritual* (Lexington: University of Kentucky Press, 1965), p. 41.

2 American Sociological Society, *Papers and Proceedings of the Third Annual Meeting of the American Sociological Society: The Family* (Chicago: University of Chicago Press, 1908), p. 132.

3 Anna A. Rogers, *Why American Marriages Fail and Other Papers* (Boston: Houghton Mifflin, 1909), p. 62.

4 Katherine G. Busbey, *Home Life in America* (New York: Macmillan, 1910), p. 149.

5 Helen Merrell Lynd and Robert S. Lynd, *Middletown in Transition: A Study in Cultural Conflicts* (New York: Harcourt Brace Jovanovich, Inc., 1937), p. 95.

6 Rogers, *Why American Marriages Fail*, pp. 174–75.

7 Mary R. Smith, "Domestic Service: The Responsibility of Employers," *Forum* XXVII (August 1899): 678–89.

8 Lucy Maynard Salmon, *Progress in the Household* (Boston: Houghton Mifflin, 1906), p. 95.

9 Barbara Ehrenreich and Dierdre English, *For Their Own Good: 150 Years of the Experts' Advice to Women* (Garden City, NY, Doubleday, 1978), p. 128.

10 Frances Parkinson Keyes, *All Flags Flying: Reminiscences of Frances Parkinson Keyes* (New York: McGraw-Hill Book Co., 1972), pp. 13, 31.

11 Mabel S. Ulrich, "A Doctor's Diary, 1904–1932," *Scribner's* (June 1933). Reprinted in *Ms.*, I (July 1972): 11–14.

12 Busbey, *Home Life In America*. p.283.

13 Ray Stannard Baker, *Following the Color Line: American Negro Citizenship in the Progressive Era* (Garden City, NY: Doubleday, Page, 1908), p. 141.

14 Helen Marot, *American Labor Unions, by a Member* (New York: Henry Holt, 1914), p. 74.

15 Theresa Wolfson, *The Woman Worker and the Trade Unions* (New York: International, 1926), p. 110.

[16] Frank Hatch Streightoff, *The Standard of Living Among the Industrial People of America* (Boston: Houghton Mifflin, 1911), p. 138.

[17] Wolfson, *Woman Worker and the Trade Unions*, p. 43.

[18] Streightoff, *Standard of Living*, pp. 138–64.

[19] Frances Donovan, *The Woman Who Waits* (Boston: Richard Badger, 1920), p. 224.

[20] State of Illinois, *Report of the Senate Vice Committee* (Chicago, 1911), p. 203.

[21] William Sanger, *The History of Prostitution: Its Extent, Causes, and Effects Throughout the World* (New York: Medical, 1927), p. 488.

[22] Massachusetts Commission for the Investigation of the White Slave Traffic, *Report of the Commission for the Investigation of the White Slave Traffic, so-called* (Boston, 1914), p. 43.

[23] Donovan, *Woman Who Waits*, p. 224.

[24] *Ibid.*, p.226.

BIBLIOGRAPHY

A wealth of material is available to reconstruct a profile of the middle-class woman during any period of her history. For the early twentieth century, one can consult newspapers and journals, diaries and biographies, contemporary analyses and novels. On the history of the family, see Carl Degler, *At Odds: Women and the Family in America From the Revolution to the Present* (New York: Oxford University Press, 1980), and Michael Gordon (ed.), *The American Family in Social-Historical Perspective*, 3rd. ed. (New York: St. Martin's Press, 1983). Arthur Calhoun, *Social History of the American Family*, 3 vols. (Cleveland: Arthur Clark, 1918), remains interesting, and Sidney Ditzion, *Marriage, Morals, and Sex in America: A History of Ideas* (1953; reprint ed., New York: Octagon, 1970), is useful on morality and sexual attitudes.

Studies by contemporary writers and later sociologists are also useful. These include Sophonisba P. Breckinridge, *The Family and the State: Select Documents*, (1934; reprint ed., New York: Arno Press, 1972); Hugh Carter and Paul Glick, *Marriage and Divorce: A Social and Economic Study* (Cambridge, MA: Harvard University Press, 1970); Ruth Shonle Cavan, *The American Family* (New York: Crowell, 1969); Lydia Commander, *The American Idea* (1907; reprint ed., New York: Arno Press, 1972); Ernest Mowrer, *Family Disorganization: An Introduction to a Sociological Analysis* (Chicago: University of Chicago Press, 1927); Anna A. Rogers, *Why American Marriages Fail and Other Papers* (Boston: Houghton Mifflin, 1909); John Sirjamaki, *The American Family in the Twentieth Century* (Cambridge, MA: Harvard University Press, 1953); and the American Sociological

Society, *Papers and Proceedings of the Third Annual Meeting of the American Sociological Society: The Family* (Chicago: University of Chicago Press, 1908).

For divorce in general, see Nelson Blake, *The Road to Reno: A History of Divorce in the United States* (Westport, CT: Greenwood Press, 1962; reprint ed., 1977). More detailed studies include Robert L. Griswold, *Family and Divorce in California, 1850–1890: Victorian Illusions and Everyday Reality* (Albany: State University of New York Press, 1982); Elaine Tyler May, *Great Expectations: Marriage and Divorce in Post-Victorian America* (Chicago: University of Chicago Press, 1980); and William L. O'Neill, *Divorce in the Progressive Era* (New Haven: Yale University Press, 1967), on the ideas of divorce reformers.

For rural women, the most comprehensive source is Joan M. Jensen, *With These Hands: Women Working on the Land* (Old Westbury, NY: Feminist Press, 1981). On working-class women, the autobiographical material is more limited than it is for middle-class women. There are, however, many studies of ethnic cultures, and recently some of them have begun to pay specific attention to women. In particular, see Charlotte Baum, Paula Hyman, and Sonya Michel, *The Jewish Woman in America* (New York: The Dial Press, 1976); Rosalyn Baxandall, Linda Gordon, and Susan Reverby (eds.), *America's Working Women: A Documentary History—1600 to the Present* (New York: Random House, 1976); Deborah Dash More, *At Home in America: Second-Generation New York Jews* (New York: Columbia University Press, 1981); Cecyle S. Neidle, *America's Immigrant Women* (Boston: Twayne, 1975); Maxine S. Seller (ed.), *Immigrant Women* (Philadelphia: Temple University Press, 1980); Virginia Yans-McLaughlin, *Family and Community: Italian Immigrants in Buffalo, 1880–1930* (Ithaca, NY: Cornell University Press, 1977); and the powerful, contemporary novel by Anzia Yezierska, *Bread Givers* (New York: Braziller, 1925). The movie, *Hester Street*, is an accurate and moving story of immigrant acculturation, family conflict, and the nature of gender in the Jewish community. It is available from Cinema 5, 595 Madison Avenue, New York, NY, 10022.

On black women, the secondary literature is thin. A useful compilation of primary source material is Gerda Lerner (ed.), *Black Women in White America* (New York: Pantheon Books, 1972). Also consult Lenwood G. Davis, *The Black Woman in American Society: A Selected Annotated Bibliography* (Boston: G.K. Hall, 1975); Claudia Goldin, "Female Labor Force Participation: The Origin of Black and White Differences, 1870 and 1880," *Journal of Economic History,* 37 (March 1978): 87–108; Sharon Harley and Rosalyn Terborg-Penn (eds.), *The Afro-American Woman: Struggles and Images* (Washington, D.C.: National University Publications, 1978); and Elizabeth H. Pleck, *Black Migration and Poverty: Boston, 1865–1900* (New York: Academic Press, 1979). The most recent study of the black family is Herbert G. Gutman, *The Black Family in Slavery and Freedom, 1750–1925* (New York: Pantheon Books, 1976).

There is also little material available on Oriental women. The best place to begin is Verna Abe et al., *Asian American Women* (Stanford, CA: Stanford University Press, 1976), and Lucie Cheng Hirata, "Chinese Immigrant Women in Nineteenth-Century California," in Carol Ruth Berkin and Mary Beth Norton (eds.), *Women of America: A History* (Boston: Houghton Mifflin, 1979), pp. 223–44. Maxine Hong Kingson's autobiographical novels—*The Woman Warrior: Memoirs of a Girlhood Among Ghosts* (New York: Alfred A. Knopf, 1976), and *China Men* (New York: Alfred A. Knopf, 1980)—are indispensable. Pearl S. Buck, *The Good Earth* (London: Methuen, 1932), is a classic exposition of the Chinese background.

On working-class women more generally, consult the works cited in the bibliography to Chapter 1 and also Leslie Woodcock Tentler, *Wage-Earning Women: Industrial Work and Family Life in the United States, 1900–1930* (New York: Oxford University Press, 1979). Studies of individual industries and labor unions can be used with profit. These include Leon Stein, *The Triangle Fire* (Philadelphia: Lippincott, 1962), and Benjamin Stolberg, *Tailor's Progress: The Story of a Famous Union and the Men Who Made It* (Garden City, NY: Doubleday, 1944). The most extensive contemporary survey of working conditions is the United States Bureau of Labor's *Report on the Condition of Woman and Child Wage-earners in the United States*, 19 vols. (Washington, D.C.: Government Printing Office, 1910). On women in the labor movement, see Nancy Schrom Dye, *As Equals and as Sisters: Feminism, the Labor Movement, and the Women's Trade Union League of New York* (Columbia: University of Missouri Press, 1980); Philip S. Foner, *Women and the American Labor Movement: From Colonial Times to the Eve of World War One* (New York: The Free Press, 1979); Foner, *Women and the American Labor Movement: From World War One to the Present* (New York: The Free Press, 1980); Meredith Tax, *The Rising of the Women* (New York: Monthly Review Press, 1980); and Barbara Mayer Wertheimer, *We Were There: The Story of Working Women in America* (New York: Pantheon Books, 1977). Several older works are also still useful. These include Alice Henry, *The Trade Union Woman* (New York and London: Appleton-Century-Crofts, 1915); Helen Marot, *American Labor Unions, by a Member* (New York: Henry Holt, 1914); and Theresa Wolfson, *The Woman Worker and the Trade Unions* (New York: International, 1926).

Progressive reformers conducted numerous surveys and exposés of working conditions for women. Among the most revealing are Elizabeth Butler, *Women and the Trades: Pittsburgh, 1907–1908* (New York: Charities Publication Committee, 1909); Helen Campbell, *Prisoners of Poverty: Women Wage-Workers, Their Trades and Their Lives* (Boston: Roberts Brothers, 1890); and Mrs. John Van Vorst and Marie Van Vorst, *The Woman Who Toils: Being the Experiences of Two Gentlewomen as Factory Girls* (Garden City, NY: Doubleday, Page, 1904).

Several interesting autobiographies of workers are also available, including Agnes Nestor, *Woman's Labor Leader: Autobiography of Agnes Nestor* (Rockford, IL: Bellevue Books, 1954); Dorothy Richardson, *The Long Day: The Story of a New York Working Girl as Told by Herself* (New York: Century, 1905); and Rose Schneiderman (with Lucy Goldthwaite), *All for One* (New York: Paul S. Eriksson, Publisher, 1967).

On women and radical movements, see Mari Jo Buhle, *Women and American Socialism, 1870–1920* (Urbana: University of Illinois Press, 1981), a work that supports the interesting case that a climate of radicalism permeated late nineteenth-century America. See also Margaret Marsh, *Anarchist Women, 1870–1920* (Philadelphia: Temple University Press, 1980). For contemporary accounts, Elizabeth Gurley Flynn, *I Speak My Own Piece* (New York: Masses and Mainstream, 1955), and Mary Jones, Mary Field Parton (ed.), *Autobiography of Mother Jones* (Chicago: C.H. Kerr, 1925), are interesting, as is Ella Reeve Bloor, *We Are Many: An Autobiography by Ella Reeve Bloor* (New York: International, 1940). On Emma Goldman, discussed more fully in Chapter 3, see Richard Drinnon, *Rebel in Paradise: A Biography of Emma Goldman* (Chicago: University of Chicago Press, 1961); Emma Goldman, *Living My Life*, 2 vols. (New York: Alfred A. Knopf, 1931); and Alix Kates Shulman, *To the Barricades: The Anarchist Life of Emma Goldman* (New York: Harper & Row, 1971).

Several scholars have recently explored the Progressive anti-vice movement and the culture of prostitution in the early twentieth century. See Mark Thomas Connolly, *The Response to Prostitution in the Progressive Era* (Chapel Hill: University of North Carolina Press, 1980), and Ruth Rosen, *The Lost Sisterhood: Prostitution in America, 1900–1918* (Baltimore: Johns Hopkins University Press, 1982). Ruth Rosen (ed.), *The Mamie Papers* (Old Westbury, NY: Feminist Press, 1977), is a fascinating selection of the letters between a prostitute and a middle-class reformer. On the breakdown in Victorian culture during this period, see Lois W. Banner, *American Beauty* (New York: Alfred A. Knopf, 1983); Lewis A. Erenberg, *New York Nightlife and the Transformation of American Culture, 1890–1930* (Westport, CT: Greenwood Press, 1981); John F. Kasson, *Amusing the Million: Coney Island at the Turn of the Century* (New York: Hill & Wang, 1978); and Albert F. MacClean, Jr., *American Vaudeville as Ritual* (Lexington: University of Kentucky Press, 1965).

3

WOMEN AS ORGANIZERS AND INNOVATORS: SUFFRAGE, REFORM, AND FEMINISM, 1890–1920

BETWEEN 1890 AND the First World War, the feminist movement was vigorous and active. Historians have often interpreted these years as an era when organized women were virtually monopolized by the woman's suffrage movement. In fact, it was a period when a variety of innovative feminist activities appeared, and women's organizations proliferated. Feminists and reformers were aware of a range of problems that women were encountering in a modernizing America, and they moved in many ways to confront them. Never before had so many women belonged to so many women's organizations; not until the 1960s was feminism again so vigorous. Most organized women were social feminists. But there were radical women, too: Some concentrated their efforts on political causes; others, on women's causes. By 1914, most of the segments of the women's movement had joined together behind suffrage. But before that time, feminism looked in many directions.

SUFFRAGISM ON THE WANE

In the first decade of the twentieth century, the suffrage movement fell on hard times. The suffrage crusade had followed a difficult path since Reconstruction (1867–1877), when Congress and the nation enfranchised blacks but would not give the vote to women. In 1868, its force had been weakened by a split in the movement between the more militant wing, led by Susan B. Anthony and Elizabeth Cady Stanton, who wanted to pressure Congress into passing a suffrage amendment, and the moderate wing, led by Lucy Stone, who wanted to concentrate on passage by the states. In 1874 in *Minor v. Happersett*, the Supreme Court had added its stamp of approval to the doctrine of disfranchisement.

But even the reunion of these two factions into the National American Woman Suffrage Association (NAWSA) in 1890 did not accomplish a great deal. If anything, in the first decades of its existence, the NAWSA achieved less than the divided organizations had before. Under the auspices of the Stanton–Anthony organization, for example, the suffrage bill had been introduced into Congress in 1868. It had reached the floor of both houses each year after that date, and hearings had

A turn-of-the-century post card pokes fun at suffragists.

SUFFRAGETTE VOTE-GETTING
THE EASIEST WAY.

been held on it each year. But the NAWSA, which was dominated by Stone's group, decided to abandon the congressional campaign to concentrate on the states. The result was that after 1890, with feminist pressure removed, Congress paid little attention to the amendment. Yet the NAWSA had no better success with its state campaigns. Between 1896 and 1910, referenda on the suffrage amendment were held in only six states and were defeated in all six. In 1910, women had equal suffrage in only four states.

These failures were partly due to vigorous antisuffrage opposition. Local antisuffrage groups, often headed by socially prominent women, appeared in the late nineteenth century. In 1911, they united to form the National Association Opposed to the Further Extension of Suffrage to Women, which claimed a membership larger than that of the NAWSA.

Antisuffrage leaders presenting their case to legislators.

The organization gained political support from three powerful groups: the liquor industry, which was afraid that suffrage for women would bring prohibition; the political bosses, who were fearful that women would vote for reform politicians; and the Catholic Church, which staunchly believed that a woman's place was in the home.

The arguments of the antisuffragists also spoke powerfully to American men and women who upheld traditional values. Politics, they believed, was no place for a woman. It was, and should be, a special male preserve, central to the public sphere of behavior reserved for men. It was an exhausting activity that required long periods of time spent away from home, and it exuded the aura of underhanded practices and barroom deals, especially since most polling places in this period were set up in saloons and barbershops (to be removed to schools, churches, and firehouses after women could vote). Politics was, as suffrage leader Abigail Scott Duniway put it in the 1900s, "sacred to the aristocracy of the [male] sex."[1] The antisuffrage argument played on all the standard fears: if women held office, they would leave the home, break up the family, and take power away from men. Woman, wrote one representative antisuffragist

> has not incorporated in her nature those qualities as mystical and as holy as the life which she transmits to the world; she has not become an inspiration and the very savior of our life, in order that she may turn traitor to herself and her ideal for a paltry bit of paper and the boast that, from being man's superior, she has now become his equal.[2]

Suffrage, according to the more hysterical antisuffragists, was a revolt against "nature." Pregnant women might lose their babies; nursing mothers, their milk. Women might grow beards or be raped at the polls.

Yet the more rational antisuffragists were not necessarily conservative on issues other than women voting. Many of them were social feminists, active in reform organizations. They added a further argument to the common objections to suffrage for women. They reasoned that without the vote and without party affiliations, women could have a greater influence on legislators because their motives could not be questioned. However naive this view of political reality, the argument had a sizable impact on women's organizations like the General Federation of Women's Clubs, which refused to endorse suffrage until 1914.

The appeal of the antisuffrage argument, however, does not entirely explain the failures of the suffrage movement in the first decade of the twentieth century. Indeed, there were problems within the leadership of the movement. Decades of unsuccessful campaigning had inevitably produced ennui and discontent. By the turn of the century, leadership had passed from the founders to a generation of more moderate women. In 1892 at the age of 76, Elizabeth Cady Stanton relinquished the presidency of the NAWSA to Susan B. Anthony, who remained in the office until 1900, when she, too, retired from active work at the age of 80. In 1893, Lucy Stone died at the age of 75. Among the moderates, Anna Howard Shaw, who had been Anthony's trusted lieutenant, assumed a dominant role. In 1904, she became president of the NAWSA, a post she held until 1915. She was an unfortunate choice. Although a brilliant orator, Shaw had limited administrative skill. She was censorious and dictatorial as president and did not inspire the confidence of her associates. Backbiting and pettiness began to

Anna Howard Shaw: minister, physician, and president of the National American Woman Suffrage Association.

emerge among the NAWSA leadership, and much time was spent in internal conflict and intrigue.

Shaw and her associates primarily wanted to maintain a moderate profile—to appear as sober seekers after justice. They held conventions each year; they circulated petitions; they issued instructions to state organizations. But rather than encouraging the membership to try new directions, they followed the traditional path of trying to educate women through reasoned pamphlets and meetings. They would have nothing to do with the kind of militancy that might associate them in the public eye with radical groups, like the anarchists or the early axe-wielding, saloon-destroying members of the WCTU whom the press derided. Nor did the moderates attempt to form alliances with working-class groups that might have been their allies in counteracting the opposition of political bosses and the Catholic Church. Harriot Stanton Blatch, daughter of Elizabeth Cady Stanton and herself a skilled suffragist in New York, judged that "the old order of

*An antisuffrage meeting of the
General Federation of Women's
Clubs at the Hotel Astor in New
York City.*

suffragists had kept youngsters 'in their place,' " "had left working
women alone," and had not " 'bothered' with men bent on politics."[3]

The position of the middle generation of suffragists was not entirely
wrong-headed. Their conservatism of action, which was matched by
equally conservative arguments in their speeches and writings, played
a large role in defusing American fears about giving women the vote.
Stanton and Anthony had argued that women deserved the vote
because, like men, they had a "natural right" to it. The next generation

contended that women, as mothers, needed the vote to protect the home and that the nation needed the votes of native Anglo-Saxon women to counteract the supposedly pernicious effects of immigrant and black males' votes. The argument from "natural right" appeared to challenge conventional male–female roles. The new "argument from expediency," as historian Aileen Kraditor has called it, suggested no such direct threat. President M. Carey Thomas of Bryn Mawr College wrote that in 1908, when she was instrumental in founding the National College Equal Suffrage League, the subject of suffrage was still so inflammatory that even college students hesitated to discuss it, while conventions of the Association of Collegiate Alumnae regularly barred the subject from their agendas. Within a few years, these reservations had vanished, and suffrage had become respectable among the academic community. Thomas suggested that the change had occurred to a large extent because the old arguments based on women's right to the vote were replaced by the argument that women needed the vote to protect the home and to become effective reformers.[4]

In any case, between 1890 and the First World War, the suffrage movement was only one woman's cause among many, and the majority of organized women probably did not support it. Before 1912, wrote Rheta Childe Dorr, the suffrage movement was dead. "No newspaper or magazine editor would have printed an article on the subject. No politician gave it a thought."[5] Dorr may have exaggerated, but her comment underscores the fact that issues other than suffrage held the attention of organized women in the early years of this century.

FEMINISM AND PROGRESSIVISM: A CASE OF GIVE AND TAKE

Central among these concerns was a renewed interest in social justice for women and the disadvantaged. This social feminism was a natural outgrowth of the new freedoms for women under the law and the new opportunities for women in education and the professions. It also stemmed from the general climate of social reform, in which people were widely questioning the benefits of unregulated industrialism and urbanization. Membership in voluntary associations formed to promote social welfare was flourishing. The debate over the nature of the American democratic order was vigorous and penetrating. Both Progressives and reformers to the left of them could not help but add women's oppression to their list of social injustices in America. Moreover, like women in the abolition movement of the early nineteenth century and in the civil rights movement of the 1960s, socialist and Progressive women came to see that their own condition was reflected in part in the problems of the disadvantaged whom they worked to help. Muckraking journals, too, were eager to print feminist exposés of the lives of working women and of prostitutes, as well as articles pertaining to the general oppression of women. The subject was fresh and vital and a stimulus to the reform impulse.

As much as Progressivism sparked feminism, feminism itself played an important role in the Progressive movement. Only recently has the participation of women in Progressivism begun to be explored. In the past, historians viewed Progressivism as a movement of status-conscious professionals attempting to re-create an older, simpler society or as an attempt on the part of certain business interests to gain favorable legislation. But from the work of historians like David Thelen, on Wisconsin Progressivism, and Allen Davis, on the settlement houses, a new interpretation of the period is emerging. This interpretation stresses reform aspects such as conservation, pure-food-and-drug acts, child-welfare legislation, kindergartens, and educational innovation, and finds a main source of the reform impulse in women's interest in expanding their roles and providing viable lives for their families in an increasingly industrial and urban America.

The Organizations: Growth and Changing Goals

Since the early nineteenth century and especially after the Civil War, women had been organizing in associations concerned with social-welfare issues. The Woman's Christian Temperance Union, for example, headed between 1878 and 1896 by charismatic Frances Willard, put reform causes at the forefront of its program. In addition to its better-known campaigns for the prohibition of alcohol and for stricter moral codes, its leadership publicized the benefits of exercise and of rational dress for women and agitated for kindergartens in the public schools, for police matrons to serve women prisoners, and for child-labor laws. Willard secured WCTU support for the Knights of Labor and for the peace movement; she herself was influential in the reform-minded Prohibition party. In 1896, Willard's conservative opponents gained control of the WCTU and made temperance its main concern.

But during Willard's years of leadership, the WCTU educated many home-bound, rural, and small-town women to a sense of social responsibility. Women often joined the WCTU and from there became involved in women's suffrage and progressive reform causes. As Willard herself put it, their "consciousness" of themselves and of their society was raised.[6]

Similarly, the women's clubs that flourished in the late nineteenth and early twentieth centuries often drew up reform platforms and took a feminist stance. Established in the 1870s as lecture and discussion clubs with an emphasis on art, literature, and travel, women's clubs were slowly drawn into social reform. This had partly to do with the influence of the widely read journalist Jane Croly, who wrote under the pseudonym Jennie June. Croly is credited with having founded the first women's club, Sorosis, in New York City in 1868, after women journalists had been excluded from a banquet in honor of the visiting English author Charles Dickens. Like Frances Willard, Croly interested many women's clubs in feminism and reform. In other cases, clubs adopted social-welfare causes in response to local conditions. In numerous clubs, a similar pattern was repeated. Lectures on art and beauty stimulated drives to beautify cities by planting flowers and grass; these drives, in turn, generated an interest in public parks and playgrounds and, ultimately, in a variety of municipal agencies and functions bearing on the health and happiness of the family. One mother's concerns over her children's schooling might lead to an investigation of the local school system or to the introduction of kindergartens—the German innovation that promised more effective education for young children and more free time for their mothers. Or, as one observer, explaining women's advocacy of improved street cleaning, commented, "It is their dresses which must sweep up the debris."[7] In 1892, Jane Croly, among others, organized the General Federation of Women's Clubs, and the national organization increased the pressure on local clubs to undertake reform causes.

Women's clubs made headway in many areas of reform between the 1890s and the First World War. The Chicago Civic Club and the Boston Women's Municipal League led successful drives in their cities to raise investment capital to buy and improve tenement houses to show that landlords could improve slum conditions and still make a profit. In New York City, as elsewhere, the Women's Municipal League acted as a watchdog group to ensure that existing laws about tenement housing

A kindergarten class, 1914.

were enforced. They also lobbied for the extension and tightening of these laws. Pressure exerted on state legislatures by federations of women's clubs in Iowa, Ohio, Pennsylvania, and Michigan was largely responsible for the creation of systems of juvenile courts. In most states, club federations worked for improvements in penal systems. Many observers credited the passage of the federal Pure Food and Drug Act of 1906 to a letter-writing campaign coordinated by women's organizations throughout the nation.

White Anglo-Saxon women were not the only women to organize for community improvement. Within the Jewish community, the National Council of Jewish Women, founded in 1893, encouraged the adoption of social service as a goal of American Jewish organizations. By the 1900s, Zionism, the movement to establish a separate Jewish state, was strong among American Jews. In 1912, Hadassah, the woman's Zionist organization, was formed to provide funds for medical services for the Jewish community in Palestine. After the Civil War, black women, too, founded local clubs, and these clubs federated into the National Association of Colored Women in 1895. Even more than among the white women's clubs (which generally excluded blacks), the primary purpose of the black organization was social welfare. The association was the first social-service agency for blacks in the nation. It was founded nearly 15 years before the better-known, male-dominated organizations—the National Association for the Advancement of Colored People (NAACP) and the Urban League.

That black women would take such a leadership role in social welfare was natural, because they often had played key roles in black churches and other voluntary organizations. Local black women's clubs established day nurseries, kindergartens, playgrounds, old people's homes, and homes for female juvenile delinquents, while they worked for better housing, schools, and employment opportunities for black women. They did what they could to challenge southern sexual mores, including the view that black women were naturally promiscuous, although southern repression dictated that most black organizations follow Booker T. Washington's accommodative position rather than assume a rebellious stance. When journalist Ida Wells-Barnett violated this principle to write a series of articles in her Memphis newspaper attacking the lynching of black men for sexual crimes they did not commit, her office was bombed. Fearing for her life, she fled to Chicago, where she became involved in social-welfare work in the black community and was one of the founders of the NAACP.

The broad spectrum of women's groups in the Progressive period included a number of associations with a variety of programs. The Young Women's Christian Association (YWCA) spent its funds on recreation and housing for working women. The Association of Collegiate Alumnae worked for municipal reform and supported the efforts of settlement-house workers. Even the Daughters of the American Revolution undertook letter-writing campaigns on behalf of conservation and child-labor reform. Voluntarism was characteristic of America's years of unsettling urbanization, immigration, and industrialization. But what was unique about the new women's organizations was the commitment of so many of them to social reform. According to one observer in 1906, this interest in the public welfare was not characteristic of men's clubs.[8]

Women's participation in social reform took many forms. An interest in cooperative housing had been a subtheme of feminist thought since the days of Robert Owen's New Harmony and other utopian communities of the 1830s, and it had been invigorated by the literary utopians of the 1890s—especially Edward Bellamy, whose *Looking*

*A meeting of the National Board
of the Young Women's Christian
Association, 1914.*

Backward powerfully influenced Charlotte Perkins Gilman. Architects
and urban planners designed ideal urban cooperative communities,
although few actually were built. The concept of providing public
kitchens in slum communities generated considerable momentum; in
many ways the settlement houses represented the most successful
achievement of the cooperationists.

Women not only supported the Progressive movement in clubs and
organizations, but they also took on leadership roles individually. For
example, Albion Fellows Bacon of Indiana, who was married and the
mother of four children, began her reform career as a volunteer member of the sanitation committee of Evansville's Civic Improvement Society
and then worked as a "friendly visitor" (the predecessor of the modern
social worker) for Evansville's associated charities. Like many Progressives, Bacon decided that inadequate housing lay at the heart of
poverty. She single-handedly launched a statewide campaign of publicity and organization for the regulation of housing, a goal she achieved
in 1913. Katherine Bement Davis, a Vassar graduate with a doctorate
in sociology, headed a Philadelphia settlement house for some years

before she became superintendent of the new Women's Reformatory in Bedford Hills, New York, in 1901. Under her superintendency, according to historian Blake McKelvey, the Bedford Hills institution was "the most active penal experiment station in America."[9] In 1914, Davis became Commissioner of Corrections in New York City, and three years later she took the job of general secretary of the Bureau of Social Hygiene of the Rockefeller Foundation; in this position, she authored studies of prostitution, narcotics addiction, and general sexual behavior.

That women like Bacon and Davis were able to pursue careers in reform is perhaps not as surprising in the long run as it might seem. Dr. Alice Hamilton (a pioneer in the field of industrial medicine, which focused on industrial pollution as the presumed source of many illnesses among workers) contended that her sex was a distinct advantage in her work. She explained that it seemed natural to most Americans that a woman should put the health of the workman ahead of the value of his product. Such impulses in a man, she contended, would have been interpreted as unmanly sentimentalism or radicalism.[10]

Women also began to assume leadership roles in male-dominated Progressive organizations. At first, men did not accept women easily into their midst. In 1894, Lillian Wald (prominent among women Progressives for founding the Henry Street Settlement in New York City and for her attempts to improve the status of the nursing profession, to which she belonged) reported that she had been dropped from the list of potential members of a New York mayoral commission on industrial safety due to the objections of male members. They feared that if a woman were present, proper etiquette would not permit them to take off their coats and roll up their shirt sleeves.[11] Within a few years, such attitudes had weakened, and women of the prominence of Wald were often appointed to reform commissions. Even the vice commissions, which dealt with the delicate question of prostitution, included at least one woman in their membership, as if the presence of a woman would legitimate their reform endeavor and earn them credibility in the eyes of women's organizations.

The Settlement Houses

Within the Progressive movement, women were often innovators. Nowhere was this more apparent than in their leadership in settlement houses. Jane Addams at Hull House and Lillian Wald at Henry

Jane Addams, who founded
Hull House (a settlement house
in the slums of Chicago),
working with neighborhood
children.

Street were the two most famous women settlement workers, but there were hundreds more. For the most part, they were first-generation college graduates, fired with a sense of dedication to women and to humanity and determined to prove to a skeptical world that educating women was not socially wasteful, that women could be as forceful and as innovative as men. Faced after college with the choices of marrying, making their way in professional and graduate schools that still discriminated against women, or taking low-status positions as schoolteachers or nurses, they responded with typical American ingenuity. They invented their own profession, founding houses in the midst of urban slums where they could live and provide social services to the poor. Almost immediately, settlement work became respectable and, unlike ordinary social work, even glamorous. It perfectly fitted women's traditional role of service—and men did not control it.

For many young women and men, settlement work was an interlude between college and marriage. Like the Peace Corps of the 1960s, it was for some a brief experiment in idealism. Some women married male co-workers and adopted more conventional life styles. Others became regular social workers or entered a profession. A few, like Jane Addams and Lillian Wald, remained at the institutions they had founded throughout their lives and reached out from these power bases to influence mayors, legislators, and the general public. Other settlement-house workers, like Florence Kelley, spent some time in settlement houses before moving into positions with other reform organizations. A few were appointed to middle-level government positions. Jane Addams's Hull House in Chicago easily held the record for such appointments. Whether inspired by Addams's example or by their own ambition and sense of mission, many of her close associates became prominent Progressive reformers. Julia Lathrop became the first woman member of the Illinois State Board of Charities and the first director of the Children's Bureau of the federal government, established in 1912. In this position, she was followed by Grace Abbott. Sophonisba Breckinridge became dean of the University of Chicago's pioneer School of Civics and Philanthropy, Mary McDowall was elected the first president of the Chicago branch of the Women's Trade Union League, and Florence Kelley was appointed head of the National Consumers' League. All of these women originally served at Hull House.

A Measure of Success

Women settlement-house workers and social feminists were particularly concerned about women, children, and the home. They were instrumental in the formation of the Children's Bureau and in the drafting of child-labor laws. The settlements in particular provided special services for women, including homemaking and visiting-nurse services, instruction in domestic skills, and nurseries and kindergartens for children of working mothers. Settlement workers, social workers, and women's clubs investigated employment agencies, assisted newly arrived immigrants, fought for better treatment of servants, and in some cities, established legal agencies to help women enforce payment of wages, prevent violations of contracts, and obtain divorces.

They worked with vice commissions to investigate prostitution and campaigned for the open discussion of sex as a way of ending both prostitution and venereal disease. Particularly through the Consumers' League and the Women's Trade Union League, they made efforts to improve working conditions for women.

To what extent social feminists succeeded in the overall area of social reform is debatable. The most recent study of Progressivism in Wisconsin leaves the impression that women revolutionized the social services of the state. However, a detailed 1909 study of services for working women in Pittsburgh, where there were numerous clubs, settlements, and YWCAs, showed that only about 2 percent of all working women were being reached.[12] The most recent study of kindergartens in Massachusetts contends that relatively few were actually opened and that they offered little more than part-time preparation for the rigid discipline to be encountered in the elementary grades.[13] Yet changing the status quo is never easy. Describing her frustration at being unable to accomplish more, Lillian Wald in her autobiography detailed the years of painstaking effort it took just to close some New York City streets to traffic a few hours each day so that children could play safely.[14]

Yet if, in the final analysis, the work of Progressive women for municipal reform, for prison relief, for pure-food-and-drug acts, for public assistance to mothers who were heads of households is judged to be minor, these social feminists nevertheless left an important legacy—the proof that women could be leaders and innovators in society.

THE RADICALS

The social feminists attempted to achieve reform within existing political and social institutions. The radical feminists, although they advocated many of the same causes, were more militant in their orientation, their ideas, and their actions. Their outspoken statements contributed greatly to the flavor of the age.

A Ferment of New Ideas

Crusaders like Margaret Sanger, who fought for birth control, and Charlotte Perkins Gilman, who called for the building of large apartment complexes with general kitchens, cleaning services, and nurseries staffed by professionals to relieve housewives' burdens, were con-

Volunteers selling copies of the
Birth Control Review.
Margaret Sanger's pioneering
publication first appeared in
1917.

tinually in the public eye. Their demands were supported by lesser-
known but no less vocal men and women who argued for the opening
of every occupation to women, for the equalization of men's and wom-
en's wages, for unrestricted divorce, for the retention of maiden names
in marriage, and for the adoption of simple, uniform clothing that
would end fashion's tyranny over women.[15] A few radicals even called
for the communalization of social institutions and espoused free sexual
relations. For example, men and women in the anarchist movement
did not marry on principle; instead, they lived in monogamous unions,
but both partners preserved the freedom to have sexual relations with
whomever they chose. In print and in public lectures, Emma Goldman
broadcast their ideas.

A scene from the 1907 production of Henrik Ibsen's A Doll's House, *starring Nazimova as Nora and Roland Young as Nils Krogstad.*

The feminist movement, then as in the 1960s, was international in scope. Major foreign writers lent their weight to native arguments. Swedish feminist Ellen Key suggested that mothers raise their children alone and that the state pay them to do. English feminist Cicely Hamilton fulminated against the structure of marriage, which she viewed as an economic arrangement for women—a trade that they entered for lack of any other. Olive Schreiner of South Africa, in her influential *Women and Labor* (1911), turned Darwinian emphases upside down by arguing that only strong and self-reliant women could bear healthy children and that the race was destroying itself by giving middle-class women nothing to do. Schreiner coined the much-used term *"sex-parasitism"* to describe the position of married women.

This ferment of feminist ideas was reinforced in the public mind by plays and novels that explored the relationship of women to men and to marriage. The realist novel was in vogue, and as presented in the novels of Susan Glaspell, Neith Boyce, and Charlotte Perkins Gilman, its message was openly feminist. Among plays, Henrik Ibsen's *A Doll's House* (1879), the portrait of a woman who slowly gains awareness of her oppression in a traditional marriage, had a striking impact on audiences in the United States and in Europe. George Bernard Shaw's plays about conflicts between strong-minded men and women—*Man and Superman, Saint Joan, Pygmalion*—also were produced and discussed throughout the United States. Many lesser playwrights imitated Ibsen and Shaw. Author and journalist Ben Hecht complained that "novelists and playwrights were knocking the wind out of the public by presenting radical heroines who had been to bed with some man before their marriage."[16] One of these plays—a minor vehicle entitled *Hindle Wakes*—was a hit on Broadway. The plot turned on a standard seduction theme. A girl spent a weekend in the country with the son of her father's employer. When discovered, the boy, in time-honored fashion, offered to marry her "to save her honor." She refused, and all were amazed. "Why did you go on the weekend?" she asked her paramour. "I'm a man," he replied. "It was just my fancy of the moment." "Well," she countered, in a statement that must have shocked audiences one step removed from Victorian prejudices, "I'm a woman. It was just *my* fancy of the moment."[17]

A New Breed of Scholars

Feminist scholars added their contribution to the battle for women's emancipation. Much like feminists in the 1970s, they scanned the past and the present for evidence of female superiority. They focused on the eras like the Middle Ages and the Renaissance, in which women played influential roles. Emily Putnam (who was allowed to retain her position as dean of Barnard College when she married but was forced to resign after she had a child) produced the prototype of such works in *The Lady* (1910), an historical analysis of the upper-class female role over the ages. Putnam explored the subtle stages of power and oppression through which woman, as cultural heroine, had passed: from Greek orientalism to medieval chivalry; from the chatelaine of the manor to the intellectual and voluptuary of the eighteenth-century European salon. Putnam ended her book with a discussion of the eighteenth-century English "bluestocking," the originator of modern feminism, and her oppressed contemporary, the lady of the southern antebellum slave plantation. The former, according to Putnam, presaged the future; the latter was an ominous reminder of the extent to which women could become the victims of a caste system.

Other feminist scholars looked beyond the discipline of history. Some authorities in the field of science argued that men, too, underwent periodic emotional disturbances based on bodily changes similar to those that occur during the menstrual cycle. On the basis of new medical and biological evidence that women were better able to resist pain and disease than men, that they lived longer, and that they had greater powers of endurance, some feminists theorized that women were, in fact, superior to men in a number of ways. It was only due to men's superior physical strength that they, rather than women, had become the world's leaders and conquerors. New anthropological knowledge about primitive societies provided some women scholars with data for a new, feminist interpretation of history. They speculated that the earliest societies had been matriarchal and that it was not the evolutionary inferiority of women that had led to the creation of patriarchal societies, but rather men's irrational and inherent drives for power and conquest. Charlotte Perkins Gilman was critical of female passivity, but she judged the male-dominated world to be an evolutionary stage that had produced a host of ills, not the least of which was warfare. In war, wrote Gilman, "we find maleness in its absurdest extremes. Here is to be studied the whole gamut of basic masculinity, from the initial instinct of combat, through every form of glorious ostentation, with the loudest possible accompaniment of noise."[18]

Feminist Action Groups: A Faint Voice

Despite their literary and scholarly endeavors, militant feminists did not translate ideology into action. There was no National Organization for Women; there were few local feminist action groups. Several groups did emerge in New York City, but they did not spread to other areas of the nation. One of these was formed by Henrietta Rodman, a schoolteacher associated with the Greenwich Village leftists of the prewar years. Her group, the Feminist Alliance, secured repeal of the prohibition against married schoolteachers in New York City. The alliance also formed committees of doctors and lawyers, who wrote lead-

Author Charlotte Perkins Gilman, who advocated that professionals take over housework.

ing law and medical schools to demand an end to restrictions on the admission of women. These feminists discussed, but never pursued, the possibility of constructing one of Charlotte Perkins Gilman's apartment houses. For the most part, their actions were piecemeal. But their membership was small, many were career women with limited leisure time, and many ultimately were drawn into the suffrage movement and were persuaded that it took priority.

A second New York feminist group, called Heterodoxy, was even less inclined toward activism than the Feminist Alliance. Its members included Charlotte Perkins Gilman, Rheta Childe Dorr, Elizabeth Gurley Flynn, and many other leading women of the day. They met to discuss their common problems and to give and gain mutual support. After attending a meeting of Heterodoxy, one observer wrote that its members seemed to be "in church, that they were worshipping at some holy shrine, their voices and their eyes were full of religious excitement."[19]

Yet many of these women were divided in their political and professional loyalties. Elizabeth Gurley Flynn was a socialist; Rheta Childe

Elizabeth Gurley Flynn addresses striking textile workers in Lawrence, Massachusetts, in 1912.

Dorr, a professional journalist active in women's suffrage. Charlotte Perkins Gilman had a limited capacity for leadership. She repeatedly suffered from depression, and although she was moderately active in the suffrage movement, she devoted her professional career to writing and to feminist scholarship. Margaret Sanger and Emma Goldman were both difficult personalities and easily clashed with other women leaders. Goldman, too, was suspicious of the women's movement, partly because her anarchist principles led her to focus on society, not on women in particular, and partly because she did not approve of the feminists' antimale rhetoric and their arguments about women's superiority. In the end, leadership to unify women around a common cause came not from the radicals, but from the suffragists.

In general, however, militant feminism was a threat to the majority of Americans. They could accept most Progressive women reformers because, as one analyst put it, most of them were "good wives and mothers" who "personally deserved public esteem" and who had not taken up such "eccentricities of base quality" as free love.[20] But Americans were suspicious of behavior and ideology that deviated from the middle-class norm. Charlotte Perkins Gilman was vilified by the press for divorcing her husband and later sending their daughter to live with him; Margaret Sanger, who underwent a similar experience, did not fare any better. Playwright Margaret Anderson invited Emma Goldman to dinner at her Chicago apartment, and the next day the manager of the building informed her of numerous complaints from other tenants. "Emma Goldman has been here. We can't allow such a thing," he admonished. "By the public," commented Anderson, Goldman "was considered a monster, an exponent of free love and bombs."[21] The support of the militant feminists added strength to the coalition of women that achieved women's suffrage and moral support to women and men who were trying to establish new roles in their own lives. But the opposition to fundamental reform for women was strong. It took Margaret Sanger, for example, 20 years of determined agitation to achieve the legalization of birth control. Besides, as so often has been true in the history of American feminism, other issues seemed more pressing than the achievement of equality for women.

SHAKY GROUNDS FOR ARGUMENT

Seen in retrospect, there were weaknesses in the ideologies and action of both the social feminists and the radical feminists. At the time, these deficiences were not readily apparent, but they contributed importantly to the decline of feminism in the 1920s. Most of these weaknesses stemmed from the fact that both groups were enmeshed in certain ingrained sexual and cultural attitudes. In their own day, these women seemed to be innovators and radicals; to a different generation after the First World War, their message was not so obvious.

Women's Frailty and Special Legislation

The attachment of many organized women of this age to the campaign for special legislation for working women provides insight into their underlying conservatism. For example, the Women's Trade Union League worked to organize women into unions, but it also lobbied for the passage by state legislatures of maximum-hour and minimum-wage laws that would apply only to women workers. Even socialist Elizabeth Gurley Flynn thought that working women needed special legislation and that an equal rights amendment, which would void this legislation, would be against their best interests. Behind this campaign lay certain pragmatic arguments. First, women were difficult to organize; second, special legislation for women might force employers to improve conditions for male workers, too; and third, the courts had overruled special legislation for men on the grounds that it violated the common-law doctrine of "freedom of contract" between worker and employer, but they might be willing to validate such legislation for women.

But behind the special legislation campaign also lay some very conservative reasoning. Those who supported it usually argued that the difficulties of factory labor were greater for women than for men, not only because women were physically weaker but also because they were potential mothers. In 1908, officials of the Consumers' League prepared the brief for lawyer Louis Brandeis on the basis of which the Supreme court rendered its first decision upholding a minimum-wage law *(Muller v. Oregon)*. They declared that "besides anatomical and physiological differences, physicians are agreed that women are in general weaker than men in muscular strength and in nervous energy."[22] Overlooking the contradictory conclusions of feminist scholars, the Consumers' League cited contemporary medical literature indicating that women who worked strained nerves and bodies and bore unhealthy children. The Court agreed with the League. Yet this argument implied that men did not need such legislation, at a time when the conditions of work were abysmal for both men and women, and also gave added weight to the arguments of those antifeminists who were convinced that a woman's anatomy was her destiny.

Housekeepers in Government—and Out

The social feminist rationale for the participation of women in reform and in government was similarly antifeminist in implication. Social feminists generally argued that women took a special interest in legislation for education, clean streets, and public parks because these issues were intimately related to successful family life. This was a central theme in the writings of Jane Addams. "As society grows more complicated," she wrote, "it is necessary that women shall extend her sense of responsibility to many things outside of her home if she would continue to preserve the home in its entirety."[23] She contended that "city housekeeping has failed partly because women, the traditional housekeepers, have not been consulted as to its multiform activities."[24]

The problem with this argument was not that it was ineffective or even untrue but that, as in the campaign for special legislation, it was based on the traditional image of the woman. Moreover, there was a counteractive side to this view of women as competent housekeepers. The belief was growing that mechanization and new scientific knowledge about, for example, child-rearing and the effective utilization of time had made homemaking itself so complex that women needed extensive training to manage it properly. The unorganized domestic-science movement of the nineteenth century was becoming the highly organized home-economics movement of the twentieth century. In the 1900s, social feminists regarded it with favor. It laid claim to being scientific in an age that celebrated science; its advocates in universities were important women who were often friends of social feminists; and it was true that most American women did not know much about proper nutrition, clothing, or time-saving housekeeping procedures.

Nor were its practitioners in those early years without a feminist rationale. Ellen Richards (the first woman graduate of the Massachusetts Institute of Technology and a founder, in 1908, and an early president of the American Home Economics Association) believed, according to her biographer, that "because women had clung to antiquated ways of doing housework . . . and had failed to take hold of their own problems in a masterful way, they were handicapped when they tried to do systematic work outside the home."[25] Yet seen in retrospect, the ultimate message that training in home economics conveyed to the general public was not that women would become so highly trained in the home that they could leave it to become involved in public affairs, but that the job of running a home was so all-encompassing that it could be mastered only over a lifetime and then with difficulty. The conservative argument of the social feminists underscored this point.

Suffrage as a Cure-All

Similar ideological weaknesses were to be found in the central arguments for women's suffrage. The argument that women needed the

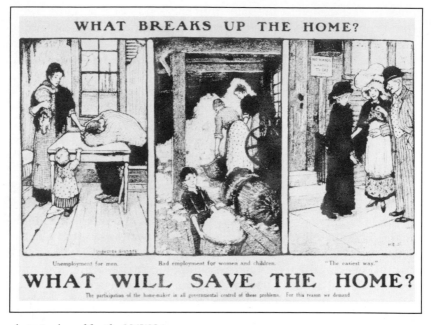

*A poster issued by the NAWSA
to gain working-class women's
support for suffrage.*

vote to protect the home undoubtedly helped to make suffrage respectable, just as it helped to disarm the opposition to women's participation in reform and to the special legislation campaign. It nonetheless implied that women's real place was in the home. "Women are the mothers of the race," wrote Inez Milholland, "and as such are admittedly more concerned than anyone else with all that goes to protect life."[26] For this reason, she argued, women should have the vote. Milholland—a young lawyer and Vassar graduate, known for her beauty—gained widespread attention in 1912 when she rode a horse at the head of a New York City suffrage parade, inviting comparisons to Joan of Arc and Helen of Troy.

Women's use of the vote to effect social change was also subject to interpretation. A central theme in the suffrage argument was that once women could vote, social reformation would ensue. What was on one level a practical argument, designed both to attract social feminists to

Inez Milholland, lawyer and journalist, leading a suffragist parade.

suffragism and to express the understanding of realistic feminists that suffrage was only a beginning step toward the emancipation of women, at times took on inflated, utopian dimensions. Thus, suffragists argued that women, as voters, would stop corruption and vice, end all discrimination against women, and prevent wars. The argument itself reflected the positions of both militant feminists and conservative antisuffragists. Both had argued that women were superior to men in gentleness and compassion. Antifeminists used this belief to support the argument that woman's place was in the home; feminists turned the argument the other way, but it still enshrined the same assumptions.

The danger in the militant assumption that women were natural reformers lay not only in its proximity to the conservative position but also in the fact that if it proved incorrect in a concrete situation, the feminists would appear to be foolish victims of irrational "feminine" logic. And insofar as feminism in general was identified with the suf-

THE POISON AND THE ANTIDOTE

A drawing in Judge *magazine in 1920 predicts the downfall of political corruption.*

frage movement—and by 1920, the identification was strong—the entire feminist movement would appear to be composed of dreamers. To a degree, this is what happened. It was apparent after the passage of the suffrage amendment in 1920 that women did not vote as a block, that they seemed to vote for the same party and candidates as their husbands and fathers, and that the suffragists had been incorrect. This failure of women to follow the feminist prediction was no small blow to feminism itself.

Sex Versus Soul

During the prewar years, feminist positions on the issues of sexuality, marriage, and motherhood were also contradictory. "We are learning to be frank about sex," Inez Milholland wrote in 1913, with seeming forthrightness. "And through all this frankness runs a definite tendency toward an assault on the dual standard of morality and an assertion of sex rights on the part of the women."[27] But what exactly did this assertion mean? To Margaret Sanger, for example, it meant women's recognition of their sensuality, of their ability to enjoy sex. Sanger was, according to Mabel Dodge Luhan (a wealthy literary patron and friend of radicals), "the first person I ever knew who was openly an ardent propagandist for the joys of the flesh."[28]

Other feminists were not so certain that sensuality was a key to woman's happiness. Many feminists, living in an age before Freudian theories interpreted sex as a human necessity, preferred celibacy. Unmarried women often found emotional fulfillment in friendships with women. Reminiscences of professional women who had never married express little regret. For romantic love and family devotion, these women substituted devotion to a cause and the close friendship of other women. They participated in the "women's separate culture" of the age.

Many feminists were suspicious of sensuality on other grounds. A major theme in the thought of nineteenth-century reformers—from free-love advocates to leaders of the WCTU—had been that excessive male sensuality lay at the heart of female oppression, that man's inability to control his sexual urges had produced extensive prostitution and widespread venereal disease. Such attitudes continued into the twentieth century. Charlotte Perkins Gilman wrote about the dangers of "excessive sex indulgence,"[29] and social feminists campaigned to make men sexually continent rather than to make women sexually free. These women wanted what they called a "single standard" of morality. It was not the monogamous marriage that they wanted to destroy or woman's sensuality that they wanted to promote; they wished to make of marriage a spiritual union.

"No one," wrote Inez Milholland, "least of all the advanced feminist thinkers, questions the imperative beauty and value of romantic love. Indeed, the hope is that marriage, far from being undermined or destroyed, can be made real and lasting."[30] Rheta Childe Dorr envisioned a time when marriage would become a matter of "soul selection" and would approach the "sacredness of a sacrament."[31] While preaching what seemed to them a revolutionary message, the feminists were also resurrecting the ideal of passionate attachment to personal relationships that had formed the core of women's romantic

THE
LADIES'
HOME
JOURNAL

ROMANCE
NUMBER

longings throughout the nineteenth century. As the feminists described the emotion of love in their writings, its ennobling qualities became clear; but translated into popular terms, the feminists' vision served to reinforce the version of sexuality found in magazines and movies, which predicated relationships on physical longing and saw woman's life as incomplete without a man's love.

Feminists of all persuasions also agreed that the chief fulfillment of a woman's life was motherhood. According to Ellen Key, "Women's best qualities . . . are inseparably bound up with the motherhood in her nature."[32] Emma Goldman wrote, "Motherhood is the highest fulfillment of woman's nature."[33] And Charlotte Perkins Gilman echoed her: Woman must "understand that, in the line of physical evolution, motherhood is the highest process."[34]

Seen from one point of view, such sentiments were indeed radical. They implied a natural superiority of women that extended beyond the traditional notions of moral superiority into the biological realm and indicated that women might embark on a permanent existence, living with children and other women separate from men. Inez Milholland asserted that the woman's movement implied the most genuinely "radical revolution . . . of all history; for the relation of the sexes is the very material out of which the fabric of life is spun and woven."[35] Ellen Key contended that the women's revolution would "finally surpass in fanaticism any war of religion or race."[36] Yet ideas about the superiority of motherhood—together with feminist advocacy of special legislation, women's moral superiority, and a "single standard" of morality—were damaging to the entire feminist position, because they adhered to the same sex stereotypes that had plagued women's reforms from the beginning.

TWO GENERATIONS

Before the First World War all feminists were not of one mind concerning the issues of organization, sexuality, and woman's nature. By 1910, two groups—one older and one younger—had emerged. The older generation, leaders of the suffrage movement and the settlement houses, subscribed to conservative ideas about sexuality and were

What more can a woman want?

primarily interested in ending discrimination against women in public spheres of activity. The younger generation—many of them dedicated careerists—were sexually more liberal and, according to one observer, used conservative arguments because they were effective, not because younger women necessarily believed them.[37]

More than anything else, however, the younger feminists were concerned with women's internal, psychological liberation. They argued that gaining the vote or entering the professions did not necessarily guarantee that women would feel differently about themselves or that they would achieve personal liberation. A psychological revolution, they argued, not only a social one, was needed. At Heterodoxy, for example, formal political papers were presented, but most of the discussions centered around the difficulties encountered in individual women's lives.

The ideas of these younger women encompassed both radical and conservative implications. Many were Socialist Party members. They seized on the new term "feminism" to describe their ideas and to differentiate themselves from the older "woman's rights" advocates. They particularly praised the writings of Ellen Key, who argued that men and women had different natures and that motherhood should be the center of a woman's life. In one of those curious interminglings of radicalism and conservatism characteristic of this era, none other than Theodore Roosevelt (who enflamed the decade's nativism by accusing educated women of engaging in "race suicide" because they were not marrying and were practicing birth control when they did) praised Key's writings, seemingly oblivious to the fact that she called for the abolition of the patriarchal family. What the "new feminists" liked about Key was her emphasis on the psychological dimensions of experience.

Yet how to combine marriage and motherhood with a career was beginning to concern them, and this question would become central to the exploration of self-development and personal life that would occupy the mainstream of American feminist thought in the 1920s. On the one hand, an emphasis on emotion and individual experience portended the possibility of a reorientation of the female psyche in America; on the other, it created the potential for diffusing women's focus on formal organization and the public sphere. In the 1920s, the latter situation would prove to be precisely the case, but women's sense of themselves in that decade underwent no particular revolution.

SUFFRAGE ACHIEVED

Such ideological weaknesses were hardly apparent as the twentieth century approached its third decade. The suffrage crusade was emerging from its doldrums, and the women's movement appeared to be stronger and more unified than ever before. Three factors were largely responsible. First, a generation of new suffrage leaders, many of whom had lived in England and had observed the militant suffragist tactics there, began to bring new ideas and new energy to the organization. Second, social feminists who believed that reform ought to receive priority found conservative suffrage rhetoric appealing; they learned that votes, not arguments, swayed politicians. Third, by the second decade of the twentieth century, Progressives increasingly came to regard women's suffrage as part of their program, and the suffrage movement gained strength from its identification with the popular reform movement. Between 1910 and 1914, six additional states—Illinois, Washington, California, Arizona, Kansas, and Oregon—gave the vote to women.

A United Front

By 1914, most activist women had united around suffrage as the central, common feminist concern. The Woman's National Committee of the Socialist party, for example, came to devote the bulk of its time to women's suffrage. In 1914, the General Federation of Women's Clubs, a last holdout, endorsed the measure. The suffrage coalition was extensive; it included women from a multitude of groups and backgrounds. Jane Addams, who was active for some years in the NAWSA, provided a vivid picture of the variety of its supporters and the reasons for their support when she wrote that the association was joined by

> a church society of hundreds of Lutheran women; . . . by organizations of working women who had keenly felt the need of the municipal franchise in order to secure for their workshops the most rudimentary sanitation and the consideration which the vote alone obtains for workingmen; by federations of mothers' meetings, who were interested in clean milk and the extension of kindergartens; by property-owning women, who had been powerless against taxation; by organizations of professional women, of university students, and of collegiate alumnae; and by women's clubs interested in municipal reforms.[38]

Tactics and Techniques

The new group of suffragist leaders first appeared in New York state in about 1910. There they revived flagging local organizations, introduced new lobbying techniques, standardized membership lists, and established a state headquarters. They actively sought out contacts with working-class groups. Above all, they introduced the suffrage parade—a striking innovation that gained national attention. Americans were accustomed to political parades and to solidarity marches of ethnic, fraternal, and religious groups. But rarely had a protest organization taken to the streets in a controlled demonstration.

In addition to the New York group (which included Rheta Childe Dorr and Harriot Stanton Blatch), Carrie Chapman Catt and Alice Paul were crucial to the new suffrage strategy. Catt, an older woman who had been president of the NAWSA between 1900 and 1904, resigned from the post to move to England due to ill health, leadership tensions in the organization, and an invitation to become president of the new International Woman Suffrage Association. By 1915, Catt had returned to the United States, where she was again elected president of the NAWSA. Alice Paul had also been living in England, as a student and an active participant in the British suffrage movement. A woman of strong will and ambition, Paul found it difficult to play a subordinate role in the NAWSA. She was also more militant in her views than Catt, and she disagreed with NAWSA tactics. Paul therefore spurned the existing suffrage organization and founded her own group, the Congressional Union, in Washington, D.C., in 1913.

Both Catt and Paul were women of considerable ability. Under Catt, the NAWSA adopted the new tactics of parades, rallies, and tight administrative coordination. Paul used them, too; but in contrast to the NAWSA, which had always concentrated on the state legislatures, Paul focused her efforts on Congress, where the suffrage amendment had lain dormant in both houses since 1893. Within one year of the formation of the Congressional Union, her group was able to pressure

Suffragists ride in a parade in New York City in 1912 (above) and march to the Capitol in Washington, D.C., in 1913 (below).

Alice Paul, founder of the   *and first woman member of the*
Woman's Party (left), *with*   *United States Civil Service*
Helen Gardener, feminist author   *Commission, 1912.*

the Senate into voting on the amendment, although the measure was
defeated in this initial attempt.

Six more years of agitation followed. Despite their differences, the
NAWSA and the Congressional Union were able to work together
effectively during those years, even though the Congressional Union
broadened its efforts to the state level and regrouped itself into a
political party, the Woman's Party, in the election of 1916. As tension
mounted and Congress repeatedly failed to pass the amendment, Alice
Paul and the Woman's Party took extreme measures. In 1917, they
organized round-the-clock picketing of the White House. Woodrow
Wilson's administration played into their hands by having them arrested
and jailed. The national press coverage they received embarrassed the
administration by exposing the harshness of their treatment, including
force-feeding the women when they refused to eat. Even this action

Picketing the White House—an innovative strategy.

did not bring an immediate victory in Congress. Not until 1919, after numerous additional state victories seemed to provide the ultimate necessary pressure, was passage of the amendment successful. Finally, on August 18, 1920, with its passage by the state of Tennessee, the Nineteenth Amendment, giving women the right to vote, became law.

The Aftermath of Victory

To what extent the militant tactics—or, indeed, the entire revived campaign after 1914—contributed to the suffrage victory is difficult to determine. Eleanor Flexner, in her study of the suffrage movement, split the difference, giving equal plaudits to the NAWSA and to the Woman's Party. Jane Addams, a close observer of the events of those years, entirely discounted the efforts of the suffrage leaders. Addams

The end of a long struggle.

thought women were given the vote because they had performed so admirably during the First World War, keeping the economy going at home while men were at war. Woman's suffrage, according to Addams, was "a direct result of the war psychology."[39] After all, in 1917, America was at war, and the nation was not sympathetic to dissent. Aliens and political radicals were regularly incarcerated, and no great public outcry was heard. It may well be that Paul's militant tactics produced a substantial reaction against feminism among an American public that was no longer responsive to the Progressive impulse by the 1920s.

The split between the NAWSA and the Woman's Party was to have grave repercussions in the future. Although the two groups seemed to agree on their goals, they differed substantially in their tactics. In 1919, Catt openly disavowed Paul's militancy. Once suffrage was

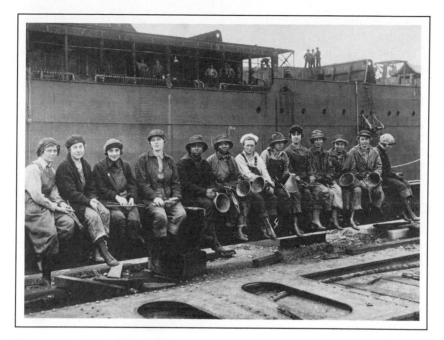

Women shipyard workers at the
Puget Sound Naval Shipyard,
1918.

achieved, the disagreement over tactics almost inevitably broadened
to include a disagreement over goals.

Yet in 1920, activist women were euphoric. Not only had women
been enfranchised; during the First World War, as the economy expanded
and men left their jobs for battle, women were promoted to the skilled-
labor and administrative positions that previously had been reserved
for men. Large-scale wars have always had the effect of increasing
employment for women. But coming at a time of extensive feminist
agitation, the expansion of women's employment during the First World
War seemed especially significant. Women were proving that they were
capable of performing jobs commonly believed to be impossible for
them; they were working as streetcar conductors, as engineers on
trains, as construction workers, and in steel factories. On the job, they

were meeting men more and more as equals, or so it seemed then. Furthermore, in 1917, the federal government formed the Women's Committee of the Council for National Defense to mobilize women behind the war effort. Both Anna Howard Shaw and Carrie Chapman Catt served with distinction on it. In 1919, the prohibition amendment—long the goal of the WCTU and of rural Protestant women, many of whom were allied with the suffrage movement—became law. It, too, gave the impression that women had the power to reform society. Viewing the scene in 1920, socialist Elizabeth Gurley Flynn was optimistic. Never before, she wrote, had women been so well-organized, so unified.[40] The future looked bright.

Flynn's optimism proved to be ill-advised. In the 1920s, the feminist movement broke into factions, and the interest of American women turned in a different direction, away from feminism and even from social-reform causes. Looking back from the vantage point of the late 1920s, when feminism was passé and conservatism dominant, one analyst of prewar feminism could write as if the movement had hardly existed. With little understanding of the scope of feminism early in the century, she passed it off as the work of "women quite remote in purpose from the millions of census breadwinners," who wanted to show that "they were as good and better than men." The growth of industrialism, she contended, had been the real reason for the changes in women's social, economic, and political positions; before the First World War, feminism had been only a "little wave" on the broader flow of events.[41] Her point of view was not at all unique.

NOTES

[1] Abigail Scott Duniway, *Path Breaking: An Autobiographical History of the Equal Suffrage Amendment in the Pacific Coast States* (1914; reprint ed., New York: Source Book Press, 1970), p. 60.

[2] Joseph Gilpin Pyle, "Should Women Vote?" in *Anti-Suffrage Pamphlets*, miscellaneous collection, Princeton University Library, p. 19.

[3] Harriot Stanton Blatch and Alma Lutz, *Challenging Years: The Memoirs of Harriot Stanton Blatch* (New York: G.P. Putnam's Sons, 1940), p. 109.

[4] Edith Finch, *Carey Thomas of Bryn Mawr* (New York: Harper & Row, 1947), pp. 249–50.

5 Rheta Childe Dorr, *A Woman of Fifty* (New York: Funk & Wagnalls, 1924), p. 148.

6 Mary Earhart, *Frances Willard: From Prayers to Politics* (Chicago: University of Chicago Press, 1944), p. 194.

7 Ida A. Harper, "Women in Municipal Governments," in May Wright Sewall (ed.), *The World's Congress of Representative Women; A Historical Resumé for Popular Circulation of the World's Congress of Representative Women, Convened in Chicago on May 15, and Adjourned on May 22, 1893* (Chicago: Rand McNally, 1894), vol. 2, p. 453.

8 "Men's Views of Women's Clubs," *Annals of the American Academy of Political and Social Science,* XXVIII (July–December 1906): 289.

9 Blake McKelvey, *American Prisons: A Study in American Social History Prior to 1915* (Chicago: University of Chicago Press, 1936), p. 214.

10 Alice Hamilton, *Exploring the Dangerous Trades: The Autobiography of Alice Hamilton* (Boston: Little, Brown, 1943), p. 269.

11 Robert L. Duffus, *Lillian Wald, Neighbor and Crusader* (New York: Macmillan, 1939), p. 71.

12 Elizabeth Butler, *Women and the Trades: Pittsburgh, 1907–1908* (New York: Charities Publication Committee, 1909), p. 332.

13 Marvin Lazerson, *Origins of the Urban School: Public Education in Massachusetts, 1870–1915* (Cambridge, MA: Harvard University Press, 1971), pp. 36–73.

14 Lillian Wald, *The House on Henry Street* (New York: Henry Holt, 1915), p. 222.

15 W.L. George, "Feminist Intentions," *The Atlantic Monthly,* CXII (December 1913): 731.

16 Ben Hecht, *A Child of the Century* (New York: Simon & Schuster, 1954), p. 48.

17 Inez Milholland, "The Liberation of a Sex," *McClure's,* XL (February 1913): 185–88.

18 Charlotte Perkins Gilman, *The Man-Made World: or, Our Androcentric Culture* (New York: Charlton, 1911), p. 211.

19 Hutchins Hapgood, *A Victorian in the Modern World* (New York: Harcourt Brace Jovanovich, Inc., 1939), p. 377.

20 Marie Theresa Blanc, *The Condition of Women in the United States: A Traveller's Notes,* (trans.) Abby Langdon Alger (1895; Freeport, NY: Books for Libraries Press, 1972), p. 88.

[21] Margaret Anderson, *My Thirty Years' War: An Autobiography* (New York: Covici, Friede, 1930), pp. 55, 74.

[22] Josephine Goldmark, "The World's Experience Upon Which Legislation Limiting the Hours of Labor for Women is Based," in Josephine Goldmark, *Fatigue and Efficiency: A Study in Industry* (New York: Russell Sage Foundation, 1917), p. 1.

[23] Christopher Lasch (ed.), *The Social Thought of Jane Addams* (Indianapolis: Bobbs-Merrill, 1965), p. 144.

[24] *Jane Addams: A Centennial Reader* (New York: Macmillan, 1960), p. 115.

[25] Caroline Hunt, *The Life of Ellen Richards* (Washington, D.C.: American Home Economics Association, 1958), p. 160.

[26] Winifred Scott Cooley, "The Younger Suffragists," *Harper's*, LVIII (September 27, 1913): 6–7.

[27] Milholland, "The Liberation of a Sex," p. 185.

[28] Mabel Dodge Luhan, *Intimate Memories* (New York: Harcourt Brace Jovanovich, Inc., 1936), vol. 3: *Movers and Shakers*, p. 69.

[29] Charlotte Perkins Gilman, *Women and Economics: The Economic Factor Between Men and Women as a Factor in Social Evolution* (1898; reprint ed., New York: Harper & Row, 1970), p. 30.

[30] Inez Milholland, "The Changing Home," *McClure's*, XL (March 1913): 214.

[31] Dorr, *A Woman of Fifty*, pp. 450–41.

[32] Ellen Key, *Love and Marriage* (New York: G.P. Putnam's Sons, 1911), p. 124.

[33] Emma Goldman, "Marriage and Love," in Miriam Schneir (ed.), *Feminism: The Essential Historical Writings* (New York: Vintage, Random House, 1971), p. 322.

[34] Gilman, *The Man-Made World: or, Our Androcentric Culture*, p. 245.

[35] Milholland, "The Changing Home," p. 208.

[36] Key, *Love and Marriage*, p. 214.

[37] Cooley, "The Younger Suffragists," 7.

[38] Jane Addams, *Twenty years at Hull House* (New York: Macmillan, 1910), p. 237.

[39] Jane Addams, *The Second Twenty Years at Hull House* (New York: Macmillan, 1930), p. 103.

[40] Elizabeth Gurley Flynn, *I Speak My Own Piece* (New York: Masses and Mainstream, 1955), p. 267.

[41] Mary Ross, "The New Status of Women in America," in Samuel D. Schmalhausen and V.F. Calverton (eds.), *Woman's Coming of Age, A Symposium* (New York: H. Liveright, 1931), pp. 545–48.

BIBLIOGRAPHY

Although historians have long focused on the women's suffrage movement (initially to the exclusion of other areas of women's experience), there is still need for a comprehensive study. Alan P. Grimes, *The Puritan Ethic and Woman Suffrage* (New York: Oxford University Press, 1967), argues that the desire for order in western states brought the early vote for women there, although he pays insufficient attention to organized suffragist activity. Aileen S. Kraditor, *The Ideas of the Woman Suffrage Movement, 1890–1920* (New York: Columbia University Press, 1965), explores the flaws in the suffrage argument, although she slights its positive aspects. The most recent study of the last years of the movement is David Morgan, *Suffragists and Democrats: The Politics of Woman Suffrage in America* (East Lansing: Michigan State University Press, 1972). Eleanor Flexner, *Century of Struggle: The Woman's Rights Movement in the United States* (Cambridge, MA: Harvard University Press, 1959), is still a useful overview, and an interesting comparative perspective is provided in Ross Evans Paulson, *Women's Suffrage and Prohibition: A Comparative Study of Equality and Social Control* (Glenview, IL: Scott, Foresman, 1973). Carl Degler, *At Odds: Women and the Family in America From the Revolution to the Present* (New York: Oxford University Press, 1980), makes a brief case for the radicalism of women's suffrage. Personal experiences in the suffrage movement are recounted in Sherna Gluck (ed.), *From Parlor to Prison: Five American Suffragists Talk About Their Lives: An Oral History* (New York: Random House, 1976).

These works should be supplemented by some of the many works of participants, including Harriot Stanton Blatch and Alma Lutz, *Challenging Years: The Memoirs of Harriot Stanton Blatch* (New York: G.P. Putnam's Sons, 1940); Carrie Chapman Catt and Nettie Rogers Shuler, *Woman Suffrage and Politics: The Inner Story of the Suffrage Movement* (New York: Scribner Book Companies, 1926); Maud Wood Park, *Front Door Lobby*, (ed.) Edna Lamprey Stentiel (Boston: Beacon Press, 1960); and Elizabeth Cady Stanton et al., *History of Woman Suffrage*, 6 vols. (New York: Fowler & Wells, 1881–1922). These volumes have been excerpted in Mary Jo Buhle and Paul Buhle (eds.), *The Concise History of Woman Suffrage: Selections from the Classic Work of Stanton, Anthony, Gage, and Harper* (Urbana: University of Illinois Press, 1978).

Studies of the many women's organizations of the period have begun to appear. On women's clubs, see Karen J. Blair, *The Clubwoman as Feminist: True Womanhood Redefined, 1868–1914* (New York: Holmes & Meier, 1980). On the WCTU, see Ruth Bordin, *Woman and Temperance: The Quest for Power and Liberty, 1873–1900* (Philadelphia: Temple University Press, 1981). The YWCA and black women's clubs still await their historians. On the DAR, see Margaret Gibbs, *The Daughters of the American Revolution* (New York: Holt, Rinehart & Winston, 1969). The only existing history of the Consumers' League, written by Maud Nathan, is *The Story of an Epoch-Making Movement* (Garden City, NY: Doubleday, Page, 1926). Material on a number of women's organizations is to be found in William L. O'Neill, *Everyone was Brave: The Rise and Fall of Feminism in America* (New York: Quadrangle, 1969). O'Neill's insights have especially informed the author's argument on the difficulties of pre-First World War feminism.

Material on women in the Progressive movement is scattered throughout the literature on the period, although Marlene Stein Wortman has provided an interesting overview in "Domesticating the Nineteenth-Century American City," *Prospects: An Annual of American Culture Studies,* III (1977): 531–572. In addition to Wortman, the most useful works are Allen F. Davis, *Spearheads for Reform: The Social Settlements and the Progressive Movement, 1890–1914* (New York: Oxford University Press, 1967); Davis, *American Heroine: The Life and Legend of Jane Addams* (New York: Oxford University Press, 1973); Kathleen D. McCarthy, *Noblesse Oblige: Charity and Cultural Philanthropy in Chicago* (Chicago: University of Chicago Press, 1982); and David P. Thelen, *The New Citizenship: Origins of Progressivism in Wisconsin* (Columbus: University of Missouri Press, 1972). For a fascinating account of the relationship between college culture and settlement-house involvement, see John P. Rousmanière, "Cultural Hybrid in the Slums: The College Woman and the Settlement House, 1889–1894," *American Quarterly,* XXII (Spring 1970): 45–66. Biographies and autobiographies are available for most major women Progressives, who themselves wrote extensively on their work. See especially Jane Addams, *Twenty Years at Hull House* (New York: Macmillan, 1910), and Lillian Wald, *The House on Henry Street* (New York: Henry Holt, 1915). For an interesting, although flawed, critique of the motives of Addams—and, by implication, the motives of other reformers like her—see Christopher Lasch, *The New Radicalism in America, 1889– 1963: The Intellectual as a Social Type* (New York: Alfred A. Knopf, 1965). Jill Conway, "Women Reformers and American Culture, 1870–1930," *Journal of Social History,* V (Winter 1971–1972): 164–77, although critical, gives a more balanced argument. Also consult Mary R. Beard, *Women's Work in Municipalities* (New York: Appleton-Century-Crofts, 1915); Suphonisba Breckinridge, *Women in the Twentieth Century: A Study of Their Political, Social, and Economic Activities* (New York: McGraw-Hill Book Co., 1933); and Rheta Childe Dorr, *What Eight Million Women Want* (1910; reprint ed., Boston: Kraus, 1971).

Several recent works underline the broad nature of the feminist movement in the early twentieth century. See Estelle B. Freedman, *Their Sisters' Keepers: Women's Prison Reform in America, 1830–1930* (Ann Arbor: University of Michigan Press, 1981), and Delores Hayden, *The Grand Domestic Revolution: A History of Feminist Designs for American Homes, Neighborhoods, and Cities* (Cambridge, MA: Massachusetts Institute of Technology, 1981).

On militant feminism in the early twentieth century, see June Sochen, *The New Woman: Feminism in Greenwich Village, 1910–1920* (New York: Quadrangle, 1972), for information on some of the New York activists. On Margaret Sanger, David Kennedy has written the most recent—although hostile—biography. To supplement his *Birth Control in America: The Career of Margaret Sanger* (New Haven: Yale University Press, 1970), Sanger's own *Margaret Sanger: An Autobiography* (1938; reprint ed., New York: Dover, 1971) ought to be read, as well as the works on birth control by Linda Gordon and James Reed cited in the bibliography to Chapter 1. On Charlotte Perkins Gilman, see Mary A. Hill, *Charlotte Perkins Gilman: The Making of a Radical Feminist, 1860–1896* (Philadelphia: Temple University Press, 1980), as well as Gilman's own autobiography, *The Living of Charlotte Perkins Gilman: An Autobiography* (New York: Appleton-Century-Crofts, 1935). For an insight into her thought, as well as a fascinating voyage into a feminist utopia, see Gilman's *Herland* (New York: Pantheon Books, 1979).

For a discussion of new biological and sociological views of women, see Rosalind Rosenberg, *Beyond Separate Spheres: The Intellectual Roots of Modern Feminism* (New Haven: Yale University Press, 1982). Two important contemporary treatises are Anna Garlin Spencer, *Woman's Share in Social Culture* (New York: Mitchell Kennerly, 1913), and Scott Nearing and Nellie Nearing, *Woman and Social Progress* (New York: Macmillan, 1912).

On the impact of the First World War on working women, see Maureen Greenwald, *Women, War, and Work: The Impact of World War One on Women Workers in the United States* (Westport, CT: Greenwood Press, 1980).

4

THE 1920S: FREEDOM
OR DISILLUSIONMENT?

MORE THAN anything else, the woman's movement of the 1920s was characterized by its splintering into a number of groups, each involved with a separate concern. True, most established women's organizations continued to function, and several major new ones were organized as the war ended and suffrage was achieved. The formation both of the National Federation of Business and Professional Women's Clubs (BPW) and of the Women's Bureau in the federal Department of Labor in 1919, as well as of the Women's Joint Congressional Committee (WJCC) and the League of Women Voters in 1920, seemed to promise further striking progress for women. But this was not to be the case. Soon after the passage of the suffrage amendment, Anna Howard Shaw remarked to Emily Newell Blair, a young suffragist who was later to become vice president of the National Committee of the Democratic Party, "I am sorry for you young women who have to carry on the work for the next ten years, for suffrage was a symbol, and now you have lost your symbol."[1] Shaw could not foresee that political conservatism and an emphasis on personal gratification would come to characterize the decade of the 1920s and that almost any reform endeavor would be doomed. But she did realize the potential for the formation of factions within the united women's movement. Essentially, these women were divided into four groups— social feminists, pacifists, professional women, and feminists.

WOMEN'S ORGANIZATIONS IN TRANSITION

The largest faction of women was clustered around social feminism. With suffrage won, the NAWSA disbanded. However, Alice Paul's Woman's Party did not succeed the NAWSA; instead, a new organization, the League of Women Voters, was formed. During the 1920s, the League concentrated on three goals: general social reform; the elimination of state laws that discriminated against women; and the education of women to their responsibilities as citizens.

As an agency of reform, the League was not without effect. Its efforts at local, state, and national levels on behalf of municipal reform, conservatism, tighter consumer laws, a Child Labor Amendment, and public support of indigent mothers were impressive. Historian Stanley Lemons argues that women's organizations, and particularly the League,

At a suffrage headquarters,
newly enfranchised women learn
how to vote.

were primarily responsible for whatever Progressive impulse still existed
in an essentially conservative decade. State chapters of the League
were successful, too, in whittling down the number of discriminatory
marriage and property laws still on the books. They also successfully
fought for the repeal of laws that prohibited women from serving on
juries or holding office—laws that a number of state legislatures passed
after ratification of the suffrage amendment. The League often served
as a training ground for women interested in politics. The career of
Lavinia Engle was not exceptional. After serving seven years as a field
secretary for the NAWSA, she became director of the Maryland League
in 1920. Later she was elected to the Maryland legislature, and in 1936,
she became an official in the federal Social Security Administration.

In function and approach, however, the League has always been
moderate. Its early history in many ways determined its destiny. As

former suffragists who had expected the vote to produce a national reformation, League leaders were shaken when the elections of the early 1920s revealed that the turnout of eligible women voters was light and that their voting patterns did not differ from those of men. Moreover, the League retained no more than a percentage of the NAWSA's membership—and it was nonpartisan, combining Republican and Democratic women whose goals were not always the same. In reaction to this turn of events, League leaders decided that the education of women for responsible citizenship must be one of their primary functions.

Expression of this concept of education took on conservative and cautious overtones. Instead of using education as a means of proselytizing, the League came to view education as study to arrive at truth. Elaborate study too often took the place of action. The League attempted, wrote one analyst, "to bring to politics the aloof detachment of the scientific method. . . . Inquiry is centered upon some definite, limited problem. Data are assembled and studied objectively. Conclusions and new ideas are tentatively held, are tested, and are revised."[2]

The problem was that lengthy inquiry delayed taking a firm stand on any issue and reinforced the belief that women were insecure in the political world and ignorant about politics. But due to its commitment to social welfare and education, the League accepted the fiction that political parties were open to women, even though representation on party-governing committees was token and few women actually ran for political office. Indeed, members of the League who became candidates for political office were required to resign from the League so that they did not jeopardize its nonpartisan stance. Moreover, although the League used the political techniques of lobbying and letter writing in social feminist campaigns, its approach was genteel. The League method was "wooing our legislators in a dignified and league-like [ladylike] manner."[3]

That another approach might challenge the political system more effectively was apparent in the striking campaigns of Florence Allen for the Ohio State Supreme Court in 1922 and 1928.* In both elections, Allen won the judgeship without party support. Instead, she formed an organization made up of women activists. The plan was simple.

---

*In 1934, Franklin D. Roosevelt appointed Allen to the Circuit Court of Appeals—the highest court below the Supreme Court.

The first United States congresswoman, Jeanette Rankin of Montana, was elected in 1917.

Her managers contacted women in every county who had been suffragists, and these women handled publicity, arranged meetings, and distributed campaign literature. But it was difficult to form an effective coalition of women around any issue in the 1920s. Many former activists were exhausted from their exertions as suffragists before the war. One former Connecticut suffragist explained: "After we got the vote, the crusade was over. It was peacetime and we all went back to a hundred different causes and tasks that we'd been putting off all those years. We just demobilized."[4] Indeed, membership in women's organizations in general dropped off, and the national leadership of the League complained of a dearth of able women willing to assume positions of leadership in local chapters.

A number of organizations active in the Progressive coalition before the war turned away from activism. Most important, local women's clubs, which had led the social-welfare coalition before the war, often developed into social organizations in the 1920s in which women played bridge or discussed fashions, gardening, and cooking. One ex-presi-

"Ma" Ferguson (seated) *was
elected governor of Texas in
1935—one of the first women to
hold the office.*

dent of a formerly flourishing suburban club in the Midwest bemoaned
the fact that her clubhouse, which had once echoed with brilliant
speeches, "now. . . rings with such terms as 'no trump' and 'grand
slam'."[5] Only with difficulty did the national leadership of these clubs
arouse the members' interest in reform legislation. This change in the
character of women's clubs was partly due to the general conservatism
of the decade; but other organizations with a social feminist emphasis,
such as the League of Women Voters, also were drawing away their
reform-minded members, and more and more professional women
were deserting them to join professional organizations.

Social workers and settlement-house workers, too, were dropping
out of the social-activist coalition. To postwar college graduates, them-

selves influenced by the conservative and individualistic tenor of the decade, settlement work—by now in its fourth decade of existence—no longer was as appealing as it had been to the first generation of settlement workers. In many cities, the Community Chest, founded in the early 1920s as a way of coordinating disparate charitable giving, became the major financial backer of settlements. Because the Community Chests were generally controlled by conservative businessmen, settlement workers became reluctant to attempt innovation. Moreover, the movement of blacks into the formerly Jewish, Italian, and Slavic neighborhoods that the settlements served made the challenge of living in the midst of their clientele ever more difficult. And settlement workers themselves were influenced by general trends within the profession of social work. After several decades of more or less uncontrolled growth, social work had entered a period of rationalization, of concern with the issues of professional standards, training, and pay. At the same time, the influence of Freudian psychology made the individual client, not the social environment, seem important to the caseworker.

Organizations like the Women's Trade Union League and the Consumers' League, still headed by Florence Kelley, remained in existence. The prewar activists in these groups were joined by vigorous lieutenants like Frances Perkins—a former Hull House resident who worked for the Consumers' League in the 1920s before becoming head of the New York State Department of Labor under Governor Franklin D. Roosevelt and, in the 1930s, Secretary of Labor in the federal government (the first woman to hold a cabinet position) under Franklin D. Roosevelt. Like the League of Woman Voters, settlement and social-welfare groups lobbied for a Child Labor Amendment, for special legislation for working women, and for federal relief for indigent mothers, among other social-welfare goals. But in the 1920s, their support and successes were limited. The old issues of Progressivism no longer prevailed.

At the same time, the primary concern of many former influential suffragists became pacifism rather than domestic welfare. Carrie Chapman Catt established the National Conference on the Cause and Cure of War, and Jane Addams became involved in the Women's International League for Peace and Freedom (WILPF). For some long-time suffragists, like Rheta Childe Dorr, internationalism promised a new and exciting crusade; their change of heart was in the nature of a "conversion." With the onset of the First World War, Dorr found herself

*Delegates to a peace mission to
end the First World War. (Jane
Addams is second from the left.)*

no longer interested in the woman's movement but concerned with
"humanity." She resigned from Heterodoxy, of which she had been a
devoted member, because "alternate Saturday lunches had no more
attractions for me." World events took precedence.[6]

For others, pacifism was a logical extension of their feminism. Organized women were outraged by the outbreak of the First World War,
which they saw as the most menacing example possible of male
aggressiveness. At the very time that the suffragists and the social
feminists were working for a national reformation, men were threatening to destroy the social order. Women as mothers, pacifist rhetoric
stressed, had a "peculiar moral passion against both the cruelty and
the want of war." To Jane Addams, pacifism meant "the replacement
of the war virtues by virtues which sublimate the heroic but anach-

ronistic energies of the soldier into aspirations towards harmony and justice in society."[7] Pacifist leaders, too, criticized preexisting antiwar societies, dominated by men, for their failure to respond quickly to the war's outbreak. By 1916, most women's organizations advocated peace.

In the 1920s, the efforts of women pacifists were not without success. The WILPF, for example, was an important pressure group behind the various disarmament and peace conferences that national governments and pacifist groups held throughout the decade. Women pacifists played no small part in pressuring the United States and foreign governments into signing the Kellogg–Briand Pact of 1927, which outlawed war as national policy. It is perhaps only in retrospect that their actions appear somewhat futile. Yet one inevitable byproduct of their praiseworthy campaign for peace was a further scattering of the feminist effort at home.

Professional women, too, were becoming an increasingly difficult group to activate behind goals other than equal pay and equal employment opportunities. During the war, the absence of men had provided women with greater opportunities for advancement, and the government, as part of its general program of bolstering citizen morale, had encouraged them to organize. These experiences heightened their consciousness of their role as professionals and of discrimination within their professions. After the war, new professional women's associations appeared in many fields, including dentistry, architecture, and journalism. In 1919, under the sponsorship of the YWCA, to which many women professionals had previously belonged, the National Federation of Business and Professional Women's Clubs was formed. Composed primarily of teachers and clerical workers, its focus was on the attainment of equal rights for women within the professions, although it often functioned more as a vehicle for socializing than for activism. In addition, a number of young, New York professional women, led by journalists Jane Grant and Ruth Hale, wife of newsman Heywood Broun, formed the Lucy Stone League after Hale was unable to obtain a passport under her maiden name. Their goal was laudatory, but again the focus was on professionalism and not on women's general oppression.

In the 1920s, the inheritors of the prewar feminist mantle split off from their sometime associates in the suffragist coalition. The Woman's Party, founded by Alice Paul in 1916, refused to endorse the League of Women Voters' program of social feminism and education for women. Instead, the Woman's Party centered its efforts on attaining an Equal Rights Amendment (ERA), which would, they believed, be the surest way of abolishing the many state and national laws that discriminated against women. In and after 1916, Paul's technique of pressuring Congress for the suffrage amendment had seemed fruitful; now, she and her associates decided to follow the same course of action. The amendment—which simply stated that "men and women shall have equal rights throughout the United States and every place subject to its jurisdiction"—was first introduced in Congress in 1923. The League, as well as most women's organizations, opposed the ERA. They did want to eliminate the legal strictures against women in such areas as marriage and property holding, but they judged that factory women still required special legislation.

The membership of the Woman's Party was small, but it contained many women of wealth and professional eminence. It was not a radical group. Crystal Eastman—socialist, pacifist, and an associate of Henrietta Rodman in the prewar Feminist Alliance and of Alice Paul in the prewar Woman's Party—charged that when she presented Paul with a list of militant demands, including the legalization of birth control, Paul refused to consider them.[8] The concern of the Woman's Party was to be the ERA. The strategy was not without effect. Even though Congress consistently refused to vote on the ERA, all commentators were impressed with the lobbying skill of Woman's Party members. Still the intransigence of the Woman's Party and its single issue campaign made unity among women's groups difficult.

If any strong sense of common purpose existed among women in the 1920s, that purpose was social feminism. In 1919, a number of women's organizations formed the Women's Joint Congressional Committee (WJCC) to work as a common lobby. At one time or another, the League of Women Voters, the National Federation of Business and Professional Women's Clubs, and the General Federation of Women's Clubs were members of the Committee, as were the National Congress of Parents and Teachers, the Woman's Christian Temperance Union, the American Association of University Women (AAUW) and the National Council of Jewish Women. In many states, similar legislative councils emerged. The national committee worked for improved education, maternal and infant health care, the Child Labor Amendment, the World Court, and increased funding for the Children's Bureau and the Women's Bureau. Its successes, however, were limited. Even its major triumph—the 1921 Sheppard–Towner Act, which provided matching federal grants to set up maternity and pediatric clinics—was overturned in 1929. Part of the difficulty lay in the fact that a woman's voting block—which might have forced Congress to pay more heed to social-welfare and feminist campaigns—had not emerged. More important, regular doctors were opposed to the community health clinics staffed by women that had been established under the act.

In addition to the WJCC, the Women's Bureau in the Department of Labor—established as the result of women's work during wartime and the vigorous lobbying of women's organizations—might have served as an agency to unify women's organization. But more than anything else, the Women's Bureau played the role of a fact-finding and publication service. It concerned itself almost exclusively with women's employment. Its first and long-term president, Mary Anderson, came from the ranks of the Women's Trade Union League. For the first decades of its existence, the bureau was a firm supporter of special legislation for women.

Throughout the 1920s, factionalism plagued the woman's movement. On the other hand, the nation's leaders and legislators were not sympathetic to reform or feminism. The wartime antiradical hysteria that culminated in the "Red Scare" of 1919, with deportations and jailings of radicals, colored the decade of the 1920s. "The business of America is business," intoned Calvin Coolidge, pointing to one of the major themes of the era. And business was a controlling element throughout the nation. In the state of Connecticut, for example, the woman's movement experienced no factionalization and remained unified under the auspices of the League of Women Voters. Its far-reaching program of women's rights (including birth control) and social reform, however, was regularly defeated by a legislature controlled by Republican businessmen. Whether or not this was the case in states throughout the nation awaits futher research.

ANTIFEMINIST UNDERCURRENTS
AND FEMINIST CONSERVATISM

Reflecting business sentiments, the general mood of the country was not receptive to feminist reform. Americans in the 1920s were tired of reform causes and dazzled by seeming prosperity and mass-produced consumer goods: automobiles, radios, and, for women in particular, washing machines, vacuum cleaners, and electric kitchens. What need was there for social service when industry was apparently fulfilling its promise of providing material prosperity to all Americans? What concerned Americans—at least of the middle class—were their cars, the availability of illicit liquor, the opportunities for stock-market and land speculation, the radio serials and the latest movies, the exploits of sports stars and cultural heroes, and the pursuit of beauty and youth. The women's clubs, which turned from social service to bridge, were indicative of the general mood of the middle class. Vida Scudder, a Wellesley College professor active in Boston settlements and in the Women's Trade Union League, concluded that "those ten exhausted years [the 1920s] were the worst I have ever known."[9]

By the mid-1920s, it had become a matter of belief—proclaimed by press and radio, businessmen and politicians—that women had in fact achieved liberation. Suffrage had been won. The number of women's organizations had not diminished. Women had been employed in large numbers during the First World War in positions of responsibility; they had become men's comrades in the office and factory, or so it seemed. Legions of Vassar and Smith graduates descended on New York City every year to become secretaries, copy editors, and management trainees in department stores. Women were smoking in public, wearing short skirts, and demanding and gaining entry into saloons, speakeasies, men's clubs, and golf courses. Female sports stars, like Helen Wills in tennis and Gertrude Ederle in swimming, were challenging any remaining notions that women could not excel in athletics. And sports promoters were promoting them as vigorously as male athletes. Even Suzanne LaFollette, author of one of the few militant feminist treatises of the decade, wrote in 1926 that the woman's struggle "is very largely won."[10]

The premise that women had achieved liberation gave rise to a new antifeminism, although it was never stated as such. In essence, it involved the creation of a new female image—certainly a more modern one than before, but no less a stereotype and still based on traditional female functions. It was subtle in argument and compelling to a generation tired of reform causes and intent on enjoying itself. By the late 1920s, numerous articles appeared in popular journals contending that in gaining their "rights," women had given up their "privileges." What these privileges amounted to in this literature were self-indulgence, leisure, and freedom from working. The new antifeminists did not openly question women's right to work. They simply made it clear that they did not think women were capable of combining marriage and a career. Women's world in the home was pictured as exotic and self-gratifying. One representative writer contended that working women simply did not have the strange and delightful experience of taking "an hour to dress," of "spending the day in strictly feminine pursuits," of "actually making the kind of cake that [now] comes from the bakery."[11]

The proponents of this new antifeminism not only borrowed the rhetoric of the prewar feminists but claimed that they were the real feminists of the 1920s. "It [the return to the home] is going to be almost as long and hard a struggle. . . as the struggle for women's rights."[12] Prewar feminists were attacked as unfeminine and asexual. In 1927, writer Dorothy Dunbar Bromley defined a "new-style feminist" who bore no relationship to "the old school of fighting feminists who wore flat heels and had very little feminine charm, or the current species who antagonize men with their constant clamor about maiden names, equal rights, women's place in the world." The new-style feminist was well-dressed, admitted that she liked men, did not care for women in groups, and was convinced that "a full life calls for marriage and children as well as a career," with the stress on the former.[13]

Other molders of public opinion spread the message far and wide. Advertising, which doubled in volume in the 1920s, found its major market in women, who spent the bulk of the family income. To sell dishwashers, refrigerators, and cleaning products, advertisers pictured the woman as the model consumer, whose existence was devoted to the improvement of family life through the purchase of new products. As the clothing and cosmetic industries began their phenomenal growth in the 1920s (a growth that was largely a product of advertising), women were shown as beings for whom fashion, beauty, and sex appeal were the most important concerns in life.

New writings on the nature of women's sexuality drove the message home. Before the First World War, a few bold feminists and doctors had suggested that women could enjoy sex; now marriage manuals advocating sexual pleasure for women and spelling out erotic techniques were readily available. Their message was underlined by the scientific theories of Sigmund Freud, who had argued as early as the 1890s that unconscious drives, and especially sex, were central forces in human behavior. A small number of doctors and Greenwich Village intellectuals had known of Freud's work before the war, but it was not until the 1920s—an age preoccupied with the notion of pleasure—that Freudian theories became popular. Yet Freud's ideas were as confining for women as they were liberating. Although Freud gave the final scientific refutation to the old belief that sex was an unpleasant duty for women, he also argued that the crucial factor in female personality formation was the female child's envy for the male sex organ—an envy that produced a lifelong dissatisfaction with being a woman. The only way to overcome this discontent, according to Freud, was through motherhood.

However, the influence of Freudian theories in the 1920s must not be overemphasized. In the later years of the decade, the behaviorist ideas of John B. Watson were in vogue. Watson played down the importance of suppressed drives as factors controlling human actions and stressed that the individual could control his or her behavior through will power. His message to women was nonetheless ambiguous. In his *Psychological Care of Infant and Child* (1928), the standard reference on childrearing for a decade or more, Watson argued that most women were failures as mothers and that they should decide either not to have children or to realize that childrearing was such a complex skill that it required extensive training and complete dedication. Unlike Freud, Watson did not view motherhood as the natural role for all women, but his prescriptions for childrearing, which centered around the conscious withholding of parental affection and the establishment of fixed schedules of activity for the child in order to nurture self-reliance, placed heavy demands on mothers who wanted to work outside the home.

Yet the theories of Freud and Watson were secondary to the fact that the notion of the pleasures of sexuality permeated the culture. Women's magazines were full of it. The films and the radio made it a stock device. Sex-story magazines like *True Confessions* exploited it and quadrupled their sales. Mabel Dodge Luhan, whose psychoanalysis in 1915 set the example for many of her wealthy and intellectual friends, laid clear the ultimate meaning of the new ideas about sexuality. "The sex act," she wrote, is "the cornerstone of any life, and its chief reality," especially for women. "It is indeed the happy woman who has no history," because she has lived for erotic gratification, for her husband or lover, and for her children.[14]

To these ideas, the feminist rebuttal was weak. The arguments of those feminists who had wanted a "single standard" of sexuality and who had attacked male sex drives seemed antiquated: Charlotte Perkins Gilman, for example, found it almost impossible in the 1920s to secure speaking engagements or to publish her books.[15] No longer did friendships among women seem as satisfying or as profound; marriage rates among women college graduates escalated strikingly in the 1920s. The argument about women's special morality, which had underlain so much nineteenth-century reform, and the reality of women's separate culture, which had defined nineteenth-century gender distinctions and given women a special place of their own, were fractured, if not completely destroyed.

Yet feminism and the new sexuality were not necessarily antagonistic. The new sexuality did represent new freedom for women, and feminists themselves took an interest in the new theories. By the mid-1920s, Gilman reported that Heterodoxy was devoting discussions to sex psychology—a topic that, she admitted, did not particularly interest her.[16] More than anything else, feminists focused on the issue of how to combine careers and marriage. It was an issue appropriate to an individualistic era in which the reality of women's work-force participation could not be denied. But it was basically a middle-class issue—one that did not address issues of class or race or more fundamental social discrimination.

Still conservatism in the 1920s ran deep. Due to the excesses of wartime antiradicalism, Emma Goldman spent the last years of her life in European exile. Moreover, the backbone of the Socialist Party was broken. The Women's Trade Union League turned from organizing and strike activities to lobbying for protective legislation. Margaret Sanger—who before the war had organized rallies, distributed mass propaganda, and courted jail sentences to achieve legalization of birth control—now confined her efforts to lobbying campaigns before legislatures and pressure groups like the American Medical Association. Greenwich Village feminists, who before the war had formed the Feminist Alliance, were dispirited as a result of the war experience and left New York City. The next generation of Greenwich Village women was primarily interested in the pursuit of pleasure. It was the experience of bohemia, not the hope of a reorganized society, that captivated them.

Finally, antifeminism was aided by extraordinary accusations of communism lodged against many feminist leaders by organizations like the American Legion and the Daughters of the American Revolution (which had evolved from a sometime advocate of social feminism into a right-wing supporter of military preparedness). Jane Addams was charged with being a communist because she was involved in pacifist causes; Florence Kelley was similarly accused because she had a socialist past and supported the Child Labor Amendment, which the extreme right saw as a socialist measure. Such charges did not create a major stir in the 1920s, but they contributed to the popular belief that feminism was foreign and dangerous.

"FLAMING YOUTH"—NEW LIBERTIES, OLD ATTITUDES

Feminism also failed to take root in the 1920s largely because it did not appeal to the young women of that generation. No movement can prosper long without attracting younger members to its ranks. In 1910, the suffrage campaign had been reactivated by a group of younger women, including Alice Paul and Rheta Childe Dorr. However, this was not true of the feminist cause in the 1920s—indeed, not until the 1960s.

Rarely before or since the 1920s has a generation of youths been so conscious of its own identity or of its perceived difference from an older generation. Their attitude was cavalier to the concerns and achievements of their elders, including the hard-won gains in women's rights. Lillian Hellman, playwright and member of this generation, has described their feelings:

> By the time I grew up the fight for the emancipation of women, their rights under the law, in the office, in bed, was stale stuff. My generation didn't think much about the place or the problems of women, were not conscious that the designs we saw around us had so recently been formed or that we were still part of that formation.[17]

Young people had other preoccupations. Foremost was their rebellion against the mores of Victorian culture, especially its sex taboos. They set the tone of the 1920s. They were the leaders in fashion, in dance, in the introduction of a freer morality. Young women were "flappers," and they lived for fun and freedom, which they defined in terms of short skirts, cigarettes, automobiles, dancing, sports, and speakeasies. Young, middle-class women began to adopt behavior already observable among the working class before the war as their percentage of the college population and the general attendance in high school rose rapidly.

*A Ford Motor Company
advertisement appeals to the
working woman.*

In the 1920s, artist John Held, Jr., captured the "flapper" for *The New Yorker* magazine in a series of drawings that were widely reprinted. Like the Gibson girl of the 1890s, Held's flapper became the symbol of her generation. With her short, straight skirt, her lean torso and her cropped hair, the rouge on her cheeks and the cigarette in her mouth, she was the epitome of youth, adventure, and healthy sex.

*Flappers compete in a
Charleston dance contest.*

To what extent such behavior constituted a true sexual revolution is debatable. Some rudimentary surveys of sex attitudes were attempted during the 1920s, but what they pointed to was a limited, rather than an extensive, change in behavior. Among her sample of about 2,000 older, middle-class women, Katherine B. Davis found that 7 percent of the married women and 14 percent of the unmarried women had had sexual relations before marriage. Among the latter group, 80 percent saw no justification for pre-marital sex.[18] In Denver, Judge Ben Lindsey, whose work among teen-agers through the Juvenile Court there gained him a national reputation, judged that before the war, young men in sizable numbers commonly had had sexual relations with prostitutes; after the war, however, their schoolmates were their sexual partners—a change produced by the vice commission's success in breaking up the red-light districts, by the war experience, and by the new permissiveness among young women. Yet Lindsey was reluc-

John Held, Jr.'s answer to the Gibson girl appears in a 1926 issue of Life *magazine.*

1896   1926

Thirty Years of "Progress"!

tant to estimate that more than 10 percent of Denver's young women were permissive when it came to sex.[19] Indeed, surveys of the incidence of premarital sex among college students in the 1930s indicated that no more than 25 percent of all women students engaged in sex before marriage.[20]

Far from all young women adopted the new standards of behavior. If they had, the "sexual revolution" would have emancipated their own generation, and their daughters and granddaughters in the generations to come would not have reported conflicts with their parents over their own desires for sexual freedom. Novelist Mary McCarthy, raised in the 1920s in a strict Catholic family, was forbidden to date until she was 18; instead she daydreamed about men. In one wild and secret flight with female friends to a distant state, she had a passionate, although unconsummated, affair with a married man who gallantly preserved her "virtue."[21] Author Anne Morrow Lindbergh has reported that she spent her time at Smith College and afterward in the classic manner of the bright college student: working hard at her studies, hoping to win the poetry prize, seeing numerous men, and worrying about whether she would ever marry.[22]

Film star Clara Bow, dubbed the "It Girl," set the style for flappers.

The path that Anne Lindbergh followed was, more often than not, a characteristic one. Sexual emancipation, if it led anywhere, led to marriage. Divorce statistics continued to rise, as they had throughout the previous decade. But the number of marriages remained equally high, and the median age of first marriage remained relatively constant. Some historians argue that the real sexual revolution occurred among married women, who began to demand sexual fulfillment in marriage and to use birth control in larger numbers than before.

Yet young women could not help but be influenced by the currents of the age. One analyst of women undergraduates wrote that "freedom" was their primary goal. It meant, on the one hand, attending countless college proms and weekends; on the other, an aversion to any rules, even to compulsory bed and meal times.[23] Many commentators agreed that the crusading spirit that had motivated the first generation of women college students had dissipated. Now, women often chose to attend college because they could not think of anything better to do.[24] Conformity to social norms and learning how to succeed in a competitive society were the major undergraduate goals; sororities and fraternities everywhere set the standards. "Freedom,"

*Charles Dana Gibson catches up
with the new attitudes of the
1920s.*

defined in sexual and personal terms, was the new value.[25] If young
women wanted power and influence over men, they could get it by
playing standard female roles—by being a temptress on the dance
floor or a companion on the gold course. They could drink, they could
smoke, they could enjoy sex. Why choose the difficult paths that Susan
Anthony and Alice Paul had followed?

Seen in retrospect, however, this generation of young women often
did not know what to do with the freedom achieved. Its rebellion was
typically adolescent, and once played out, its adherents fell back on

*A page from the 1927 issue of
the* Vassarion, *showing
sophomore students.*

the standards of their parents and their culture—marriage and motherhood. In no way had this generation overcome women's greatest difficulty: the sex-role conditioning that was an integral part of their upbringing.

Then, as before and after, little girls played with dolls; their brothers, with cars. Boys were encouraged to run and jump and to suppress their emotions; girls, to be ladylike and to express their emotions. Girls who stepped out of line were considered "tomboys." Pilot Amelia Earhart's husband, in his biography of her, emphasized that Earhart's childhood had been strikingly different from that of most girls of her age; along with her brothers, she was permitted, even encouraged, to experiment, to build, to explore the out-of-doors. He traced her later "masculine" spirit of adventure to this deviant upbringing. Psychologist Floyd Allport, writing in 1929, called for an end to the subtle indoctrination of sex roles in home and school. Woman, he wrote, "not through nature but by early training. . . . becomes a reflection of a feminine image which men carry about in their heads."[26]

Progressive women had risen above such conditioning because to do so was new and challenging and because they and their culture had played down the importance of sex in people's lives. But the generation of the 1920s was overwhelmed by it. Writing in the early 1930s, one participant in the youth culture of the 1920s remembered that they had debated free love and companionate marriage, that they had bobbed their hair and carried hip flasks—but that there the rebellion had stopped. Ten years later, these women were respectable citizens, "worried about the interest on the mortgage; making poor Aunt Ida feel she really isn't a burden; and fervently hoping Junior will escape the epidemic of measles ravaging the fourth grade."[27]

Those women who did try to combine marriage and a career still found it difficult. Yet the number of married women in the work force continued to rise—from 5.6 percent in 1900 to 10.7 percent in 1910 to 11.7 percent by 1930. Moreover, the number of professional women who were married was also rising—from 12 percent in 1910 to 27 percent in 1930. Many of these women worked due to economic necessity or the influence of the decade's consumerism. "The two-car family," noted economist Lorine Pruette, "demands the two-wage family."[28] Still the increasing participation of married women in the work force constituted one of the major long-term trends in the employment of women and directly challenged the traditional beliefs that linked women with the home and defined masculinity partly in terms of a man's ability to provide unaided for his family.

But such work on the part of married women was not so easily pursued. Late in the decade and early in the 1930s, popular journals featured a number of revealing "autobiographies" and "confessions" by self-styled "ex-feminists." The revelations were similar. Even "liberated" women found it impossible both to work and to have a family. All began marriage with their husbands' agreement that family responsibilities were to be shared, but faced with reality and given their upbringings, husband and wife soon reverted to their conventional roles. One woman realized that the problem was partly her own lack of strength but also blamed her husband. "He has given lipservice to my aspirations," she wrote, "but when it has come to the difficulty of putting them into practice, he has not helped me."[29] Another woman, who married a socialist she met while working in Norman Thomas's office, had the same problem: lack of support from her husband. Bitterly she wrote, "Feminism as a personal religion was as interesting to him as Mr. Thomas's socialism," but not when it interfered with his own aspirations and comfort. For the many women who wanted, as one "ex-feminist" admitted, "the rich domestic life of husband, home, and babies that my mother's generation enjoyed" and a career as well, the problem was indeed profound.[30]

WOMEN AT WORK: PROGRESS AND SETBACKS

Professional Women

The popular evidence of women's emancipation in the 1920s—the number of women at work, the freer sexuality, the new clothing styles—masked the discrimination against women that still existed. At the height of women's employment during the First World War, for example, only 5 percent of all women workers had not been in the labor force before the war. What seemed to reflect new employment actually reflected the fact that women who were already members of the work force were promoted to higher-paying, higher-skilled jobs during the war. In some cases, this meant a permanent transfer into clerical work. In other cases, women who had replaced men were demoted or fired when the war ended. In Cleveland, Ohio, the women who became streetcar operators were cultural heroines for a time but were laid off when returning male operators went on strike against the women's

After the First World War, many working women were demoted, fired, or permanently *transferred into clerical work when the men they had replaced returned to their jobs.*

continued employment. In some industries, like automobiles or iron and steel, women had registered permanent gains by 1920. But according to Women's Bureau analysts, the opening of some new industries to women and the advancement of a few women to skilled positions were offset by the wage discrimination that existed in every category of women's employment.[31]

Similarly, the common assumption that the proportion of women who worked increased during the 1920s is fallacious. It is true that an additional 2 million women had jobs, but this was primarily a reflection of the general population growth. In fact, whereas 23 percent of American women were employed in 1920, 24 percent were employed in 1930—an increase of only 1 percent. This stability in employment figures was partly due to the fact that the immigration restriction acts of the early 1920s cut off the flow of Eastern European families into the nation.

Furthermore, with the exception of their movement into clerical work, women did not substantially improve their position in the labor force in the 1920s. Although the number of women increased in most professions, women still held jobs that were less prestigious and lower-paying than men did. For example, although women received about one-third of the graduate degrees awarded annually, only 4 percent of the full professors in American colleges were women. Few colleges would promote women beyond the lower ranks: Mary Ellen Chase, novelist and distinguished scholar of English literature, left the University of Minnesota in 1926 for Smith College, because it was clear that Minnesota would not promote a woman beyond assistant professor. Smith, however, preserved enough of its feminist origins to deal more fairly with its female faculty.[32]

In medicine, the proportion of women to men actually declined. Dr. Alice Hamilton thought that it had been easier for a woman to become a doctor earlier in the century, when feminism was still a powerful force and "a woman doctor could count on the loyalty of a group of devoted feminists who would choose a woman [doctor] because she was a woman."[33] Few medical or law schools refused admission to women, but most applied quotas on female admission. (Until 1945, the quota was about 5 percent.) Most women lawyers and doctors continued to perform the less lucrative and challenging services in their fields or to minister principally to women and children. The few women who were dentists were primarily children's orthodontists, but they predominated in that lucrative field only temporarily; by the 1950s, most children's orthodontists were men.

Even the expanding fields of business administration and advertising offered limited opportunities for women aside from clerical work. Female Horatio Algers, it is true, could always be found to bolster the nation's success mythology and its belief that feminism had achieved its goals. Often, these businesswomen made their money by marketing products designed for women. Industries like fashion and retailing have always been open to determined career women. And during these years, shrewd female entrepreneurs recognized the immense potential of the market created by the new sex consciousness. Helena Rubinstein, who parlayed her mother's home beauty cream into a gigantic cosmetics empire, was only of a number of such women. Another was her competitor, Elizabeth Arden.

Making their way in the masculine world of business was not easy. M. Louise Luckinbill, a secretary at the Schultz–McGregor Advertising Agency in New York City, declined a promotion to a vice presidency. Businessmen, she wrote, "would throw up their hands in horror at the idea of a woman being. . .vice-president of an [advertising]

*Helena Rubinstein, to whom
personal beauty was a source of
both power and profit.*

agency which served them."[34] Edith Mae Cummings, who built her
job as an insurance saleswoman into a firm of her own, contended
that any woman could succeed in business through self-reliance and
perseverance. Yet, she admitted, businessmen were hostile to businesswomen because they were afraid that women so employed would
lose their "feminine daintiness."[35] Helena Rubinstein recalled, "It was
not easy being a hard-working woman in a man's world." To survive
in the business world, she became a tyrant. Her rages were legendary.
She married a count, lived in lavish style, and was known as "madame." For "added courage," she wore elaborate and expensive jewelry.
To Rubinstein, the quest for beauty, which was central to her business
and her life, did not represent enslavement, but was a "force. . .to
make you feel greater than you are."[36]

In keeping with women's continuing professional participation in
the 1920s, women writers and artists appeared in greater numbers
and received more and more critical acclaim. In the late nineteenth
century, Emily Dickinson and Edith Wharton developed complex personal styles, initiating a trend away from the sentimentalism that characterized the writings of Harriet Beecher Stowe and the scores of best-
selling women authors who dominated popular fiction in that century.

In the 1920s, poet Edna St. Vincent Millay, with her candle burning "at both ends," became the symbol of the nihilism and emancipated life style that characterized writers in those years. Willa Cather continued her distinguished career as a writer of frontier fiction and a critic of the technological society. Dorothy Parker dominated the New York intellectuals and wits who gathered at the famed "round table" at the Algonquin Hotel. Gertrude Stein's Parisian salon was a center for important American artists abroad. Jessie Fauset and Zora Neale Hurston were central figures within the Harlem Renaissance—the outpouring of black writings that established blacks' claim to a powerful literary imagination.

Yet for most women artists and authors, difficulties still existed. In the 1920s, for example, painter Georgia O'Keefe began her distinguished career, which has spawned the last seven decades. But gaining recognition was not easy. Her friendship with Alfred Stieglitz, the famed photographer and promoter of new talent, was initally important in securing New York shows for her and in attracting the critics' attention. Even then, her work was judged more in terms of her sex than her artistic ability. Her huge canvases filled with enormous, surrealistic flowers confounded critics; the paintings violated the canons that women were expected to do small and fragile works of art and that flowers were particularly appropriate subjects for them. O'Keefe's flowers were deemed expressions of a female "eroticism" and of woman's greater "emotionality."

O'Keefe's work would eventually receive universal acclaim, but artists in other fields were not so fortunate. Major symphony orchestras contained virtually no women musicians (despite a lengthy tradition that identified amateur music with women), and the field of conducting was especially closed to them. When conductor Antonia Brico returned to the United States in the 1930s after an acclaimed European debut, few orchestras were willing to engage her; ultimately, she founded her own orchestra of women players. What woman, it was said, possessed either the authority or the musicianship to mold 80 or more instrumentalists into an effective ensemble?

Working-Class Working Women

Working-class working women faced obstacles during the 1920s. On the surface, the decade seemed to be a time of economic prosperity, but it was a prosperity in which many workers did not participate.

Vast sectors of the economy were in a state of depression; at least 50 percent of all farm and industrial workers earned barely enough to survive. Prominent among this group were black workers, whose migration North increased substantially after the passage of immigration restriction legislation in the early 1920s, and Mexican workers, who were not included in the terms of the restrictive legislation because powerful farmers and industrialists in the Southwest wished to use them as cheap laborers.

The increased demand for processed food due to urbanization had vastly stimulated farm production and the canning industry in the West and the Southwest after the First World War. Mexicans were an obvious source of cheap labor for these enterprises, especially since Chinese and Japanese laborers, as well as immigrants from Eastern Europe and the Mediterranean regions, were restricted by this point. Among Mexican migrants, entire families worked—picking the crops at piecework rates and living in substandard housing provided by their employers. Without citizenship, they could easily be exploited and used as a divisive wedge against native workers and their threats of unionized labor. At a time when the federal government considered an annual income of $800 to be the subsistence minimum for a family, many Mexican families made less than $100 a year.

Such exploitation would remain characteristic of Mexican employment, which would wax and wane from the 1920s to the 1980s in tune with government attention and economic conditions on both sides of the border. The depression of the 1930s, which brought U.S. immigration restriction and the end of the economic incentive to move North, stimulated the replacement of Mexican workers by the Oklahoma migrants celebrated in John Steinbeck's *Grapes of Wrath*. Labor shortages during the Second World War produced the so-called "bracero program," under which the U.S. government's oversight of labor contracts to ensure equitable working conditions for Mexican workers, who were in demand in a time of labor shortages, was largely undermined by the power of local employers. More recently, desperate economic conditions in Mexico and, more generally, in Latin America have once again, as in the 1920s, resulted in a massive Hispanic immigration to the United States—an immigration that has been welcomed by employers as a source of cheap labor but that has created a major strain on government and social resources.

During the 1920s, most unskilled laborers—not just immigrants—

experienced difficult economic conditions. Sizable wage increases went primarily to skilled laborers. The income of many unskilled workers, which included the majority of women workers, rose hardly at all. If anything, the relative position of these women worsened. According to one major study, the differential between the hourly wages paid to unskilled male and female workers rose from 6.3 cents in 1923 to 10.2 cents in 1929.[37]

Working-class mothers who worked away from home faced particular difficulties. For the most part, they left young children with relatives or neighbors and their older children often fended for themselves after school.[38] In 1930, one study revealed, there were approximately 800 nursery schools in the nation.[39] Despite the fact that most of these schools were run by charitable organizations specifically for lower-income working women, most mothers were suspicious of them—a suspicion that stemmed partly from the fact that welfare agencies only too readily placed the children of indigent mothers in asylums and foster homes. Furthermore, many social workers opposed the further establishment of nursery centers, arguing that what was needed was extensions of existing county and state relief programs to mothers with children so that they could stay at home. However, such programs, which many states had mandated in the late 1910s and early 1920s, were badly underfunded and poorly administered.[40]

In some respects, these conditions of low pay and little relief for working mothers reflected the fact that the union movement was in disarray in the 1920s. Membership had plummeted, and there was not much significant strike activity. Women workers, as well as men, were reticent to challenge employers, who promised (but generally did not deliver) a new welfare capitalism under which employers would assume responsibility for the welfare of their workers. But workers were constantly threatened by unemployment during the decade and chastened by the defeats that unions suffered in a series of major strikes after the end of the war. By 1919, for example, telephone operators in New England, who were primarily women, had finally managed to form a union, but an unsuccessful strike in 1921 proved to be its undoing. Membership in the union evaporated, and former members were fired and blacklisted by the telephone companies. No further attempts at organization or strike activity were made during the 1920s.

Even the International Ladies' Garment Workers' Union (ILGWU) fell on hard times. The rise in demand for ready-to-wear clothing for women was a boon to the garment industry, but individual companies became alarmingly dependent on the caprice of fashion. When a dress style failed, the company that had created it and the workers who had made it suffered accordingly. Such worker insecurity made organization difficult. Even more disastrous for the ILGWU was the appearance of a strong communist faction among its membership in the 1920s. Instead of concentrating on organization and agitation, the union spent the decade engaged in bitter infighting for control. By 1930, the communists were defeated, but the struggle had nearly destroyed the union. Its membership had dropped from 250,000 to 40,000; its treasury was over $2 million in debt.

Those progressive organizations that had focused on working women—the Consumers' League and the Women's Trade Union League, in particular—continued operations in the 1920s, but they, too, were beset by problems. The WTUL, dependent on the regular unions for its funds, was no more successful in organizing workers than these unions were. Its budget was $20,000 yearly, and the bulk of these funds went to lobbyists for special legislation. The Consumers' League continued to focus on special legislation for working women, but the 1921 Supreme Court decision in *Adkins v. Children's Hospital*, which outlawed federal minimum-wage laws for women, made advances in special legislation difficult.

Moreover, it was difficult to persuade well-to-do women to support progressive programs for working women. They were busy with other activities and willing to believe businessmen's propaganda. In 1926, Maude Nathan, a wealthy founder of the New York Consumers' League, wrote that there had been a "complete metamorphosis" over the years in working conditions for women in urban department stores. Consumers' Leagues, she implied, were no longer necessary, at least not for women in this category. Yet the improvements, she had to admit, were only relative. Although pay had risen, it was still low; women worked a 12-hour rather than a 16-hour day; and they had won the right to sit down on occasion and to take a week's vacation a year. All of this, according to Nathan, proved that the merchants were "vying with each other in giving humane attention" to their employees. The problem, in short, had been solved.[41] Nathan's attitude was representative of the popular view that women were achieving equality on a wide variety of fronts and that society need do little more for them.

Amelia Earhart, whose solo flight on a Lockheed Vega monoplane from Newfoundland to Ireland in 1932 made her one of the most celebrated women of her time.

THE NEW HEROINES

Every age has its heroines, and those chosen by the 1920s generation tell us much about the prevailing attitudes toward women. In the 1910s, Jane Addams had been the national heroine—the secular saint whose deep compassion and forceful personality endeared her to a generation of humanitarian Americans. The heroines of the 1920s were strikingly different. Among them, pilot Amelia Earhart, movie actress Mary Pickford, and the "vamp," a standard film character, stand out as representative. Although their careers seemed to give weight to women's emancipation, together they signaled the demise of feminism as the prewar generation had known it.

In her way, Amelia Earhart was a feminist *manqué.* Her early career was peripatetic, split between devotions to social feminism and to flying. A graduate of Barnard College, Earhart tried a number of jobs before she became a settlement worker in Boston. Meanwhile, she learned to fly. She searched out women instructors, because she found male pilots insulting, hostile, or overprotective. In 1927, representatives of Amy Phipps Guest, a wealthy New York flying enthusiast, contacted Earhart with the proposition that she make a solo flight across the Atlantic, as Lindbergh had done the year before. With Guest's financial backing, Earhart made the flight, was welcomed by impressive crowds, and vaulted to national prominence.

Earhart's life was an eloquent testimony to women's abilities. But in the long run, her fame and her achievements had a limited feminist impact. Part of the difficulty was that she was shy and self-effacing—a female counterpart to the boyishly appealing Lindbergh. She was popularly known as "Lady Lindy" (she bore a striking physical resemblance to Lindbergh), and there were those who said that this was the reason she had been chosen for the flight. Despite her membership in the Woman's Party, her feminism was modest. She wrote, "probably my greatest satisfaction was to indicate by example, now and then, that women can sometimes do things themselves if given the chance." But it was flying above all that thrilled her and that she publicized; her books described each of her flights in detail and celebrated the dangers and glories of aviation.

Earhart's last flight, on which she disappeared, took place in 1937. After her presumed death, there were other women flyers, but none captured the public imagination in the same way. As aviation became professionalized, men flyers came to dominate the career. Finally, in 1931, an innovation was added to commercial air flights that made the future position of women in aviation clear. Airline stewardesses—who were then called "hostesses" and were required to have a nursing degree—made their appearance. Now, as doctors had their nurses and businessmen their secretaries, pilots had their helpers, too. Once again, women were to perform the traditional role of service.

If the public of prewar America made the social worker the heroine of the 1910s, the public of the 1920s thrilled to the individual feats of courage and daring that Earhart provided in abundance. Mary Pickford and the "vamp" gave expression to two other sides of the American character—both antifeminist in implication. Pickford was the virginal child–woman incarnate, "America's Sweetheart," its "Little Mary"; the vamp was the eternal temptress, the Eve, who led men astray and lived for sex.

The world's first airline
stewardesses—"hostesses" hired
in 1930 to fly the Chicago to
San Francisco run.

Between the First World War and the 1930s, Pickford triumphed.
Golden-haired and impish, she played adolescents on the verge of
maturity—roles similar to those that Shirley Temple would play at a
younger age in the next decade. Often, she was portrayed as athletic
and rebellious; sometimes, as a working woman. To this extent, she
mirrored trends of the age, but Pickford was no feminist. However,
she was iron-willed and shrewd; she was the first in her profession
to demand and receive the high salaries that have become standard
in the movie industry. She was less successful in convincing the public
to accept her as something other than the personification of pure youth—
a role she came to hate. When, in the late 1920s, she cut off the long
blonde curls that had been her trademark, she almost lost her audience. As much as it thrilled to the *femme fatale* and the sex dramas of

"America's Sweetheart," Mary Pickford, in Rebecca of Sunnybrook Farm.

the 1920s, the movie audience wanted Pickford to show them an idyllic America, where women never grew up.

The opposite character, the "vamp", appealed to the nation's new fascination with sexuality. Her origins can be traced to the days of prewar burlesque and vaudeville, to music-hall stars like Lillian Russell and the Florodora girls, who bared shoulder and ankle to beguile the male public. As was often the case, the war simply speeded up a trend that was already underway. As a type, the "vamp" underwent several transformations during the course of the decade. For a time, she was the seductress, pure and simple; with the rise of the youth cult and the appearance of censorship codes that restricted open sexuality on the screen, she became the "flapper." Finally, she emerged as the *femme fatale*, who remained a major screen character into the 1930s, particularly as personified by Greta Garbo and Marlene Dietrich.

The vamp first appeared in 1915 in a movie entitled *A Fool There Was*. It starred Theda Bara, who became famous overnight for her brand of sultry sexuality. Press agents transmogrified her typical

Theda Bara, the star of
Cleopatra, *was promoted as the*
"wickedest force in the world."

American background into a saga of Egyptian illegitimacy and sexual
license: She was the daughter of an Algerian soldier and an Egyptian
dancer; she was kidnapped and raised by a band of Egyptian cut-
throats; she had occult powers. Bara supposedly played the role in
real life as well as on the screen. (Bara was also the first screen personality to wear eye makeup; Helena Rubinstein invented it for her as
a way of creating a new cosmetic market.) After the war, the mantle
of "sex queen" was passed on to Gloria Swanson. She was more sleek
and sophisticated than Bara, but Swanson fulfilled the same role of
seductress. In her films, surprisingly, wives were sometimes allowed
to philander and to divorce their husbands and women of easy virtue
often escaped punishment. In the beginning, before censorship was
imposed, the movie industry endorsed women's new sexual freedom.
    The flapper was different; she was the flirt—the sex tease who eter-
nally promised sex play but not mature passion. There were overtones
of the Pickford role in her character, the flapper was the virginal,
healthy adolescent, grown a bit older and wiser. Although the flapper

Marlene Dietrich personifies the femme fatale—*subtle and sophisticated, mysterious and ageless.*

smoked, danced, and went to petting parties, she was honest of heart and deserved the hero's love. The *femme fatale*, however, returned to the tradition of the vamp. Whereas the flapper had been flighty, the *femme fatale* was sophisticated, ageless, and often tragic; but whereas the vamp had been open and brazen, the *femme fatale* was subtle and mysterious. Whether vamp, flapper, or *femme fatale*, the end in life for all three was a man.

That another screen image for women might have been possible is illustrated by the popularity of the prewar serials that often starred a woman as the main character. The most famous of these was the *Perils of Pauline*, starring Pearl White. These women were capable of finding their own way out of a given predicament without the assistance of the strong and handsome hero. The early Pauline could ride and shoot as well as any man. And in *The Goddess*, made in 1915, the heroine

Pearl White, the "Pauline" of the film serial The Perils of Pauline, *could take care of herself.*

Margaret Gorman, Miss Washington, D.C., becomes the nation's first "Miss America" in 1921.

was a modern Joan of Arc, raised on a desert island in the belief that she was a goddess destined to solve the world's ills.

Such feminist themes were inappropriate to the decade of the 1920s, which wanted its women soft and pliant and accepted aggressiveness only in sex or sports. The emblem of change became the "beauty queen." In 1920, hotel owners in Atlantic City, New Jersey, concocted a promotional scheme to lengthen the summer season at the beach. Their idea was to host a beauty contest late in September, when most vacationers would normally have gone home—a contest to select America's reigning beauty, its "Miss America." These promoters raised the beauty contest to a level of national attention and enshrined it as a typically American institution. And more than anything else, they provided the ultimate symbol of what the America woman in the 1920s was supposed to be.

NOTES

1 Emily Newell Blair, "Wanted—A New Feminism," *Independent Woman* (December 1930): 499.

2 Sara Barbara Brumbaugh, *Democratic Experience and Education in the National League of Women Voters* (New York: Teachers College Press, 1946), p. 45.

3 Martin Gruberg, *Women in American Politics: An Assessment and Sourcebook* (Oshkosh, WI: Academia Press, 1968), p. 91.

4 Marion K. Sanders, *The Lady and the Vote* (Boston: Houghton Mifflin, 1956), pp. 141– 42.

5 Anna Steese Richardson, "Is the Women's Club Dying?" *Harper's*, CLIX (October 1929): 607.

6 Rheta Childe Dorr, *A Woman of Fifty* (New York: Funk & Wagnalls, 1924), pp. 280*ff.*

7 Marie Louise Degen, *The History of the Woman's Peace Party* (Baltimore: The Johns Hopkins Press, 1939), p. 20.

8 June Sochen, *The New Woman: Feminism in Greenwich Village, 1910–1920* (New York: Quadrangle, 1972), pp 115–16.

9 Vida Scudder, *On Journey* (New York: E.P. Dutton, 1937), p.300.

10 Suzanne LaFollette, *Concerning Women* (New York: Albert and Charles Boni, 1926), p.10.

11 Elizabeth Onatavia, "Give Us Our Privileges," *Scribner's*, LXXXVII (June 1930): 593–94.

12 *Ibid.*, p. 597.

13 Dorothy Dunbar Bromley, "Feminist—New Style," *Harper's*, CLV (October 1927): 552–60.

14 Mabel Dodge Luhan, *Intimate Memories* (New York: Harcourt Brace Jovanovich, Inc., 1936), Vol.3: *Movers and Shakers*, p. 263.

15 Charlotte Perkins Gilman, *The Living of Charlotte Perkins Gilman: An Autobiography* (New York: Appleton-Century-Crofts, 1935), pp. 332–33.

16 *Ibid.*, p. 313.

17 Lillian Hellman, *An Unfinished Woman: A Memoir* (Boston: Little, Brown, 1969), p. 35.

18 Katherine B. Davis, *Factors in the Sex Life of Twenty-Two Hundred Women* (New York: Harper & Row, 1929).

19 Ben B. Lindsey and Evans Wainwright, *The Revolt of Modern Youth* (New York: Boni and Liveright, 1925), pp. 66–67.

20 Dorothy Dunbar Bromley and Florence Britten, *Youth and Sex: A Study of Thirteen Hundred College Students* (New York: Harper & Row, 1938).

[21] Mary McCarthy, *Memories of a Catholic Girlhood* (New York: Harcourt Brace Jovanovich, Inc., 1957).

[22] Anne Morrow Lindbergh, *Bring Me a Unicorn: Diaries and Letters of Anne Morrow Lindbergh, 1922–1928* (New York: Harcourt Brace Jovanovich, Inc., 1972).

[23] Dorothy Waldo, "College or Not?" in Mabelle Babcock Blake *et al.*, *The Education of the Modern Girl* (Boston: Houghton Mifflin, 1929), pp. 99–118.

[24] Jessie Bernard, *Academic Women* (University Park: Pennsylvania State University Press, 1964), pp. 36–37.

[25] Phyllis Blanchard and Carolyn Manasses, *New Girls for Old* (New York: Macauley, 1937), p. 175.

[26] Floyd Allport, "Seeing Women as They Are," *Harper's*, CLVIII (March 1929): 406.

[27] Maxine Davis, *The Lost Generation: A Portrait of American Youth Today* (New York: Macmillan, 1936), pp. 25–26.

[28] Lorine Pruette, "The Married Woman and the Part-Time Job," *Annals of the American Academy of Politial and Social Science* (1929): 302.

[29] "Confessions of an Ex-Feminist," *New Republic*, XXII (April 14, 1926): 218*ff.*

[30] Worth Tuttle, "Autobiography of an Ex-Feminist," *The Atlantic Monthly*, CLII (December 1933): 645.

[31] Alice Rogers Hager, "Occupations and Earnings of Women in Industry," *Annals of the American Academy of Political and Social Science* (1929): 65–73.

[32] Mary Ellen Chase, *A Goodly Fellowship* (New York: Macmillan, 1939), p. 285.

[33] Alice Hamilton, *Exploring the Dangerous Trades: The Autobiography of Alice Hamilton* (Boston: Little, Brown, 1943), p. 268.

[34] *Women of Today* (1926): 235.

[35] Edith Mae Cummings, *Pots, Pans, and Millions: A Study of Women's Right to Be in Business; Her Proclivities and Capacity for Success* (Washington, D.C.: National School of Business Science for Women, 1929).

[36] Helena Rubinstein, *My Life for Beauty* (London: Bodley Head, 1964).

[37] Irving Bernstein, *The Lean Years: A History of the American Worker, 1920–1933* (Boston: Houghton Mifflin, 1960), p. 69.

[38] Gwendolyn Hughes Berry, "Mothers in Industry," *Annals of the American Academy of Political and Social Science* (1929): 315–24.

[39] The White House Conference on Child Health and Protection, *Nursery Education* (New York: Century, 1931).

[40] Katharine Anthony, *Mothers Who Must Earn* (New York: Survey Associates, 1914).

41 Maude Nathan, *The Story of an Epoch-Making Movement* (Garden City, NY: Doubleday, Page, 1926), pp. 105–109.

BIBLIOGRAPHY

Historians disagree as to whether the position of women and the feminist movement advanced or declined in the 1920s. The classic argument for improvement is contained in J. Stanley Lemons, *The Woman Citizen: Social Feminism in the 1920s* (Urbana: University of Illinois Press, 1973). Lois Scharf, *To Work and To Wed: Female Employment, Feminism, and the Great Depression* (Westport, CT: Greenwood Press, 1980), takes the opposite point of view. Lemons' position has been restated from a broader perspective by Susan Ware, *Holding Their Own* (Boston: Twayne, 1982). Also consult Susan Becker, *The Origins of the Equal Rights Amendment: American Feminism Between the Wars* (Westport, CT: Greenwood Press, 1981), and Carole Nichols' interesting "Votes and More for Women: Suffrage and After in Connecticut," *Women & History* (Spring 1983).

On the social-work profession, the settlement houses, and social reform in general, see Jane Addams, *The Second Twenty Years at Hull House* (New York: Macmillan, 1930); Clarke A. Chambers, *Seedtime of Reform: American Social Service and Social Action, 1918–1933* (Minneapolis: University of Minnesota Press, 1963); and the 1929 issue of the *Annals of the American Academy of Political and Social Science*, "Women in the Modern World." On cultural attitudes, Frederick Lewis Allen, *Only Yesterday: An Informal History of the 1920s* (New York: Harper & Row, 1931), and Helen Merrell Lynd and Robert S. Lynd, *Middletown: A Study in Contemporary American Culture* (New York: Harcourt Brace Jovanovich, Inc., 1929), are still indispensable. Walter Lippman, *A Preface to Morals* (New York: Macmillan, 1929), is insightful.

There are as yet no comprehensive studies of advertising, of the impact of Freudian ideas, of the participation of women in the peace movement, or of the exact dimensions of the youth "rebellion" in the 1920s. On each of these subjects, consult Otis Pease, *The Responsibilities of American Advertising: Private Control and Public Influence, 1920–1940* (New Haven: Yale University Press, 1958); Grace Adams, "The Rise and Fall of Psychology," *Atlantic,* CLIII (1934): 82–92; Lucille C. Birnbaum, "Behaviorism in the 1920s," *American Quarterly,* VII (Spring 1955). 15–30; and Gertrude Bussey and Margaret Tims, *Women's International League for Peace and Freedom, 1915–1965* (London: Allen & Unwin, 1965). The culture of college students in this period has been explored by Paula Fass, *The Damned and the Beautiful: American Youth in the 1920s* (New York: Oxford University Press, 1977).

To what extent the 1920s witnessed a change in sexual attitudes has caused considerable debate. Many historians (the author included) think that the pre-

First World War era was the crucial period and that the changes originated first among the working class. Fass, *Damned and the Beautiful,* provides a thoughtful statement of the limitations of the "sexual revolution." Elaine Showalter, *These Modern Women: Autobiographical Essays from the Twenties* (Old Westbury, NY: Feminist Press, 1978), has reprinted a set of moving autobiographies by contemporary women indicating the depths of the difficulties individual women experienced in this decade. The popular impression of striking change in the 1920s is partly based on the well-publicized exploits of several well-known women. In many ways, Zelda Fitzgerald, the wife of F. Scott Fitzgerald, became a symbol for the abandoned behavior of the age. The story of the triumph and ultimate tragedy of her life is told by Nancy Milford, *Zelda: A Biography* (New York: Harper & Row, 1970). For contemporary points of view on morality, see Phyllis Blanchard and Carolyn Manasses, *New Girls for Old* (New York: Macauley, 1937); V.F. Calverton, *The Bankruptcy of Marriage* (New York: Macauley, 1928); and Ben B. Lindsey and Evans Wainwright, *The Revolt of Modern Youth* (New York: Boni & Liveright, 1925). Also consult V.F. Calverton and S.C. Schmalhausen, *Sex in Civilization* (New York: Macauley, 1929); Floyd Dell, *Love in the Machine Age; A Psychological Study of the Transition from Patriarchal Society* (New York: Farrar & Rinehart, 1930); and Freda Kirchway (ed.), *Our Changing Morality: A Symposium* (New York: Albert & Charles Boni, 1924).

On women and work, see Irving Bernstein, *The Lean Years: A History of the American Worker, 1920–1933* (Boston: Houghton Mifflin, 1960); William H. Chafe, *The American Woman: Her Changing Social, Economic, and Political Roles, 1920–1970* (New York: Oxford University Press, 1972); Philip S. Foner, *Women and the American Labor Movement: From World War One to the Present* (New York: The Free Press, 1980); Alice Kessler-Harris, *Out to Work: A History of Wage-Earning Women in the United States* (New York: Oxford University Press, 1982); Winifred D. Wandersee, *Women's Work and Family Values, 1920–1940* (Cambridge, MA: Harvard University Press, 1981); and the studies of this subject by the Women's Bureau of the Department of Labor. On Mexican–American women, the available literature is slim. Consult Roberto Cabello-Argandoña, Juan Gomes-Quinones, and Patricia Herrera Duran, *The Chicana: A Comprehensive Bibliographic Study* (Los Angeles: University of California at Los Angeles Press, 1975); Alfredo Marandé, *La Chicana: The Mexican–American Woman* (Chicago: University of Chicago Press, 1979); and Rosalinda M. Gonzáles's article on the subject in Lois Scharf and Joan M. Jensen (eds.), *Decades of Discontent: The Women's Movement, 1920–1940* (Westport, CT: Greenwood Press, 1983).

On women and music, see Christine Ammen, *Unsung: A History of Women in American Music* (Westport, CT: Greenwood Press, 1980). A moving film study of the career of Antonia Brico, *Antonia: A Portrait of a Woman* (1977), has been made by Judy Collins and Jill Bodmilow and is available from Phoenix Films, Inc., 470 Park Avenue South, New York, NY 10016. On women and art, see Eleanor Munro, *Originals: American Women Artists* (New York: Simon & Schuster, 1979). For information on Georgia O'Keefe, see Laurie Lisle, *Portrait of an Artist: A Biography of Georgia O'Keefe* (New York: Harper & Row, 1980).

On Amelia Earhart, see George Palmer Putnam, *Soaring Wings: A Biography of Amelia Earhart* (New York: Harcourt Brace Jovanovich, Inc., 1939). On women in sports, see Stephanie L. Twin (ed.), *Out of the Bleachers: Writings on Women and Sport* (Old Westbury, NY: Feminist Press, 1979). On women in films, see Molly Haskell, *From Reverence to Rape: The Treatment of Women in the Movies* (New York: Holt, Rinehart & Winston, 1973); Lary May, *Screening Out the Past: The Birth of Mass Culture and the Motion Picture Industry* (New York: Oxford University Press, 1980); Marjorie Rosen, *Popcorn Venus: Women, Movies, & the American Dream* (New York: Coward, McCann & Geoghegan, 1973); Mary P. Ryan, "The Projection of a New Womanhood: The Movie Moderns in the 1920s," in Jean E. Friedman and William G. Shade (eds.), *Our American Sisters: Women in American Life and Thought*, 2nd ed. (Boston: Allyn & Bacon, 1976), pp. 366–84; and Robert Sklar, *Movie-Made America: A Cultural History of American Movies* (New York: Random House, 1976).

On women and films, also see Cecil B. DeMille, *Autobiography,* (ed.) Donald Hayne (Englewood Cliffs, NJ: Prentice-Hall, 1959); Jim Harmon and Donald F. Glut, *The Great Movie Serials: Their Sound and Fury* (Garden City, NY: Doubleday, 1955); and Mary Pickford, *Sunshine and Shadow* (Garden City, NY: Doubleday, 1955). The autobiography of actress Louise Brooks, *Lulu in Hollywood* (New York: Alfred A. Knopf, 1982), addresses broad cultural issues, as does Betty H. Fussell in her biography of Mabel Normand, *Mabel: Hollywood's First I-Don't-Care-Girl* (New York: Ticknor & Fields, 1982).

A compilation of interesting articles pertaining to material in this chapter and succeeding ones is contained in Lois Scharf and Joan M. Jensen (eds.), *Decades of Discontent: The Women's Movement, 1920–1940* (Westport, CT: Greenwood Press, 1983). For an argument that women's "separate culture" was seriously undermined in the 1920s, see Estelle Freedman, "Separatism as Strategy: Female Institution Building and American Feminism, 1870–1930," *Feminist Studies*, V (Fall 1979): 512–29.

5

WOMEN IN DEPRESSION AND WAR: 1930–1945

THE ADVANCES WOMEN made during the First World War and the 1920s were of secondary importance. Their new freedom to compete in organized sports, to wear comfortable clothes, to expect sexual fulfillment represented no inconsiderable progress. But underlying these gains was the traditional concept that home, husband, and the attainment of beauty were still woman's paramount goals. During the 1930s and 1940s, these basic attitudes about women remained constant, but some countervailing forces appeared. The federal government was starting to concern itself with the plight of working women. Labor unions began to make a genuine commitment to the organization of women workers. Major women's organizations, after a long period of factionalism, began to unite around advocacy of the Equal Rights Amendment. And the Second World War, like the First, opened up extensive employment opportunities to women. Once again, it seemed that war might bring women the liberation that peace had not provided.

FEMINISM AND WOMEN'S ORGANIZATIONS

On the whole, feminist causes were not the central concern of organized women during these years. The depression cut across class and gender divisions and refocused attention on society rather than on the individual. Thus, social feminism came to the fore. The League of Women Voters, for example, was responsible for state and national laws extending the civil service merit system and was a major promoter of both the 1936 Social Security Act and the 1937 Food, Drug, and Cosmetic Act. "We of the League are very much for the rights of women," wrote one leader, "but . . . we are not feminists primarily; we are citizens."[1] The General Federation of Women's Clubs remained moderate in its approach. In response to the economic hardships of the time, it allied itself with the home economics movement in a campaign to make labor-saving devices and efficient housework techniques familiar to housewives. Moreover, many women activists continued to work for pacifist groups like the Women's International League for Peace and Freedom. They did achieve some token successes. In 1931, Jane Addams won the Nobel Peace Prize (sharing it with Columbia University President Nicholas Murray Butler). The 1934–1935 congressional investigation, conducted by Senator Gerald Nye, of the munitions industry was largely the result of the lobbying of women's pacifist groups.

Women's groups did not entirely abandon feminist efforts, however. For a time in 1936, it appeared that the major women's organizations might unify around a charter of women's rights promoted by Margaret Anderson of the Women's Bureau. But this idea floundered due to the continuing division between supporters of special legislation and of the ERA. Most women's organizations came together to protest and lobby against state bills prohibiting the employment of married women who were not heads of households and federal legislation that disallowed the employment of both husband and wife in the federal civil service. "The apprehensions caused by this assault," writes historian Lois Scharf, "created a unity among women's organizations and institutions unmatched since the passage of the 19th amendment."[2] But the arguments advanced in opposition to this legislation were conservative. The League of Women Voters' primary objection to the federal nepotism legislation was not that it discriminated against women but rather that it violated the merit principle. Other groups characteristically argued for women's right to work on the basis of need or family interest, not on the feminist principle of equal employment opportunities.

In contrast to women during the Progressive era, reformers in the 1930s were content to work through existing organizations and to place their emphasis on influencing government legislation. An exception to this generalization was the extraordinary Association of Southern Women for the Prevention of Lynching, founded in 1930. Since Reconstruction, the lynching of black men by white mobs in southern rural communities had been a grievous social ill and a major means of social control of blacks. This vigilantist action implicitly involved women as well as men, because the crime invariably and incorrectly charged to the black victim was the rape of a white woman. Lynching revealed the sexual attitudes that lay at the heart of southern race and gender control. Blacks were oversexed, and white women had to live in constant fear of them; white men could be vigilantist in guarding the virtue of white women but violated no mores in taking their pleasure with black women.

Since the late nineteenth century, black and white southern women had organized, particularly through the medium of their churches, and had taken tentative steps toward cooperation, especially in regard to the issue of lynching. From 1920 on, through the auspices of the Methodist Women's Missionary Council and the black YWCA, annual women's interracial conferences were held. In 1922, in connection with the National Association of Colored Women, the National Association for the Advancement of Colored People (NAACP) had formed a women's group called the Antilynching Crusaders to mobilize support for its antilynching bill before Congress. The most important group, however, was the Commission on Interracial Cooperation, which had been formed in response to post-First World War race riots. Texan Jessie Daniel Ames, a widowed mother of three who supported her family after her husband's death by operating a local telephone exchange, was the catalyst for change, and it was through the Women's Committee of the Commission on Interracial Cooperation that Ames particularly worked.

Ames and her Association of Southern Women for the Prevention of Lynching mounted a massive educational campaign to reach women's organizations. These women sent out speakers, wrote articles, passed out pamphlets, and lobbied legislatures for antilynching legislation. By 1933, the incidence of such mob violence, which had been on the increase with the onset of the depression, began to decline. In 1942, the antilynching association was disbanded, its mission apparently accomplished. Yet before its demise, its achievements were impressive. Not only had it played a role in ending a brutal form of violence, but also it had persuaded white southern women to stand up against the sexual intimidation that kept them in their place—"the crown of chivalry which has been pressed like a crown of thorns on her head," as Jessie Daniel Ames put it.[3] Moreover, it was an important forerunner of the organizations that would fight the civil rights battles of the 1950s and 1960s.

ELEANOR ROOSEVELT: EXEMPLAR OF HER ERA

The social-welfare concern of the 1930s, prominent particularly during the New Deal administration of Franklin Delano Roosevelt, did not exclude women. The primary spokesperson for women both inside and outside the government was Eleanor Roosevelt. Through her radio broadcasts, newspaper columns, books, and speeches, aided by her position as the President's wife, she molded public opinion at the same time that she reflected it.

Eleanor Roosevelt was a feminist of the traditional sort. Above all, she felt that women's concerns should be focused on providing the qualities of compassion and self-abnegation that were lacking in male-dominated institutions. Her thinking was influenced by the traditional view that men functioned best as hard-headed patriarchs and professionals; women were sensitive homemakers and volunteer workers. Women had "understanding hearts," wrote Eleanor Roosevelt; men had "ability and brains." Still, in a crisis situation, men had the alarming propensity to always feel "that they must fight," and the natural pacifism of women was needed to moderate male aggressiveness.[4] Such reasoning resembled that of Jane Addams and other Progressive women of a social feminist point of view—and gained from the same strengths and suffered from the same deficiencies theirs had. Like Addams, Eleanor Roosevelt accepted the popular belief that a woman's primary responsibility was to her family. Again like Addams, she argued that the complexities of the modern world necessitated that women, with their special gifts, take part in public affairs to preserve the home. By appealing to the nation's prejudices, Eleanor Roosevelt offered compelling justifications for widening women's sphere. Yet she ran the risk of appearing to give support to those who, arguing from the same premises, would deny women any positions of real responsibility outside the home.

Eleanor Roosevelt's attitudes reflected her Victorian upbringing and early marriage. Although the Roosevelts from whom she descended were a wealthy New York family, her father was a ne'er-do-well. After her mother died at a young age, she was raised by her strict grandmother. She married her cousin Franklin Roosevelt, who was dominated in domestic matters by his own mother. For the first 15 years of her marriage, Eleanor Roosevelt was a shy and dutiful wife, regularly bearing children, acceding to the wishes of her mother-in-law, and remaining in the background while her husband served as Assistant Secretary of the Navy between 1913 and 1920 and ran for vice president on the unsuccessful Democratic ticket of 1920.

Two events provided the key to what would be the transformation of her life. The first was her discovery in 1917 of her husband's love

Eleanor Roosevelt at the age of 23, holding one of her children.

for another woman; the second was his crippling attack of polio in 1921. The first experience disillusioned her with Franklin and drove a wedge between them. Against her better judgment, she continued the marriage so that she would not endanger his political career and because she did not believe in divorce. The attack of polio gave her a new role to play in her husband's life: that of political adviser. She now found the strength to defy her mother-in-law, to persuade her husband to return to public life, and to play a public role in her own right. She gave up the round of social activities that occupied the leisure time of the typical wealthy matron to become active in the League of Women Voters, the Consumers' League, the Democratic party, and especially the Women's Trade Union League. Through her, many women leaders came to know Franklin Roosevelt and to counsel him on labor and social-welfare decisions.

*Eleanor Roosevelt opens the
Grandmothers' War Bond
League campaign.*

The transformation of her life and behavior was not easy for Eleanor Roosevelt. By nature, she was retiring. She had a high voice and a nervous giggle; she did not speak well in public, and throughout her life, she deprecated her looks. But she was faced with the probability that if she herself did not maintain her husband's position in politics while he was ill, they would permanently retire to his wealthy mother's estate and live under her domination. Eleanor Roosevelt found experts to coach her in public speaking and in politics, and she learned through practical experience. In the end, she developed into a capable speaker and a skilled politician.

Eleanor Roosevelt's problems did not end once her own difficulties had been conquered and her husband had reentered public life. During FDR's first two terms as President, the press pilloried her for playing an activist role while she was the President's wife. Cartoonists caricatured her prominent teeth and her patrician manner. But managing the household and arranging ceremonial occasions—the standard routine of a President's wife—took only a fraction of her time. Instead, she used her tremendous energy to lecture, write articles and books, and work for the Democratic Party as well. She was FDR's unofficial adviser on domestic matters and his frequent representative on public business.

For emotional support throughout her trials, she turned to other women, to whom she wrote passionate letters and with whom she spent important personal time. Estranged from her husband, she demonstrated a pattern of behavior typical of women in the nineteenth-century culture in which she had grown up and which had molded her opinions. Her writings were permeated with the idea of separate spheres for the sexes; her personal behavior reflected the earlier era's de-emphasis on heterosexuality and extolling of friendships among women. Like Jane Addams and others, she was not afraid to turn to women for enduring affection as well as for political and reform support.

By the end of the 1930s, polls began to show that Eleanor Roosevelt was very popular among the public. After her husband died in 1945, there was talk of her running for the Presidency. But like other social feminists, her interest turned to internationalism and the United Nations; she served as the U.S. representative to the United Nations General Assembly in 1946 and as U.S. representative to the United Nations Human Rights Commission and the Economic and Social Council from 1947 to 1952.

During her years of public life, Eleanor Roosevelt, the idealist, stressed women's duty to humanity—counsel that she consistently followed in her own work. Aside from her formative role in the Federal Theatre Project (the government's first extensive subsidy to the arts) and in conceiving the building of planned communities in rural areas, she was not involved in the central planning of New Deal programs. Rather, she became a special lobbyist for those groups—blacks, the poor, and women—whose interests were overlooked in power-oriented Washington. She personally served as a clearing agent of project proposals initiated by women under the auspices of agencies like the Works Projects Administration (WPA), and she lobbied for numerical guidelines for women's employment in New Deal programs. Democratic Party chairman James Farley estimated that Eleanor Roosevelt was personally responsible for the appointment of over 4,000 women to post-office jobs, many of which were then patronage positions. She

After FDR's death, Eleanor Roosevelt's interest, like other social feminists, turned to internationalism and the United Nations, where she served from 1946–1952.

would admit only female reporters to her press conferences, hoping thereby to generate more newspaper jobs for women. She regularly appeared at NAACP gatherings, and in a celebrated 1939 incident, publicly resigned from the Daughters of the American Revolution when that organization refused to allow famed black singer Marian Anderson to appear in Constitution Hall. Meanwhile, she arranged a public concert at the Lincoln Memorial.

Largely due to Eleanor's influence, Franklin Roosevelt appointed a number of women to important government offices, including the first women ministers to foreign countries (the rank directly below ambassador) and the first woman judge on the Circuit Court of Appeals (the court directly below the Supreme Court). Ruth Bryan Owen, daughter of William Jennings Bryan, served as minister to Denmark; Florence

*Eleanor Roosevelt confers with
U.S. Army officers at a
redistribution station prior to
visiting with returnees.*

Jaffray Harriman, widow of the railroad magnate, served as minister
to Norway; Florence Allen was elevated from the Ohio Supreme Court
to the Circuit Court of Appeals. Women from the Consumers' League
and the Women's Trade Union League were found in every New Deal
agency. In New Deal agencies, women constituted about one-third of
the administrators; in the regular bureaucracy, they constituted about
one-sixth. In addition to Eleanor Roosevelt's influence, these percentages also reflected the fact that women dominated the profession of
social work, from which New Deal welfare bureaucrats were largely
recruited.

Throughout the 1930s, Eleanor Roosevelt was an important symbol
of social activism. Prominent throughout the decade, she set a new
standard of justice for politicians in the fair treatment of women and

blacks. For several decades, she served as the conscience not only of her husband (allowing him to act the part of the consummate politician) but also of the nation: She would not let the dispossessed be forgotten. And more than any President's wife before or since, she carved out a career for herself that could serve as an important model of endeavor for women.

THE WOMEN'S NETWORK AND NEW DEAL PROGRAMS

In addition to Eleanor Roosevelt, prominent New Deal women came together to advance the participation of women in New Deal programs. So constant were the connections among 32 of them that historian Susan Ware contends they formed an informal "network" of activist women similar to the networks male professionals and politicians have always formed. The network included Eleanor Roosevelt; Mary Dewson, head of the women's division of the Democratic Party; Frances Perkins, Secretary of Labor and FDR's most important female

Frances Perkins, FDR's
Secretary of Labor and the first
woman cabinet member.

appointee; and Ellen Woodward, head of Women's and Professional Projects for the Works Projects Administration, the New Deal's major employment program. Other activist women were involved in the Democratic Party, New Deal agencies, and the Women's and Children's Bureaus of the Labor Department. They mobilized women within the Democratic Party, furthered relief programs for women, and were influential in attaining Social Security legislation.

On the periphery of the women's network was Mary McCleod Bethune—the most important black woman leader during this decade. The daughter of slaves, Bethune became a prominent educator, president of the National Association of Colored Women, and founder, in 1935, of the National Council of Negro Women, which pursued a more militant program of protesting discrimination than the Association's moderate self-help program. Identifying herself with black concerns in particular, as Director of Negro Affairs under the National Youth Administration, Bethune founded the Federal Council on Negro Affairs—the so-called "black cabinet," which safeguarded black concerns under the New Deal administration as the women's network safeguarded women's concerns.

The social and economic reforms of the New Deal directly affected women. In 1933, Eleanor Roosevelt and other administration women worked with the Women's Trade Union League, the League of Women Voters, and the Consumers' League to call a White House Conference on the Emergency Needs of Women, which publicized women's economic problems and set priorities for relief. The earliest 1933 relief agencies—the Federal Emergency Relief Administration (FERA) and the Civil Works Administration (CWA)—included women in their programs; by 1935, WPA rolls contained about 350,000 women, which represented about 15 percent of the agency's total employment. Under FERA and later under the National Youth Administration (NYA), resident job-training camps were set up for unemployed women, which paralleled the Civilian Conservation Corps camps for young men. In addition to old-age pensions, the 1935 Social Security Act provided federal funding for state and local aid-to-dependent-children programs and funds for state programs for maternal and pediatric care reminiscent of the 1920s Sheppard–Towner clinics.

Moreover, most of the special WPA employment projects for out-of-work artists and writers also took care to employ women. Although women were not especially included in the Federal Music Project (renowned for its attempts to preserve and transcribe indigenous folk music), they formed an important part of the Federal Art Project and the Federal Theatre Project. The former was dedicated to enriching the nation's public artistic heritage through instructive and decorative murals in post offices, train stations, and other public buildings. The latter attempted, through its productions, to make theater accessible to all classes, not just to the elite. Louise Nevelson was employed by the Federal Art Project; Tillie Olsen, by the Federal Writers' Project. In an age fascinated by documentary accounts of social conditions that might render the era's social breakdown more comprehensible, the Farm Security Administration employed photographer Dorothea Lange to document the grim conditions of rural Americans. Her brilliant photographs have become a famed and moving exhibit of human dignity in the midst of economic despair.

Any attempt to describe the New Deal's attention to women must also include the National Industrial Recovery Act of 1933. This Act provided that representatives of labor and management in each industry meet with government negotiators to draft production codes and also set up the National Recovery Administration (NRA). Under the National Industrial Recovery Act, maximum-hour and minimum-wage standards were established for both men and women workers. In 1938, after the Supreme Court declared the NRA unconstitutional, Congress passed the Fair Labor Standards Act, which reaffirmed maximum-hour and minimum-wage legislation for interstate industries, and state legislatures followed suit for intrastate commerce.

Such legislation represented a complete change in the way in which unions and the government viewed the worker. For all workers, the old common-law doctrine of the inviolability of contract between worker and employer was overruled. For women, the implications of the new laws were additionally significant. The massive unemployment during the depression had threatened male as well as female labor, thereby offering compelling support to those who argued that the government must protect all workers, not just women and children. The New Deal laws did just that, and in one blow, the campaign for special legislation for women, which had divided organized women for over a decade, was brought into question. By 1933, even the Women's Trade Union League had reversed its historic stand to join other reform groups in advocating general labor legislation for minimum wages and maximum hours. Although the general labor movement supported special legislation until the 1970s, the way was now open for an eventual rapprochement of numerous women's groups around the Equal Rights Amendment.

Antifeminism had not, however, been exorcised, nor had the unequal treatment of women been ended. Sex segregation in work opportunities characterized most New Deal work programs. In keeping with the general New Deal discriminations against minorities, the Works Projects Administration and other work-relief agencies barred women from construction jobs—the major employment they offered—and shunted them into sewing and other traditional types of women's work. In comparison with the male CCC camps, the women's resident camps were small in number and their purpose was never entirely clear; the kinds of reforestation and conservation projects the young men engaged in were not deemed appropriate for women. Nor was the welfare aid offered under the aid-to-dependent-children provision of the Social Security Act necessarily of immediate benefit to the women who qualified for it. Once it was available, many local WPA officials fired all women with children from the higher-paying WPA jobs, despite the women's vociferous protests.

Moreover, many of the codes drawn up by the NRA permitted industries to pay less to women workers than to men employed in similar jobs. In general, the minimum wages established by NRA codes did operate to increase women's salaries. Yet fully one-fourth of these codes contained some measure of salary discrimination, particularly the codes written for industries that employed large numbers of women. This had, of course, long been the unofficial practice. And the Fair Labor Standards Act of 1938 specifically exempted from its provisions many job categories, like domestic service, in which women were clustered. The argument was that such marginal work might disappear completely if wages were raised; on the other hand, the lack of regulation invited serious exploitation. Furthermore, despite the protest of women's organizations, the federal government ruled that only one member of a family could work in the federal civil service, arguing that additional jobs thereby would be made available to heads of families. The result was that thousands of women with civil service jobs, who usually earned less than their husbands, did resign. Bills categorically prohibiting the employment of married women were introduced in the legislatures of 26 states, and it took the determined resistance of women's organizations to defeat them. Louisiana actually passed such a law, but the courts declared it unconstitutional.

Whether or not Eleanor Roosevelt or other women in the administration could have done anything about these discriminatory New Deal measures is debatable; they did reflect the traditionalistic views about women that dominated mainline New Deal thinking. Grace Abbott, historian of New Deal welfare programs and herself head of the Children's Bureau for some years, contended that the women in New Deal agencies had a difficult time. Most male administrators, according to Abbott, were prejudiced against women. They took the advice of women lightly, and when a woman displayed incompetence, they drew conclusions about the performance of all women from an individual case.[5] Rose Schneiderman, a WTUL official and FDR's female appointee to the Labor Advisory Board of the National Recovery Administration, never accepted the monthly dinner invitation issued to members of the labor board by the employer's advisory board. She thought that the presence of a woman among these men would "cramp their style" and prevent them from being "chummy" with one another.[6]

Frances Perkins hit these prejudices head-on. Fearful of arousing the special enmity of the business community and of losing the support of organized labor, which distrusted her not only because she was a woman but also because she had risen through social-welfare rather than labor ranks, Perkins hesitated when it came to issues specifically involving women. She may have had good reasons for doing so. According to Eleanor Roosevelt, businessmen and politicians who did not like the pro-labor legislation of the New Deal consistently accused Perkins of being a typically incapable woman, "bewildered, rattlebrained, befuddled," and "scared" of John L. Lewis, the militant labor leader. Moreover, Congress took special pains to require Perkins to testify before their committees. "Dragging Frances Perkins up to the Hill before congressional hearings, with accompanying ballyhoo in the press," according to Eleanor Roosevelt, "became a kind of game."[7]

On the other hand, Perkins, like Eleanor Roosevelt and other New Deal women, was basically a traditionalist. She had followed the typical social feminist career path—from settlement work through paid employment with a voluntary agency (the Consumers' League) to government bureaucracy. Yet she did not really want to be held up as an example to women. Perkins "never recommends a public career"

Socialites distribute bread and
canned goods to the jobless
during the depression.

for women, reported the BPW national journal, because she believes that "the happiest place for most women is in the home."[8] By and large, New Deal women leaders were silent on the issue of New Deal discrimination against women. They were social feminists, not feminists, and they were willing to compromise on issues of full-gender equality. As long as programs included women, discriminatory practices did not seem to trouble them.

More than that, they did not seem cognizant of their crucial position as the transmitters of the Progressive social-feminist tradition to later generations. Born in the 1880s and 1890s, many of them had worked in Progressive reform as young women. When they entered New Deal agencies, most of them were in their 50s and a decade or so away from retirement. They had lived through the 1920s; they had witnessed the self-involvement of the generation that followed them. Yet they did little to ensure the survival of their network—or of social feminism more generally—by recruiting younger women to it. For the most part married and with families, they neither challenged prevailing traditionalism nor ensured that their efforts on behalf of women within the federal government would continue. Still, these social feminists were crucial to the New Deal's social-welfare legislation, and their contribution must be recognized. Before Frances Perkins accepted her assignment as Secretary of Labor, she demanded and received FDR's support for a full Social Security program, for which she worked assiduously throughout her tenure in office. Women had been central to the direction and success of Progressive social-welfare reform; they played a similar role during the New Deal.

CHANGES FOR THE WORKING WOMAN: UNEMPLOYMENT, NEW UNION STRENGTH

During the 1930s, working women encountered severe difficulties. It is true that unemployment figures were higher for men than for women until the late 1930s. Yet this situation partly reflected the fact that the consumer-goods industry and the clerical field, both employers of large numbers of women, were initially less affected by the economic downturn than industries that employed primarily men. Ironically, in this situation, the sex-segregated work force helped women retain their jobs. However, the unemployment figures, which included only individuals who were actively seeking work, may not have provided a true statistic; women may have been more prone than men to retreat from the work force into the home when securing employment seemed impossible.

Throughout the depression, official unemployment statistics rarely rose above 30 percent, although they sometimes were much higher in hard-hit urban and rural areas. The percentage of unemployed women was dominated by older and minority women, who had the least resources. Many companies, for example, refused to hire women over 35 years of age, which made the campaign for Social Security legislation especially compelling. And even single women encountered difficulties; although they were often given preference over married women in employment, they were often passed over for direct-relief payments in favor of families. According to one observer in 1934, there were 75,000 homeless, single women in New York City alone. The pattern of their lives was similar. They spent the mornings making

Attracted by federal relief jobs, more than 5,000 unemployed workers line up at the state labor bureau building in New York City in November 1933.

the rounds of employment agencies; afternoons they rested in the train stations; at night, they rode the subways. They ate in "penny kitchens," cheap eateries spawned by the depression.[9] Some of them—like the poor and the unemployed more generally—began to organize. An Association of Unemployed Single Women was formed, which, although small in membership, put pressure on government agencies. However, one study of the many teen-age girls who had left home to join the legions of tramps who roamed the nation concluded that prostitution was often their only livelihood.[10]

For black women, the situation was especially severe. Employment on federal work-relief projects was often closed to them. Traditional discriminatory practices in employment still existed. A Women's Bureau study in 1938 found that only 10 percent of black working women were employed in manufacturing—only a 7 percent gain over the statistic for 1890. Clerical labor and office work were equally closed to them; social worker Ellen Terry remembered that in 1930 in Harlem all the salesclerks in the stores on 125th Street, the black shopping center, were white. [11] Black workers remained farm laborers and domestic workers, and the only remotely mitigating factor in their situation was that they were accustomed to the economic deprivation that was a new experience for whites. Even so, whites were far better off economically; in 1939, the median annual earnings for nonwhites were 38 percent of those for whites.

Even women who were employed encountered hardships. In occupation after occupation, wages and hours were cut and the possibilities of advancement became severely limited. Professional women were especially affected by this trend. On one hand, men entered the feminized professions of teaching, librarianship, and social work in larger numbers than ever before. On the other, women's gains in male-dominated professions decreased. During the 1930s, the number of male librarians grew from about 9 percent of the profession to 15 percent; the number of male teachers, from 19 percent to about 24 percent; the number of male social workers, from 20 percent to over 35 percent. More than ever before, men dominated the high-level administrative positions in all these fields. With regard to the male-dominated professions, the representation of women remained fairly stable. But these figures masked a deeper reality in which women were often demoted from high-level positions and replaced by men. In business, positions held by two women were often combined into one, and the new post was given to a man. In university teaching, the numbers of women faculty declined precipitously. This was especially true at women's colleges, which had been founded partly as places where talented academic women who had been disregarded elsewhere could find permanent appointments.

By and large, professional women accepted the discriminatory situation and themselves began to seek less prestigious professional jobs. Women scientists, for example, gave up vying for academic work and found employment in government agencies or as research assistants. Personnel managers became secretaries; secretaries became file clerks. Clerical occupations did increase 24 percent during the decade, but advancing technology and increased business size considerably less-

*Over 1,000 women storm an
office building in St. Louis in
answer to a newspaper
advertisement for 150 jobs as
soap demonstrators.*

ened the need for education and skills in the positions available. Private secretaries, for example, were often replaced by stenographers who used dictating machines. Although women seemed to accept such demotions without protest, many internalized their discontent. Forced unwillingly to lower their expectations and experiencing the humiliation of downward mobility, many of them, according to recent analysts, lost self-confidence and acceded to a masculine domination of the professions that would not be challenged until the 1960s.

As a group, women schoolteachers were especially affected by attitudes against married women working. By 1940, only 13 percent of communities nationwide hired wives as teachers and only 30 percent retained women who married. Such discrimination against a group highly visible in local communities and supported by public funds seems to indicate the strength of traditional attitudes not only about working women but also about domesticity as women's primary role. In fact, surveys showed that such was the case. A 1936 Gallup poll found that nearly four out of every five Americans felt that wives should not work if their husbands were employed. Among women, this statistic was 75 percent. Indeed, the argument was not uncommon in the 1930s that women had caused the depression by going to work and taking needed jobs away from men. Or by leaving home, the argument went, they had weakened the moral fiber of the nation and rendered inevitable a crisis of the spirit.[12]

As the economic situation worsened, one unexpected avenue of relief appeared. Massive unemployment and government sympathy produced a new, more militant labor movement that was more responsive to women workers than the conservative American Federation of Labor (AFL). The International Ladies' Garment Workers' Union (ILGWU)—a powerful prewar AFL affiliate which, by 1930, had nearly ceased to exist—underwent a transformation within a few years. The passage of the 1933 National Industrial Recovery Act, which specifically recognized labor's right to organize, prompted the union's leadership to call a series of successful strikes. Throughout the clothing industry, hours were reduced and wages were increased by as much as 50 percent. During 1934, union membership increased from 45,000 to over 200,000.

Most important for women workers was the formation by a faction within the AFL leadership of the Committee for Industrial Organization in 1935, which emerged in 1938 as the Congress of Industrial Organizations (CIO). The militant CIO abandoned the skilled-craft orientation of the AFL to focus on all workers in a given industry, and under its leadership, mass-production industries like the automobile and steel industries, which employed small numbers of women workers, were finally organized. Inroads were even made in the textile industry, in which 40 percent of the workers were women. Through effective and often bloody strikes, as well as through the mediation of the National Labor Relations Board, established in 1936, employers

The wives of United Auto Workers strikers back up their husbands' demands during the 1936–1937 steel and automobile strikes.

were forced to recognize worker demands. Women were involved in many of these strikes. When police fired into a mass picket line during the famed 1937 "Memorial Day Massacre" at the Chicago Republic Steel plant, women were at the head of the line. In the Flint, Michigan, strike which finally resulted in the unionization of the automobile industry, women formed an Emergency Brigade and armed themselves with clubs and blackjacks. In department stores, hosiery mills, restaurants, and hotels, women adopted the tactic of sit-down strikes, which proved to be the most effective strike weapon yet devised and which would be a major influence on civil rights protesters in their "sit-in" demonstrations during the 1960s.

It was precisely because working women were clustered in the mass-production industries that the new labor movement became valuable to them. The CIO cannot be credited with any extensive feminist sentiment; it was simply that for the CIO to gain majority control in many industries, women had to be included as members. Not surprisingly, few women breached the leadership ranks of the new labor organization. Men dictated local and national policy then, as they do today. Nor was the new union organization among women workers in general ever very extensive. Even in 1973, only one-third as many women as men belonged to unions; women clerical workers, domestic servants, and many schoolteachers have never been unionized. Nor was the new union structure any more willing to support the WTUL than the predepression AFL had been. In 1947, the WTUL was dissolved; the reason given by its leaders was that the sympathetic attitude of the unions toward women made its existence unnecessary. But WTUL official Rose Schneiderman, for one, contended that the real reason for its demise was the unwillingness of the male-dominated unions to allot it any additional funding.[13] Working women profited greatly from the organization of the CIO, but its appearance did not lead to extensive feminist support among unions or within the working class.

The impact of the Communist Party on unionization in the 1930s deserves mention here. Dedicated to the class struggle, Communists were iron-willed union activists, and the contrast between apparent economic success in Stalinist Russia and the breakdown of the world capitalist system increased Communist Party membership, particularly among intellectuals. Communists encouraged the discussion of women's issues: Elizabeth Gurley Flynn joined the Party in 1936 and subsequently wrote a regular feminist column on politics for the *Daily Worker*. But even more than for early twentieth-century socialists and anarchists, feminism was not a Communist priority; class issues were what mattered. Communists focused on union organization, on aiding the black cause, and on forming associations of the unemployed and of community groups to fight high prices and rents.

Communist authoritarianism and Soviet Russia's control of the American Labor Party cannot be discounted. By the 1940s, knowledge of Stalin's purges and his disingenuous dealings with western allies would disillusion American members, and Party membership would plummet, reducing the organization to an unimportant influence in American society. But during the 1930s—at a time when the Socialist Party, headed by intellectual Norman Thomas, was only a shadow of its former self—Communists seemed willing to confront the issues of poverty and discrimination head-on when other groups often avoided them.

THE SECURITIES OF MARRIAGE IN AN INSECURE AGE

One of the most significant trends in women's employment during the depression was the increased employment of married women. Despite widespread hostility against their leaving the home to work, the percentage of their employment increased from 11.7 percent in 1930 to over 15 percent in 1940, continuing trends that had begun to emerge during the 1920s and would become dominant by the 1950s. By and large, economic motives, not feminist ones, dictated the employment of married women. Unless their income was severely reduced, most families did not reduce the consumption standards they had established during the affluent 1920s. That gasoline sales and automobile registrations did not diminish during the decade is an indication that the automobile—once viewed as a luxury—was now considered a necessity. At the same time, due to compulsory-education laws and state regulations prohibiting child labor, in addition to psychological theories stressing the fragility of childhood, families were much less willing—or able—to put their children to work. All of these factors placed great pressure on wives to supplement the family income.

Contrary to conservative predictions that working wives would destroy the home, the family generally seemed to become stronger during the decade. After all, as Gallup polls demonstrated, the vast majority of married women still defined domesticity as their primary responsibility. And in this time of economic insecurity, the family assumed a new importance in the social structure; the home was, after all, one place where the individual could find emotional sustenance. The number of divorces declined during the early 1930s, as did attendance at public events, travel, and club memberships. In part, people were staying home and staying married because they could not afford to do otherwise. Also, the radio had become a popular form of home entertainment. In their study of Muncie, Indiana, for example, Helen and Robert Lynd found an increasing incidence of teen-age marriage,

A West Virginia coal miner and
his wife spend an evening
listening to the radio.

motivated, they thought, by the search for emotional security that the
depression stimulated in all Americans.[14]

Many sociologists who studied the response of families to the
depression were surprised to find that economic adversity did not, as
they had expected, destroy families. On the contrary, it often welded
them together into more closely knit units. Families who were unaf-
fected by unemployment often gave money to indigent relatives and

shared living space with them. One city editor in the Lynds' *Middletown* expressed a general sentiment when he wrote, "More families are now acquainted with their constituent members than at any time since the log-cabin days of America." And, he continued, in a characteristically antifeminist vein, "Society is not made poorer because mother is now neglecting the encyclopedia from which sprang full blown the club papers with which she formerly bored her fellow clubwomen, and is devoting more of her time to cookbooks."[15]

Severe economic adversity, however, often contributed to the undermining of traditional family roles and relationships. According to one analyst, a long-term loss of income could create an "epic demoralization" within the family.[16] Sometimes wives could find jobs when husbands could not, and this situation often increased the relative power of women in the family. One psychiatrist who observed long-unemployed miners in Pennsylvania found that the entire structure of the family there had shifted. The men hung out on the street corners and dreaded returning home. Within their culture, a jobless man was considered worthless—by himself and by his family. Wives punished their unemployed husbands by withholding themselves sexually, and, according to this observer, "by belittling the men . . . [and] undermining their parental authority."[17] One thinks, however, of the Joad family in John Steinbeck's *The Grapes of Wrath*, torn apart by the process of migration from Oklahoma to California and by the terrible conditions of work for migrant families there, yet held together by the strength of the mother, who emerged in this case as a loving matriarch.

The Lynds identified a similar pattern in Muncie, Indiana. The lives of the majority of the wives were much less disrupted by the depression than were their husbands' lives. For women who remained at home, the household routine remained intact. Women who worked often gained increased status within the family. Men who were out of work "lost much of their sense of time and dawdled helplessly and dully about the streets." In such situations, women became the centers of stability within the family and often the arbiters of family decisions. In general, the Lynds concluded, "All sorts of temperamental variations have appeared, with women showing perspective and steadfastness under stress and men sometimes dissolving into pettiness . . . and personal rancor."[18]

Given women's increased authority within the family and in response to lowered incomes and unemployment, the birth rate dropped during

This photograph of the mother and two children of a migrant family en route to California in search of work was taken by Dorothea Lange for the Farm Security Administration.

the 1930s. More couples were using contraceptive measures, and every state in the union with the exceptions of Massachusetts and Connecticut, had legalized the dissemination of birth-control information by 1940. At the beginning of the decade, there were 28 family-planning clinics in the nation; by 1941, there were 746, and almost one-third were receiving government assistance.

The increasing availability of contraceptives probably did not lead to an increase in sexual promiscuity. Among the young, the vanguard of liberated sexual attitudes in the 1920s, most studies showed that premarital intercourse was on the increase but that both men and women expected it to lead to marriage and fidelity. The "emancipated" young women in Mary McCarthy's novel *The Group* provide an example—knowledgeable about sex but shocked by the one member of the group who had lived with her lover before marriage; expectant that a sexual encounter ought to eventuate in a permanent liaison, if not marriage; using condoms and douches as the only means of birth control.

Birth-control advocates at a House Judiciary Committee hearing in 1934; (seated, left to right) Katharine Houghton *Hepburn, mother of the actress; Representative Walter Pierce of Oregon; and Margaret Sanger.*

The 1930s witnessed the demise of America's so-called "flaming youth." Concerned about jobs and housing, people lost interest in the rebellion of youth and the new moral standards. What concerned people was that a generation of young Americans could not find jobs, that these future citizens might become despairing and embittered. Young middle-class women did not demand liberation. Caroline Bird, author of several studies of the women of the 1960s, has written regarding her college class at Vassar in the 1930s that "we did not think we had a right to a private life until we had first straightened out society."[19] A 1936 *Fortune* magazine survey of college campuses found that economics had replaced liquor, sex, and religion as the dominant issue of campus debate.[20] Reflecting the increased nationwide strength of communism, leftist movements emerged on many college campuses. Critic Pauline Kael, a student at the University of California at Berkeley in the late 1930s, remembered that the college was then a "cauldron" of radical discontent.[21]

But the majority of the younger generation probably was not so oriented. While acknowledging student discontent, Kael also recalled that the conservative fraternities and sororities were immensely powerful and regularly acted in conjunction with the university administration to quell radical dissent. The *Fortune* study showed that three out of every five college women wanted to marry immediately after graduation. Writer Doris Fleischman agreed. The "charming and lovable fire-eating youngsters" of the 1920s were gone, she wrote. The young women of the 1930s, Fleischman thought, were tired of the "sport of their elder sisters." But in her view, they had not found much to take the place of the older interests. "They go to college in great numbers, but they are ashamed of being regarded as highbrows. They enter the professions and place an enormous compensation emphasis on their social activities. They seem to be stabilizing their interest into a feminine preoccupation with the essentials of marriage and motherhood."[22]

Author Pearl Buck thought that in the face of the depression, women in general—old as well as young—more than ever before were retreating into domesticity and femininity. "Women's interest in work and a profession," wrote Buck, "has not been lower in the last half century than it is now."[23] In contrast to the Chicago Columbian Exposition of 1893, the New York World's Fair of 1937 contained no separate women's building. Rather, in keeping with a decade of feminist retreat, the emphasis on the integration of women's cultural contributions throughout the displays resulted in exhibits of women's fashions and culinary skills and not much else. Based on such evidence, some historians argue that the retreat to marriage and motherhood which dominated the 1950s was already evident in the 1930s, that an earlier return to prosperity would have ended the decade's low family fertility rates and precipitated a "baby boom" two decades before that phenomenon occurred in the 1950s.

Still, this was the decade in which Nancy Drew—the forceful detective whose skillful sleuthing was to become favorite reading for adolescent girls in the coming decades—was invented and in which Blondie—the daffy housewife who dominated Dagwood, her incapable, worried, frail husband—first appeared in comic strips. How do we interpret Scarlett O'Hara, the most famed fictional character of the age, renowned in print and on the screen in Margaret Mitchell's *Gone with the Wind*? Her tempestuous involvement with two men (one a fair and gentle cavalier and the other a virile, dark-haired rogue) mirrored the standard theme of women's romantic fiction. But during the Civil War—a time of economic and emotional crisis not without resonance to the 1930s—Scarlett cast off traditional conceptions of womanhood to pursue any path necessary for survival and success. Identifying with her self-made immigrant father, she became a successful businesswoman and the main financial support of a family unable to cope with the horrors of wartime. Of indomitable spirit, she was calculating and ruthless, as much masculine as feminine, and a nation of women assessing conflicting models of domesticity and assertiveness adored her.

FASHIONS AND MOVIES: OLD AND NEW IMAGES

Among all women, working or not, a return to tradition was clearly evident in their dress. The "ladylike look" once again became the cynosure of the American woman. Women no longer wore the short skirts and the flat-chested frocks of the 1920s. Although their clothes remained loose and free-flowing, skirts became longer and, above all, bosoms reappeared. Indeed, to look just right, well-groomed women again donned some form of figure-molding undergarment. In the 1927 spring–summer Sears Roebuck catalogue, the source of fashion for thousands of rural women and other mail-order customers, corset advertising had been directed to the overweight woman, to the woman who wanted the "stylish 'un-corseted' effect without allowing [her] figure to spread."[24] By the fall of 1930, however, corset advertising was directed to all women. According to the Sears catalogue: "The new mode calls for a definitely higher indented waistline, long tapering hips and the molded bust. To wear the new frocks, you must wear the smart, new corsetry."[25] During the next two decades, as defined bosoms and small waistlines became increasingly fashionable, the corset once again emerged triumphant. Its name was changed to "girdle,"

Jean Harlow in Dinner at
Eight: *the sales of peroxide
skyrocketed.*

but its function remained the same. Its apogee would be reached in
that much-treasured possession of the young lady of the 1950s, the
"merry widow" waist-cincher.

That the new fashions, with their emphasis on traditional models,
emerged as a specific response to the emotional insecurity fostered by
the depression is difficult to prove. Styles follow a cyclical pattern all
their own, and what looked new and chic in 1920 looked old and
boring by 1930. Yet for several years before the 1930s, Parisian design-
ers had tried to lower skirt lengths and reintroduce closer fitting clothes.
The new styles did not catch on until 1929. In 1920, American women
thumbed their noses at a Victorian past; by 1930, they were willing to
accept a new concept of elegant femininity that in some ways drew
from a Victorian model. So Paris, finally, had its say.

The most influential model for the change in fashion was the movie star. Author Maxine Davis found that in every section of the country and within every social group, the most common subject of conversation was the cinema queen.[26] Particularly in a time of social despair, people were living their lives vicariously through films. Unlike other types of entertainment, movies still attracted sizable audiences. First, Greta Garbo was the rage; then, Marlene Dietrich and Bette Davis. And when Jean Harlow dyed her hair blonde, it started a fad that has lasted for decades. In the 1910s and 1920s, the vamps all had dark hair, and the virginal heroines were blonde—a literary convention that was actually a holdover from an earlier age. But by the 1930s, this image had changed. Now the real temptresses, the true vamps, were as blonde as they could possibly be. In combining the old image of innocence with a new image of guile, the movie industry created a powerful sex symbol—a symbol that would reach its apogee in Marilyn Monroe.

In general, the films of the 1930s continued the trends started in the 1920s. There was the vamp turned temptress, such as Marlene Dietrich in *The Blue Angel*, and the sweet virginal blonde, such as Janet Gaynor in a series of films beginning with her best-known *Seventh Heaven* (1927). A new twist was the "good–bad girl," who was both temptress and angel and whose good qualities, through the help of a man, always triumphed in the end. Yet during the 1930s, a strict film-censorship code was in force, and although violence was not prohibited, any hint that immorality was condoned could bring down the wrath of the powerful censorship board. Endings almost invariably had to be happy; adultery had to lead to marriage or be strictly punished, particularly when it was on the part of the woman.

One female film star of the 1930s, however, paid little attention to the canons about woman's proper role. Big and buxom, Mae West mimicked contemporary standards of feminine beauty; she even padded her hips to make them larger. In voice and movement, she exuded sexuality, and no man could resist her. No man could manipulate her, either. Her attitude toward sex was masculine: sex did not imply any commitment to a man; marriage she could take or leave. A range of men from Cary Grant to W.C. Fields chased her; and to Grant's question, "Haven't you met a man who could make you happy?," her answer was classic West, "Sure, lots of times." She was strong and confident, always in command. Her sardonic, salacious dialogue (much of which

*Mae West, the voluptuous,
independent siren of the 1930s,
was an exception to the rule
about immorality.*

she wrote herself, just as she took a hand in directing and editing some of her films) was so cleverly worded that, for a time, it even slipped by the strict censors of the day.

Mae West movies were, however, exceptions. The prevailing movie plots continued to deny women any real power outside of sex. In some ways, this message became even more heavily underscored than before. In the gangster film, a favorite genre of the 1930s, leading ladies were regularly mistreated by their gangster lovers. In 1931, James Cagney established the fashion by hitting Mae Clark in the eye with a grapefruit in the movie *Public Enemy.* Critic Gilbert Seldes attributed the stir created by this scene to its effect in reinforcing the male image of masculinity, which, he contended, feminism and the depression had undermined.[27] By 1938, one analyst of movie trends thought that the mistreatment of women stars had become a stock device. "Today, a

A 1936 movie billboard in
Atlanta, Georgia: women
controlled by violence.

star scarcely qualifies for the higher spheres," she wrote, "unless she
has been slugged by her leading man, rolled on the floor, kicked
downstairs, cracked over the head with a frying pan, dumped into a
pond, or butted by a goat."[28]

One of the most consistent themes of the 1930s, 1940s, and 1950s involved a hard-nosed professional woman or a wealthy woman who was taught by a strong man that sex and marriage were all that really mattered in life. The movie was made again and again. Occasionally, as in the sophisticated 1936 comedy *Wedding Present*, with Cary Grant and Joan Bennett, marriage itself was satirized and the professional woman was sympathetically portrayed. More often, the opposite was the case. In *Take a Letter, Darling* (1942), Rosalind Russell gave up a lucrative and glamorous career as head of an advertising agency to travel around Mexico in a trailer with Fred McMurray. In *Lady in the Dark* (1944), magazine executive Ginger Rogers relinquished all to marry her assistant, Ray Milland, after her psychoanalyst had convinced her that only through marriage could she really find fulfillment. Spencer Tracy and Katharine Hepburn waged the war of the sexes in eight films; in most of them, the battle was charmingly intense until Hepburn capitulated in the last frames. And in one of the most successful films of the 1930s, *It Happened One Night* (1934)—which catapulted Clark Gable to fame—wealthy Claudette Colbert found Gable, the virile journalist of indeterminate origins and low income, irresistible.

Although still antifeminist in their viewpoint, these films did strike a new note. The women in them were portrayed as strong-minded, quick-witted, even aggressive. Despite the fact that Bette Davis, Rosalind Russell, and Katharine Hepburn regularly gave in to men on screen, their intelligence and strength showed through. They were women of character and force, and it is impossible not to recognize this when watching their movies today. In fact, so much does the personality of these women dominate their films that their ultimate surrender seems almost irrelevant to the triumph of their character. In *Middletown*, the Lynds provided an example of the effect of one of these early film stars on the first generation of young women who viewed her. Joan Crawford, they wrote, "has her amateur counterparts in the high-school girls who stroll with brittle confidence in and out of 'Barney's' soft-drink parlor, 'clicking' with the 'drugstore cowboys' at the tables; while the tongue-tied young male learns the art of the swift confident comeback in the face of female confidence."[29]

The high-school girls at Barney's in Middletown became the WACS and the war workers of the Second World War, and then the wives and mothers of the postwar era of the 1940s. Joan Crawford and Bette Davis did not open the vision of a feminist future to them. But these

In movies like Mildred Pierce, *Joan Crawford offers women a new kind of prototype.*

(Also pictured: Eve Arden, Chester Clute)

actresses became part of the mythology of the culture. Their movies continued to be shown, and the emergence of the feminism of the 1960s is not unrelated to the image these women projected.

BLACK WOMEN AND POPULAR CULTURE

The complexities of the movie image of white women in the 1930s were abandoned in the case of black women. Consistent with older stereotypes and in keeping with the age's persistent racism, black women in films were invariably servants, the "mammies" of yore, content to be caretakers and domestics, simple in affection and intellect, loyal to white employers, massive of build and round of body. Hattie McDaniel was the most famous movie mammy; she won an academy award for her portrayal of the character in the film version of *Gone with the Wind*, which faithfully reproduced Margaret Mitchell's racist views of blacks just as it did her complex portrait of Scarlett O'Hara.

Another type of black entertainer was popular in the 1930s, although she did not appear on the screen. On records and in roadhouses, in nightclubs and on the vaudeville stage, black female vocalists bellowed and crooned jazz and the blues—the shouts, laments, and often ribald rhapsodies that grew out of the reality and tragedy of the black experience in America as well as of their own lives. Ma Rainey began the tradition of the female black folk singer in the 1900s; Bessie Smith continued it in the 1920s; Ethel Waters and Ella Fitzgerald carried it into the 1930s. Many of these women had fought their way out of the ghetto from poverty, often through a period of prostitution. Extravagantly dressed, often overweight by white standards, they mirrored a nouveau-riche prosperity and sang songs of pathos and female strength that contrasted sharply with the idealized love refrains of white popular music: "I'll Build a Stairway to Paradise," "My Blue Heaven," "You're My Everything," "Lover Come Back to Me."

Exactly what role these women played in an emerging black consciousness is hard to say. As much as they by implication challenged oppression, they offered an escape from it. But the advent of the Second World War, which increased employment opportunities for blacks, and the acceleration of their movement to the North and to cities due to the final mechanization of cotton picking, which brought an end to southern tenant farming, both underlay what would become a revolution in their expectations and a civil rights movement of epic dimensions. By the 1940s and 1950s, light-skinned women like Lena Horne and Dorothy Dandridge were being allowed some latitude in film roles; by the 1960s, blacks were proclaiming that "black is beautiful," even as the racist and sexist attitudes of Americans were beginning to erode on many levels.

WOMEN AS PART OF THE WAR EFFORT

Both world wars created major changes in the female work force. However, whereas few additional women entered the work force during the First World War, more than 6 million women went to work for the first time during the Second World War. The proportion of women in the labor force increased from 25 percent in 1940 to 36 percent in 1945. This increase was greater than that of the previous four decades combined. That the Second World War had a sizable impact on women's employment when the First World War did not is not surprising. The United States participated in the First World War for only 19 months; the Second World War, and thus the shift in women's roles, lasted for four years, from 1941 to 1945.

Initially, it was not easy to persuade women that they ought to violate traditional mores and fill the jobs vacated by men. To this task, the molders of public opinion in newspapers, magazines, and radio turned their considerable power. They created "Rosie the Riveter," who became the lauded symbol of the woman temporarily at work. In all the media, women at work were pictured and praised, and the woman who did not at least raise a "victory garden" or work as a volunteer for the Red Cross was made to feel as guilty as the working woman had been made to feel in times past. Even the movies joined in. As part of their effort to bolster national morale, moviemakers churned out a steady stream of pro-allied propaganda films. In these films, the wife or sweetheart who stayed behind and went to work in a regular job or for an agency like the USO became as familiar a figure as the valiant soldier-lover for whom she waited.

Behind the propaganda for the employment of women stood official government policy. During the war years, four times as many women as men found employment in the federal bureaucracy. The War Manpower Commission, established to utilize labor resources more effectively, sponsored local vocational-training programs in high schools, in storefronts, and on the job, and actively encouraged women of all ages to enter these programs. State governors and legislatures suspended protective legislation for women so that they could take over the kinds of skilled labor and higher-paid jobs previously denied them. The non-combatant Women's Army Corps, the Navy WAVES, the Women Marines, and the Coast Guard's SPARS were founded, and Americans saw women in military uniform—a traditional symbol of masculinity. The government, too, at least paid lip service to the idea that women and men should receive equal pay and that child-care centers should be established throughout the nation. The War Manpower Commission repeatedly urged a policy of equal pay, and the National War Labor Board, established to mediate labor disputes, for a time applied this principle in discrimination cases. By 1945, 100,000 children were enrolled in federally supported child-care facilities.

Although women were courted to join the work force, it was primarily to fill clerical and factory jobs, particularly in war-related industries. Some additional opportunities were available in medicine and law, but few women moved into professional careers during the war years. Women were not hired for high-level positions in business or in government; these were left for men. For example, a shortage of teachers and school administrators was caused, not so much because male instructors and supervisors went off to war, but because industry and business, desperate for administrative talent, lured men away with higher salaries. As for government directives that women's wages should be the same as men's, inexplicit wording and lack of continued strict enforcement by the National Labor Relations Board made it relatively easy for employers to disregard them. And, although FDR supported the principle of federally funded day-care centers, little money was actually allocated for them, despite the fact that Women's Bureau studies showed that a large proportion of working mothers had inadequate provisions for child care while they were on the job. Federal funds supported day-care facilities for 100,000 children in 1945, but this figure represented only 10 percent of the total number of children who needed such care. Finally, women leaders charged that the government showed little interest in their recommendations. The War Manpower Commission, for example, composed entirely of men, shunted them into a Woman's Advisory Committee, which was rarely consulted.

The concern for women lacked impetus because, for the most part, no one really expected women to continue working after the war ended. The unstated assumption was that women, like men, were enlisting in the national service during a time of crisis and that, like men, they would take up their "normal" roles again when the crisis ended. Thus, factory labor was often described in government and private prowork propaganda as analogous to housework. Women, it was said, could adapt to factory machines "as easily as to electric cake-mixes and vacuum cleaners."[30] The implication was that the transition back to domesticity would be equally easy. Added to this reasoning was the

"Rosie the Riveter"—an arc welder at the Bethlehem-Fairfield Shipyards in Baltimore, Maryland, May 1943.

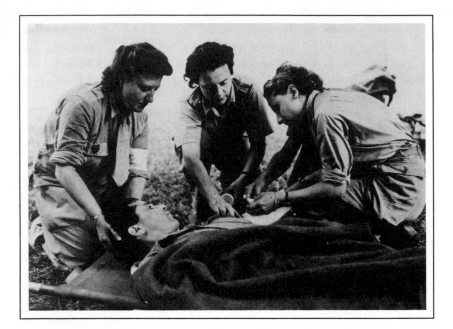

*Three American nurses
recruited for the Free French
Army Service treat a wounded
French soldier near Eschouche,
France, in 1944.*

memory of the depression, as well as the recollection that many of
the women who had gone to work returned to their homes or went
back to unskilled "women's work" after the First World War. Typical
of the national attitude, all federal funds for day-care facilities were
discontinued in 1946. Few were the commentators who, like the Wom-
en's Bureau staff, suggested to the public and to the government that
many women might not want to return to domesticity or to lower
salaries and that arrangements ought to be made to accommodate their
desires in terms of equal opportunities for advancement, equal pay
for equal work, and publicly funded day-care centers. The Second
World War produced women of strength, but it did not produce militant feminists.

When the war ended, many women happily left jobs in factories, farms, and offices to return to the homes and marriages denied them during the war years. Others were not so content to return to the home. A Women's Bureau study in 1944 showed that 80 percent of the women who had worked throughout the war wanted to continue in their jobs. After all, many women had moved into high-paying men's work as railroad switchmen, precision toolmakers, blacksmiths, and even lumberjacks. Black women in particular had been aided by the manpower crisis; the number of black women who worked as servants fell from 72 percent to 48 percent, while the proportion of black women working in factories grew to nearly 19 percent. According to historian William Chafe, the war represented for them almost a "second emancipation."[31]

Yet cutbacks among women workers, particularly in industry, began as soon as peace was declared. This was not unexpected; in the period of conversion from wartime to peacetime production, businesses and factories simply did not need as many workers. What was surprising was the large number of women who were laid off in comparison with men. For example, in aircraft-engine plants, women had made up 39 percent of the workers but comprised 89 percent of those who were laid off; in the truck and agricultural-implements industry, women had made up 13 percent of the work force but comprised 51 percent of those who were laid off. In harmony with these trends, the percentage of women in the labor force in general dropped from 36 percent in 1945 to 28 percent in 1947.

After 1947, the number of working women again began to rise. By 1951, the proportion had reached 31 percent. In general, then, women either remained in the work force after the war or reentered it after a brief hiatus. Conditions in clerical work, long defined as "women's work," remained essentially stable throughout the war and the postwar years. But in manufacturing, women were often either demoted to lower-paying jobs, or rehired under such a classification that their seniority was denied them. Without definite equal rights legislation, there was little they could do; state protective laws, suspended only temporarily during the war years, could easily be interpreted as meaning that women were not capable of performing whatever labor was defined as "men's work." Or state provisions like those for special rest periods for women could be used to justify lower wages. In some instances, the unions were willing to aid women members; the movement of women into war industries had caused their membership in the CIO to quadruple. During the war years, for example, the automotive unions had negotiated an agreement with General Motors, which the National War Labor Board had approved, that specified there should be no difference in pay between men and women. But the male-dominated unions were only too willing, once the war ended, to acquiesce or even to institute agreements that reserved higher paying positions for men. General Motors, as did other industries, reinstituted its discriminatory practices simply by changing the job classifications of "male" and "female" to "heavy" and "light," respectively. In the late 1940s, some women filed court suits demanding back pay as a result of these practices. Most of these suits were denied, but 31 women won a retroactive wage settlement of $55,000 from the Chrysler Corporation in 1948 because the company had laid them off in violation of their seniority.

Despite the discriminations imposed on women during and after the Second World War, a striking number of women remained at work. After 1951, the percentage of women in the labor force steadily continued to increase; by 1973, it had reached 42 percent. The percentages of employed married women and older women continued to rise accordingly. Thus, many women retained their tie to a world outside the home. The experiences of depression and war had lasting effects on the lives of women—at least on the lives of those who were now relatively permanent members of the work force.

NOTES

[1] William H. Chafe, *The American Woman: Her Changing Social, Economic, and Political Roles, 1920–1970* (New York: Oxford University Press, 1972), p. 115.

[2] Lois Scharf, *To Work and To Wed: Female Employment, Feminism, and the Great Depression* (Westport, CT: Greenwood Press, 1980), pp. 59–60.

[3] Quoted in Jacquelyn Dowd Hall, " 'A Truly Subversive Affair': Women Against Lynching in the Twentieth-Century South," in Carol Ruth Berkin and Mary Beth Norton (eds.), *Women of America: A History* (Boston: Houghton Mifflin, 1979), p. 366.

[4] Eleanor Roosevelt, *It's Up to the Women* (New York: Frederick A. Stokes, 1933), pp. 202, 206.

5 Grace Abbott, *From Relief to Social Security: The Development of the New Public Welfare Services and Their Administration* (Chicago: University of Chicago Press, 1941), pp. 361–62.

6 Rose Schneiderman (with Lucy Goldthwaite), *All for One* (New York: Paul S. Erickson, Publisher, 1967), p. 197.

7 Eleanor Roosevelt and Lorena A. Hickok, *Ladies of Courage* (New York: G.P. Putnam's Sons, 1954), p. 192.

8 *Independent Woman* (April 1933): 123.

9 Grace Hutchins, *Women Who Work* (New York: International Publishers, 1934), p. 191.

10 Thomas Minehan, *Boy and Girl Tramps of America* (New York: Farrar, Straus, & Giroux, 1934), pp. 75, 139–40.

11 Ellen Terry, *The Third Door: The Autobiography of an American Negro Woman* (New York: David McKay Company, 1955), p. 88.

12 Margaret Culkin Banning, "They Raise Their Hats," *Harper's*, CLXXI (August 1935): 355; Alma Lutz, "Why Discharge Women First?," *Independent Woman* (December 1931): 534.

13 Schneiderman, *All for One*, p. 246.

14 Helen Merrell Lynd and Robert S. Lynd, *Middletown in Transition: A Study in Cultural Conflicts* (New York: Harcourt Brace Jovanovich, Inc., 1937), p. 152.

15 *Ibid.*, p. 146.

16 Paul L. Benjamin, " The Family, Society, and the Depression," *Annals of the American Academy of Political and Social Science*, CLX (March 1932): 142.

17 Studs Terkel, *Hard Times: An Oral History of the Great Depression* (New York: Pantheon Books, 1970), pp. 196–97.

18 Lynd and Lynd, *Middletown in Transition: A Study in Cultural Conflicts*, pp. 178–79.

19 Caroline Bird, *The Invisible Scar* (New York: David McKay Company, 1966), p. 139.

20 Dorothy Dunbar Bromley and Florence Britten, *Youth and Sex: A Study of Thirteen-Hundred College Students* (New York: Harper & Row, 1938), p. 20.

21 Terkel, *Hard Times*, p. 346.

22 Doris E. Fleischman, "Women: Types and Movements," in Fred J. Ringel, (ed.), *America as Americans See It* (New York: Literary Guild of America, 1932), p. 117.

23 Pearl Buck, *Of Men and Women* (New York: John Day, 1941), p. 91.

24 *Sears Roebuck Catalogue*, CLIV (Spring/Summer 1927): 88.

25 *Sears Roebuck Catalogue*, CLVII (Fall/Winter 1930): 79.

26 Maxine Davis, *The Lost Generation: A Portrait of American Youth Today* (New York: Macmillan, 1936), p. 87.

27 Gilbert Seldes, "The Masculine Revolt," *Scribner's*, XCV (April 1934): 279– 82.

28 Margaret Thorp, *America at the Movies* (New Haven, CT: Yale University Press, 1939), p. 76.

29 Lynd and Lynd, *Middletown in Transition: A Study in Cultural Conflicts*, p. 262.

30 Leila J. Rupp, *Mobilizing Women for War: German and American Propaganda, 1936–1945* (Princeton, NJ: Princeton University Press, 1978), p. 152.

31 Chafe, *The American Woman*, p. 142.

BIBLIOGRAPHY

For the history of women in the 1930s, see Lois Scharf, *To Work and to Wed: Female Employment, Feminism, and the Great Depression* (Westport, CT: Greenwood Press, 1980), and Susan Ware, *Holding Their Own* (Boston: Twayne, 1982). Also insightful are Richard Lowitt and Maurine Beasley (eds.), *One-third of a Nation: Lorena Hickok Reports on the Great Depression* (Urbana: University of Illinois Press, 1981), and Jeanne Westin, *Making Do: How Women Survived the '30s* (Chicago: Follett Publishing Co., 1976). Also consult with profit Mary Beard, *America Through Women's Eyes* (New York: Macmillan, 1933); Caroline Bird, *The Invisible Scar* (New York: David McKay, 1966); Doris E. Fleischman, "Women: Types and Movements," in Fred J. Ringel (ed.), *America as Americans See It* (New York: Literary Guild of America, 1932); Helen Merrell Lynd and Robert S. Lynd, *Middletown in Transition: A Study in Cultural Conflicts* (New York: Harcourt Brace Jovanovich, Inc., 1937); Studs Terkel, *Hard Times: An Oral History of the Great Depression* (New York: Pantheon Books, 1970); and Dixon Wecter, *The Age of the Great Depression, 1929–1941* (New York: Macmillan, 1948).

Information on the League of Women Voters and women's political behavior can be found in Martin Gruberg, *Women in American Politics: An Assessment and Sourcebook* (Oshkosh, WI: Academia, 1968). On this subject, Eleanor Roosevelt and Lorena A. Hickok, *Ladies of Courage* (New York: G.P. Putnam's Sons, 1954), is also useful. On women's role in the New Deal administration, see Susan Ware, *Beyond Suffrage: Women and the New Deal* (Cambridge, MA: Harvard University Press, 1981). The standard biography of Frances Perkins is George Martin, *Madame Secretary: Frances Perkins* (Boston: Houghton Mifflin, 1976). Mary Anderson's autobiography, *Women at Work: The Autobiography of*

Mary Anderson, as Told to Mary N. Winslow (Minneapolis: University of Minnesota Press, 1951), sheds light on the inner workings of women in the FDR administrations. Studies of New Deal programs, including Grace Abbott, *From Relief to Social Security: The Development of the New Public Welfare Services and Their Administration* (Chicago: University of Chicago Press, 1941); Josephine Chapin Brown, *Public Relief, 1929–1939* (New York: Henry Holt, 1940); and Clarke A. Chambers, *Seedtime of Reform: American Social Service and Social Action, 1918–1933* (Minneapolis: University of Minnesota Press, 1963), give some information.

Numerous biographies of Eleanor Roosevelt are available. Among the best are Tamara Hareven, *Eleanor Roosevelt: An American Conscience* (New York: Quadrangle, 1968); James R. Kearney, *Anna Eleanor Roosevelt: The Evolution of a Reformer* (Boston: Houghton Mifflin, 1968); and Joseph Lash, *Eleanor and Franklin: The Story of Their Relationship* (New York: W.W. Norton, 1971), and *Eleanor: The Years Alone* (New York: W.W. Norton, 1972). None, however, fully analyzes Eleanor Roosevelt's relationship to women's organizations and concerns or her personal involvements with women. On the latter issue, see Doris Faber, *The Life of Lorena Hickok: Eleanor Roosevelt's Friend* (New York: William Morrow, 1980). For a representative sample of her ideas, see *It's Up to the Women* (New York: Frederick A. Stokes, 1933). On her international involvements, see Jason Berger, *A New Deal for the World: Eleanor Roosevelt and American Foreign Policy, 1920–1962* (New York: Columbia University Press, 1982).

On women at work and the labor movement in the 1930s, see Irving Bernstein, *Turbulent Years: A History of the American Worker, 1933–1941* (Boston: Houghton Mifflin, 1970); Philip S. Foner, *Women and the American Labor Movement: From World War One to the Present* (New York: The Free Press, 1980); Grace Hutchins, *Women Who Work* (New York: International Publishers, 1934); Alice Kessler-Harris, *Out to Work: A History of Wage-Earning Women in the United States* (New York: Oxford University Press, 1982); and Women's Bureau studies of the subject. Several excellent movies are also available. *Union Maids* (1977) focuses on an exploration of the work situation for women of various ethnic backgrounds in Chicago. *With Babies and Banners* (1977) is a moving exploration of women's participation in the 1937 sit-down strikes in the automobile industry in Flint, Michigan, and of the later lives of some of these women. Both films are available from New Day Films, P.O. Box 315, Franklin Lakes, NJ 07417.

The subject of women's involvement in radical movements in the 1930s awaits its historian. Two insightful autobiographies of women radicals are Ella Reeve Bloor, *We Are Many: An Autobiography* (New York: International Publishers, 1940), and Dorothy Day, *The Long Loneliness: The Autobiography of Dor-*

othy Day (New York: Harper & Row, 1952). Day was a leading exponent of Catholic radicalism. Bertha Thompson, *Sister of the Road: The Autobiography of Box Car Bertha, as Told to Dr. Ben L. Reitman* (New York: Macaulay, 1937), tells the story of a woman on the road.

On the family and the depression, numerous studies undertaken by sociologists at the time and later are particularly useful. See, for example, *Annals of the American Academy of Political and Social Science* (March 1932); Robert Cooley Angell, *The Family Encounters the Depression* (New York: Scribner's Book Companies, 1936); Glen Elder, *Children of the Great Depression* (Chicago: University of Chicago Press, 1974); Mirra Komarovsky, *The Unemployed Man and His Family: The Effect of Unemployment Upon the Status of the Man in Fifty-Nine Families* (New York: Institute of Social Research, 1940); Winona Morgan, *The Family Meets the Depression: A Study of a Group of Highly Selected Families* (Minneapolis: University of Minnesota Press, 1939); Samuel Stouffer and Paul Lazarsfeld, *Research Memorandum on the Family in the Depression* (New York: Social Science Research Council, 1937); and Winifred D. Wandersee, *Women's Work and Family Values, 1920–1940* (Cambridge, MA: Harvard University Press, 1981).

On youth during the depression, see Dorothy Dunbar Bromley and Florence Britten, *Youth and Sex: A Study of Thirteen-Hundred College Students* (New York: Harper & Row, 1938); Maxine Davis, *The Lost Generation: A Portrait of American Youth Today* (New York: Macmillan, 1936); and Thomas Minehan, *Boy and Girl Tramps of America* (New York: Farrar, Straus & Giroux, 1934). For a study of an important southern group during the period, see Margaret Jarman Hagood, *Mothers of the South: Portraiture of the White Tenant Farm Woman* (Chapel Hill, NC: University of North Carolina Press, 1939). On the women's crusade against lynching in the South, see Jacquelyn Dowd Hall, *Revolt Against Chivalry: Jessie Daniel Ames and the Women's Crusade Against Lynching* (New York: Columbia University Press, 1979), and Lillian Smith, *Killers of the Dream*, 2nd ed. (Garden City, NY: Anchor Books, 1963).

On changes in fashion and other matters pertaining to physical appearance, see Lois W. Banner, *American Beauty* (New York: Alfred A. Knopf, 1983). On women in films, the studies listed in the bibliography to Chapter 4 pertain, as well as Andrew Bergman, *We're in the Money: Depression America and Its Films* (New York: Harper & Row, 1971). However, nothing is an adequate substitute for viewing the films themselves. On blues singers and black women in films, see Donald Bogle, *Brown Sugar: Eighty Years of America's Black Female Superstars* (New York: Harmond, 1980).

On black women during this period, see Zora Neale Hurston, *Their Eyes Were Watching God*, a 1937 novel, and Maya Angelou, *I Know Why the Caged Bird Sings* (New York: Random House, 1969), a superb autobiography.

On women in the Second World War, there is a large literature, including studies at the time and more recent works. Especially important are Karen Anderson, *Wartime Women: Sex Roles, Family Relations, and the Status of Women During World War Two* (Westport, CT: Greenwood Press, 1981); Susan M. Hartmann, *The Home Front and Beyond: American Women in the 1940s* (Boston: G.K. Hall, 1982); Leila Rupp, *Mobilizing Women for War: German and American Propaganda, 1936–1945* (Princeton, NJ: Princeton University Press, 1978); and Sheila Tobias and Lisa Anderson, "Whatever Happened to Rose the Riveter?", *Ms.*, 1 (June 1973): 94. Also consult with profit Katherine Glover, *Women at Work in Wartime* (New York: Public Affairs Committee, 1943), and Elizabeth Hawes, *Why Women Cry: Or, Wenches with Wrenches* (New York: Reynal & Hitchcock, 1943). A superb film on this subject, *Rosie the Riveter,* is available from Clarity Educational Productions, P.O. Box 315, Franklin Lakes, NJ 07417.

6

FEMINISM COMES
OF AGE: 1945–1984

WOMEN'S LIVES WERE influenced by two central and divergent trends during the decade that followed the Second World War. The first was their continued participation in the work force—a participation which reflected changing economic, demographic, and medical factors. The second was a resurgent cultural emphasis on domesticity and femininity as woman's proper roles.

A GENERAL CONSENSUS ON WOMAN'S ROLE

Women Under Attack

In contradistinction to the movement of women into the work force, and partly as a result of it, an emphasis on the importance of marriage and motherhood became widespread in the late 1940s and the 1950s. In the immediate postwar years, antifeminist rhetoric was especially virulent. During the war, the nation lauded women for their participation in the national effort, and they emerged from the war, in the words of a contemporary, "noble, impeccable, and shining."[1] But within months, many opinion makers had turned against women, criticizing them not only for having gone to work during the war but also for having, as they saw it, destroyed the American family in the process. The attack was blatant and resembled nothing so much as the inflated antisuffrage rhetoric early in the century. The antifeminism of the 1920s and 1930s had been extensive, but subtle, and it had only rarely depicted women as evil. But the antifeminism of the postwar 1940s held women responsible for society's ills—either because they were failures as mothers or because they had left the home for work.

As early as 1942, in his best-selling *Generation of Vipers*, Philip Wylie accused American women of being tyrants in their homes and emasculating their husbands and sons. Taking the opposite tack in *Modern Woman: The Lost Sex* (1947), sociologist Marynia Farnham and historian Ferdinand Lundberg argued that the problems of modern society—including war and depression—could be traced to the fact that women had left the home. In their view, women had given up their femininity to compete in a futile battle with men, causing their children to become delinquents or neurotics and their husbands to become alcoholics or sexually impotent. Wylie, Farnham, and Lundberg based their case, as did most antifeminists of this period, on studies that seemed to

*GIs being welcomed on their
return home at the end of the
Second World War.*

show high rates of neurosis among army draftees and career women and increasing alcoholism and impotence among American men. They concluded that the career woman was neurotic because she had rejected her natural role and that the other evils were traceable to the neurotic housewife.

Their arguments, however, grew directly out of their ideological biases. Farnham and Lundberg, for example, were Freudians. In the 1920s, Freudianism had begun to have a major influence on Americans. But the advent of behaviorism, which offered a compelling alternative, and the onset of the depression, which made it difficult for anyone to afford psychoanalysis, had diluted the Freudian impact.

*In the postwar 1940s, women
were expected to return to the
home. Those who did not were
branded by antifeminists as
responsible for society's ills.*

Also, by the 1930s, psychiatrists like Karen Horney had begun to attack
Freudian views about women. But among psychiatrists in the postwar
years, Freudianism prevailed. The Freudians argued that women could
attain emotional stability only through domesticity and motherhood.
Women who worked denied their deepest needs and risked being
unable to experience love or sexual satisfaction. This, in turn, threatened the family, and, according to the most apocalyptic thinkers, the
whole of Western civilization. Moreover, Freudians emphasized the
importance of the early years of life on total personality development.
The message to mothers was clear; they ought to stay at home to
oversee their children's development.

Expert Opinion: Freud and Functionalism

The bitter antifeminism of the immediate postwar years was a transitory phenomenon, but its arguments, and particularly the Freudian ideas on which it was based, echoed throughout the 1950s, forming a body of thought that few analysts could avoid. As late as 1956, sociologists Alva Myrdal and Viola Klein commented that conferences of school headmasters, juvenile magistrates, probation officers, and welfare workers invariably blamed mothers, especially working mothers, for the problems of their youthful charges.[2] Child-care experts universally recommended that mothers stay at home with their preschool children and be available when their older children returned from school. Dr. Benjamin Spock, whose book *Baby and Child Care* (1946) became the standard authority on the subject, recommended that the federal government pay women to raise their children so that mothers would not leave the home.[3] College educators argued for the adoption of new curricula for women that would stress courses on marriage and the family.

Within the disciplines of sociology and anthropology, the technique of analysis known as functionalism, itself partly an outgrowth of the conservative postwar years, was predominant. Functionalism stressed the value-free analysis of existing institutions and left little room for criticism of them. Not all sociologists, however, were functionalists or Freudians. In her influential book *Women in the Modern World: Their Education and Their Dilemmas* (1953), sociologist Mirra Komarovsky criticized the Freudians and the functionalists and argued that female personality traits and women's relative lack of accomplishment in comparison to men's was due to their cultural conditioning, not to their biological inferiority. She did not deny women the right to work, and she counseled that men as well as women needed training for marriage and childbearing. Komarovsky criticized the then-current concern about the threat to men's masculinity that competition with women posed. But she clearly implied that wives, not husbands, bore the major responsibility for the home and the family. "Everything we know and believe today about the development of the child points to the importance of mother–child relations."[4] In childrearing, the father was a secondary figure. And, while cataloging the biological evidence that women were constitutionally superior to men and counseling that the male world of work needed the woman's influence, anthropologist Ashley Montagu, in his popular *The Natural Superiority of Women* (1952), wrote that a large part of women's superiority lay in their greater gentleness and humanity, while, echoing the argument of the traditionalists, he stressed the importance of "mother love" to successful human development. Even anthropologist Margaret Mead was ambivalent. In studies like *Male and Female* (1955), she criticized the rigid sex-role definitions of American culture; at the same time, she glorified woman's role as mother and homemaker.

The Evidence from Popular Culture

On a popular level, the new emphasis on domesticity was everywhere apparent. In newspapers and magazines, on radio and billboards, the homemaker replaced "Rosie the Riveter" as the national feminine model. Advertisers in particular were quick to exploit the expanded market for domestic products that the return to a peacetime economy and the appearance of a new affluence offered. It was predictable, as before, that the model woman they projected would be either a housewife eager to buy the latest home products or a seductress whose appearance suggested special pleasure from the product she displayed. In addition, according to feminist Betty Friedan in *The Feminine Mystique* (1963), Freudian attitudes infused most articles in the mass-circulation women's magazines; the majority of the heroines in the short stories were housewives, and nonfiction articles were devoted almost exclusively to cooking and child care.[5]

Reinforcing society's belief that women functioned best as sweethearts, sirens, or wives, female film stars of the 1950s were either sweet, innocent, and characterless, like Debbie Reynolds and Doris Day, or projected a complex blend of innocence and aggressive sexuality, like Marilyn Monroe. In addition, by the mid-1950s, television was beginning to beam its message into countless American homes, also portraying the woman either as a sex object or a contented homebody, often flighty and irresponsible. The emphasis on domesticity was pronounced in long-running, popular shows like "I Love Lucy" and "Father Knows Best."

Women's dress styles reflected the same female images. During the war, women had worn mannish clothes: Skirts were narrow; suits

*Marilyn Monroe at the premiere
of her film* The Seven-Year
Itch.

were popular; padded shoulders were in vogue. But in 1947, Parisian designer Christian Dior introduced the "new look," and women abandoned their masculine garb in a rush to femininity. The "new look" featured long, full skirts and emphasized a defined bosom and tiny waist, which required wearing foundation garments. By the early 1950s, these fashions reached their height in the "baby doll" look, characterized by a cinched-in waist, a full bosom, and bouffant skirts held out by crinoline petticoats. Shoe styles emphasized ever higher heels and ever more pointed toes until, ultimately, women had difficulty walking. Not since the Victorian era had women's fashions been so confining.

The Back-to-the-Home Movement

The new arguments and styles could never have gained widespread favor had not women—and men—been willing to accept them. After the war, traditionalism was in vogue, and the patriarchal past took on a romantic hue. The deprivation of the war years made a close family life attractive; women eagerly responded to the returning soldiers' desire to recreate a secure environment within the family. Rates of marriage and of remarriage after divorce remained high, and the age of first marriage dropped. In 1900, the average age of first marriage

Out of slacks and back into skirts: Christian Dior's 1947 "new look."

for women was 22 years; by 1940, it had lowered to 21.5 years. The Second World War and the postwar era occasioned the most rapid decrease over the course of the century; by 1962, women's average age of first marriage was 20.3 years. In addition, the size of families increased. Families with four and five children were common; the 1940s and the 1950s witnessed the most rapid family formation in the history of the nation. Within a brief number of years, the trend toward smaller families that had been in evidence since the early nineteenth century was reversed. In keeping with these developments was the widespread influence of two movements that exalted the joys of motherhood. One, the La Leche League, was dedicated to helping mothers nurse their infants. The other movement promoted the LaMaze method of natural childbirth, which combined a humanitarian desire to free women from the pain of childbirth with a fervor to make it the most important experience of their lives.

Even college-educated women continued to see marriage as their most important goal in life. From her vantage point at Barnard College, Mirra Komarovsky noted that, far from taking a militant feminist position, college women were defending marriage and motherhood with Freudian arguments.[6] Betty Friedan estimated that by the mid-

*A relaxation technique for labor
is demonstrated to a natural
childbirth class in San Francisco
in 1978 by childbirth educator
and author Shelia Kitzinger.*

1950s, 60 percent of female undergraduates were dropping out of college to marry.[7] One educator presciently explained this development as the result of the overwhelming influence of movies, television, and popular magazines, with their glorification of romantic love and marriage. To the young, marriage seemed both a haven and an escape from parental and social restraints.[8]

The desire to marry and to create a stable life around a romanticized version of the family (in many ways, a middle-class luxury made possible by postwar affluence) was reinforced by other factors. The fear that the decrease in population due to the war had weakened the nation prompted some government officials and scientists to call for a return to large families. The superficially tranquil postwar decade had its own tensions and pressures. International affairs were char-

*A suburban ritual: waiting at
the station for the commuter
train.*

acterized by a series of crises and wars, including the Korean conflict,
and by the perceived threat of a newly resurgent communism. A virulent anticommunism, led by the vituperative Minnesota Senator, Joseph
McCarthy, flourished. Recurring cycles of inflation and depression cast
an air of unease over the new affluence. As early as 1945, one analyst
contended that the postwar attack against women was a classic case
of scapegoating—of blaming vague fears on a definable villain.[9] Shortly
thereafter, woman as virtuous wife replaced woman as villain as the
central image within the cult of domesticity. But to a nation that had
undergone an exhausting war and was living in a troubled peace,
home as a refuge was welcome.

Also, affluent Americans increasingly clustered in suburban areas,
where jobs for women were limited and domestic help was in short

supply. Husbands were away from home longer because they had to commute to work, leaving wives to bear the complete responsibility for the family—including the sometimes overwhelming task of transportation. With schools, stores, and the train station rarely within walking distance, the suburban housewife could spend her day behind the wheel of the station wagon, suburbia's solution to the transportation problem. The American dream of affluence in a natural, bucolic setting away from urban squalor often made it impossible for women to be anything other than housewives and mothers.

Sex and Childrearing The new emphasis on Freudianism also was central to the return to the home. Americans have always respected experts, particularly when "science" is their justification and when sexuality is the issue. Marriage manuals and sex handbooks have never wanted for sales in the twentieth century. After the Second World War, as after the First, Americans were captivated by the notion of sexual liberation, eager to learn the style and techniques of physical gratification. To this drive, Freudian theories provided a rationale: Sex was a necessity of life that ruled human development. But Freudians also argued that the real sexual gratification for women lay in motherhood, and they incorrectly advised that proper orgasms were vaginal, not clitoral. The message of marriage manuals was that men were to play the dominant role and women were to be submissive. Child-care experts like Benjamin Spock told women that they must stay at home to raise their children.[10] More than at any time since the Victorian era, the American woman became a domestic being.

Feminism in the 1950s

In response to the arguments of Freudians and traditionalists, the feminist rebuttal was weak. True, bold statements appeared from time to time. Simone de Beauvoir's *The Second Sex* was published in the United States in 1952. More typical of the feminism of the 1950s was Mirra Komarovsky's stated purpose for writing *Women in the Modern World:* to steer a course between feminism and antifeminism.[11] In studying feminism during the 1950s, sociologists Arnold Green and Eleanor Molnick encountered few radicals. Those they did meet felt it was futile to issue manifestoes or to organize because the majority of Americans had become conservative in opinion and life style. Militant feminism in the American past had often coincided with times of general reform sentiment. But such was not the climate in the 1950s.

Old-line women's organizations continued their activities, but many had declined in strength, and disagreement over the ERA made a unified campaign difficult. The Women's Joint Congressional Committee, for example, an important agency of social feminism in the 1920s, was serving as an information clearinghouse for liberal organizations by the 1950s. The Consumers' League was rarely heard from; the Women's Trade Union League had disbanded in 1947. Even the Lucy Stone League, founded in 1921 to end legal restrictions against women using their maiden names after marriage and to persuade women to do so, had little impact in the 1950s. "The present young generation is not interested," wrote an early leader of the organization, despairingly.[12]

The Woman's Party, the National Federation of Business and Professional Women's Clubs, and the National Federation of Women's Clubs supported the ERA, but the League of Women Voters, the Women's Bureau of the Department of Labor, and women in the labor movement still considered it to be against the best interests of working women. In 1950 and again in 1953, the Senate passed the ERA. But in both years, a coalition of 43 national organizations, known as The Committee to Defeat the Unequal Rights Amendment, successfully lobbied for the attachment of riders to the bill that exempted state protective laws for working women from its provisions. Yet despite the differences, the major women's organizations were instrumental in the passage of equal-pay legislation in many states. Although the Fair Labor Standards Act of 1938 had established the principle of equal pay, the government and the courts had been unwilling to apply it with any consistency. At the same time, women's organizations pressed for a broader federal law.

The Reemergence of Domestic Feminism

Given the climate of the 1950s, it is not surprising that the domestic feminist argument, in evidence throughout the century, attracted numerous adherents. Even the conservative analysts of woman's role were aware that many women were discontented at home, that they were frustrated about working at an all-demanding job for which they were paid no salary and received little recognition. But the solution of the traditionalists was not that women could rearrange their lives to accommodate their own ambitions or creative drives, but that women should be educated to find satisfaction in domesticity and that society should recognize housework as a real profession. "Many a girl marries unprepared either intellectually or psychologically for the lifetime job she is undertaking," wrote one supporter of professional training programs for future wives.[13] In a variation on the theme, journalist Agnes Meyer revived the idea of women's superior morality and, like Eleanor Roosevelt, chided women for not organizing on their own behalf. But Meyer was not interested in community concerns; she wanted women to organize behind the goal of raising the status of the housewife.[14]

The aim of these "domestic feminists" was admirable: Unquestionably homemakers, whether male or female, ought to enjoy greater recognition. But these publicists of domesticity, like those before them, had little impact on popular attitudes. They were successful in expanding training in home economics, in introducing new courses on marriage and the family in high schools and colleges, and in generating public debate on the issue. These successes, however, did not alter what feminists and antifeminists alike diagnosed as the cause of American women's discontent. They did not modify the American belief that housework was menial, nor did they change the fact that a wife's social status was determined by her husband's occupation rather than by her achievements as a homemaker.

The feminists of the 1950s did not envision a vastly altered future. They believed that women could achieve equality with certain modifications in the existing social structure. Many contended that there were biological differences between men and women, and they did not want to tamper with them. Writing in the May 1947 issue of *The Annals of the American Academy of Political and Social Science*, Margaret Bruton, a housewife and part-time historian, outlined the moderate feminist position:

> Former generations smothered a girl's intellectual capacities; the feminists and most of her teachers today ignore her emotional needs . . . Each woman must still learn for herself and often too late the necessity for managing somehow to find outlets for her dual needs with the limitations imposed on her by society and by her biological function.[15]

It is difficult to decry the honest endeavors of the postwar feminists on behalf of women; what seems to have been lacking were methods adequate to force the issue. By 1964, Alice Rossi, sociologist and feminist, found that the overt antifeminism of the immediate postwar years had ended, but at the same time "there was practically no feminist spark left among American women."[16] Her judgment as applied to the moderate feminists of the 1950s was harsh but basically not incorrect.

EVIDENCE TO THE CONTRARY

New Economic, Demographic, and Medical Factors

At the same time that militant feminism was in decline and traditional attitudes were prevalent among Americans, more and more women were entering the work force. Thoughout the twentieth century, the expanding American economy had absorbed increasing numbers of women workers, largely into low-paying, part-time work. In addition, by the 1950s, changing patterns in the lives of American women had made work outside the home increasingly possible. In 1900, the average woman married at 22 and had her last child at 32. With a life expectancy of 51 years, it was probable that childrearing would take up most of her adult life. By 1950, however, the average woman married at 20, bore her last child at 26, and had a life expectancy of 65 years. Even if she remained at home until her children were grown, she still had at least 20 years of life at home without children. For many women, the reasonable alternative was to go to work, and the employment figures of married women increasingly reflected this demographic dispensation. The proportion of married women employed outside the home was about 15 percent in 1940, about 30 percent in 1960, and over 50 percent in 1968.

Medical science, too, was helping women gain more control over their lives. By 1960, with the marketing of oral contraceptives for women, birth-control technology made an epic advance. A relatively inexpensive and almost foolproof method of contraception was now available to women, and its popularity was attested to by the sizable number of them who began to use it. Women who chose to use the pill finally seemed to be free to have sexual intercourse without fear of pregnancy, to plan their children around their lives and not their lives around their children.

During the 1950s, it was evident that the experience of depression and war had eroded older notions that work for married women violated the fulfillment of their role as wives and mothers. The substantial lowering of the average age of first marriage was not only an indication of a new traditionalism but also proof that the old stigmas against working wives were ending; because wives could work, young couples no longer felt that they had to postpone marriage. Marriage rates among professional women also began to rise substantially. In 1940, 26 percent of all professional women were married; in 1960, among a sampling of approximately 50,000 professional women, 45 percent were married.[17] Most significant was the increasing percentage of working mothers with dependent children. In the mid-1950s, 25 percent of all women with young children had jobs; by 1969, this statistic had risen to 40 percent. Moreover, between 1960 and 1969, the category of workers that increased most rapidly was that of mothers with preschool children. By 1969, 33 percent of these women were employed outside the home.

The New Trends—Revolutionary or Not?

To what extent this movement of women into the work force represented a revolutionary force is debatable. The old discriminations against women were in evidence everywhere. Women did not continue to move into higher-paying, skilled-labor or professional jobs after the war years. Rather, as it had during most of the century, clerical labor offered working women their greatest opportunity. Reflecting the labor shortages of the war years, the proportion of women in most professions increased somewhat between 1940 and 1950, but by and large, these gains were not retained during the 1950s. Moreover, the postwar years spawned a new consumerism, and inflationary cycles created instabilities in husbands' salaries and increased the costs of items like cars and college educations for children. As they had during the 1930s, many women worked out of a sense of financial responsibility. They did not regard themselves as full-fledged members of the labor force, and they did not readily join unions. They accepted part-time work with a lower pay scale than full-time work; as late as 1980, only about 40 percent of all working women were employed in full-time, year-round jobs.

It is also difficult to determine to what extent employment produced a change in family roles. Some sociologists have argued that a major realignment took place, and, indeed, news commentary carried stories about husbands who washed dishes and diapered babies. Other analysts contended that despite any readjustment in relationships, the

*Sharing the housework—more
than "playing the part of a
volunteer aide"?*

old masculine–feminine models remained dominant. "Wives still have
the main responsibility for the home," wrote sociologist David Reisman, "the husband playing the part of a volunteer aide, and . . . the
women have made a tacit bargain with their husbands not to compete
with them professionally or in career terms."[18] Yet as early as 1957,
before the birth-control pill was marketed, the national birth control
rate had begun to decline—an indication of the waning of 1950s traditionalism and of a new upsurge in the reassertion of identity among
women.

Moreover, a 1962 Gallup poll showed that only 10 percent of the
women surveyed wanted their daughters to have the same lives they
had had. This statistic in particular seems to show a dissatisfaction
with traditional life styles that could become fertile ground for the
feminist movement. "The problem that has no name," Betty Friedan

Rosa Parks, the black woman
who refused to give up her seat
to a white man, rides in the
front of a city bus in
Montgomery, Alabama.

called women's discontent. But until the advent of the new feminists of the 1960s, there was little outspoken protest. It would take the agitation of a small group of determined women to alert the nation to the unseen inequality in its midst.

THE SHIFT TO MILITANCY

In the face of the virulent antifeminism of American society in the immediate postwar years and the strong appeal of domesticity in the 1950s, the rise of a militant feminism in the 1960s is surprising. Given the long-standing ambivalence of most women about feminism, why were so many willing to embrace a radical ideology at this time?

A New Reform Climate

Most significant in the emergence of the new feminism was the appearance of a new reform mentality. In the late 1950s and early

*Betty Friedan: her message
"spread like a nuclear chain
reaction."*

1960s, studies showing the growth of crime, poverty, juvenile delin-
quency, and drug abuse appeared in abundance, and these problems
became dominant public issues. The civil rights movement burst on
America following the Montgomery, Alabama, bus boycott of 1956,
begun when a black woman, Rosa Parks, refused to give up her seat
when a white man demanded it. The mid-1960s witnessed the advent
of a new radicalism among the young, inspired by the civil rights
protest and by increasing dissatisfaction with America's long-term
involvement in the Vietnam war.

These new trends made Americans receptive to controversial exposés.
Thus, when Betty Friedan's polemic, *The Feminine Mystique*, was published in 1963, it captured a mass audience. Friedan's prose was powerful, and her argument gave no quarter to the defenders of women's
traditional role. In Friedan's view, women were discontented not because
they were untrained to be housewives and mothers, but because
homemaking was boring. If women contributed to the ills of society,
it was precisely because they stayed at home, inflicting their dissatis-

faction on husbands and children. Friedan saw little justification for the argument that women had a special ability to raise their own children. She refused to give any credit to the Freudians. Rather she launched the kind of bitter attack against Freud that became standard in feminist writings of the 1960s.

The new interest in social reform led to gains for women during the administration of John F. Kennedy. Kennedy was no feminist, but he was willing to listen to the suggestion made by women both inside and outside his administration that he appoint a commission to study the position of women in the United States and to make recommendations for change. The concept of such a commission had been discussed since the 1940s, when it appeared that the ERA might be passed out of gratitude for women's war efforts. But Women's Bureau directors during the 1950s were opposed to the idea, and Presidents Harry S. Truman and Dwight D. Eisenhower fulfilled what seemed to be the necessity of giving a symbolic reward to women voters and the many women workers of both parties to whom had fallen the unrewarding task of local canvassing and vote-getting through a few appointments of women to executive offices. By the end of the 1950s, however, personnel shortages were occurring in important feminized professions like nursing and teaching, and some influential analysts called for specific government attention to make this kind of work more attractive to women through, for example, equal-pay legislation and federal funds for child-care facilities.

President Kennedy's appointee to head the Women's Bureau, Esther Peterson, was responsive to these needs, and she, more than anyone else, put the necessary pressure on Kennedy to assemble a commission. Then, too, Eleanor Roosevelt's influence was not absent. She was shocked that only nine women were included among Kennedy's first 240 appointees to office, and she sent him a three-page list of women she judged qualified for government service. Kennedy, anxious to gain support from the Adlai Stevenson wing of the Democratic Party, which Eleanor Roosevelt led, appointed her chairperson of the Commission on the Status of Women, which he created in 1960.

Eleanor Roosevelt, with John F. Kennedy, who appointed her to chair the Commission on the Status of Women, which he created in 1960.

The commission's report, issued in 1963, was not a radical document. It supported the nuclear family and recommended that women be specially trained for marriage and motherhood. It withheld support from the Equal Rights Amendment on the grounds that the Fifth and Fourteenth Amendments provided sufficient constitutional guarantees for women's rights. But among other recommendations, the report called for equal job opportunities and equal pay for women, for the end to laws discriminating against women, and for the expansion of child-care facilities outside the home. Its debates and its recommendations stimulated some important action on behalf of women. In 1963, Congress passed the Equal Pay Act—a measure that had been a priority item for women's organizations for some time. After 1963, the states began to appoint commissions similar to the national one. Several presidential advisory groups composed of private citizens and government officials also were formed. Title VII of the 1964 Civil Rights Act prohibited all discrimination on the basis of sex as well as on the basis of race. (Title VII was introduced by a Southern congressman— not out of feminist sentiment, but as a strategy to block passage of the entire bill. The plan backfired, and the amendment passed together with the bill.)

The pressure of old-line women activists was instrumental in persuading Kennedy to establish the presidential commission and the subsequent committees. The composition of the Committee on Civil and Political Rights under the 1960 commission offers a graphic example of their involvement. Members of the committee included presidents of the League of Women Voters, the General Federation of Women's Clubs, the National Federation of Business and Professional Women's Clubs, and a vice president of the International Ladies' Garment Workers' Union. Esther Peterson, who had risen through the ranks of labor to become, as head of the Women's Bureau and later Assistant Secretary of Labor, Kennedy's highest-ranking female appointee, served as vice chairman of the commission under Eleanor Roosevelt. Peterson herself had been a powerful advocate within the administration for convening such a commission. Over the years, the national women's organizations represented on this commission had taken an increasingly feminist position. By 1960, for example, even the League of Women Voters had become much more sympathetic to the Equal Rights Amendment, although the League did not officially endorse it until 1972. Such action, however, did not imply any increased radicalism on the part of these groups. The League, for example, did not give up its concern for social welfare. And the National Federation of Business and Professional Women's Clubs refused to take a strong leadership role in the post-1966 women's movement because the organization did not want to be identified by the public as "feminist"—a stance it considered too radical.[19]

New Faces and the Formation of NOW

In addition to old-line activists, a second group of women, more militant in style and demands, emerged in the mid-1960s. Generally young, these women often turned to radical feminism as a result of their disillusioning experiences in the civil rights and student movements, where they found that male leaders relegated them to housekeeping and clerical chores and often demanded sexual favors of them. Black leader H. Rap Brown's renowned statement that the proper position of women in the movement was "prone" expressed the extreme sexism women often encountered. And, like many nineteenth-century feminists who turned from reform to feminism, they began to identify with the disadvantaged for whom they worked and to ask if they, too, were not objects of discrimination. At the same time, young women activists often found powerful role models among local black women in community-action projects in the South. "In every southwest Georgia county," wrote one activist, "there is always a 'Mama.' She is usually a militant woman in her community, willing to catch hell, having already caught her share."[20]

The feminist issue was first raised in the civil rights movement during the summer of 1964, when whites and blacks worked together to help disfranchised blacks register to vote in Mississippi. It first surfaced in the student antiwar movement that same fall at the University of California at Berkeley—a center of student protest led by veterans of that Mississippi summer. As student activists began to move into community organizing in ghetto areas in northern cities that same year, they encountered the same combination of sexism from male coworkers and powerful local female role models that they had experienced in their civil rights work in the South. Again the experience drew them in the direction of feminism.

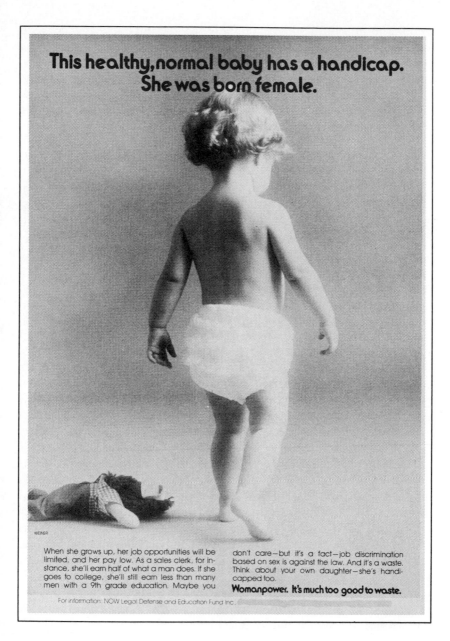

This healthy, normal baby has a handicap.
She was born female.

WEINER

When she grows up, her job opportunities will be limited, and her pay low. As a sales clerk, for instance, she'll earn half of what a man does. If she goes to college, she'll still earn less than many men with a 9th grade education. Maybe you don't care—but it's a fact—job discrimination based on sex is against the law. And it's a waste. Think about your own daughter—she's handicapped too.

Womanpower. It's much too good to waste.

For information: NOW Legal Defense and Education Fund Inc.

Old-style feminists worked through the existing women's organizations and through the government commissions dealing with women. New-style feminists moved in a different direction; they formed their own groups, often modeled after those they had recently left. They opted for small, loosely structured, informal groups, deemphasized leadership, and stressed equality; they issued manifestoes and, like the left in general, published their own newspapers. They conducted "consciousness-raising" meetings, where they employed the techniques of group therapy to heighten women's sensitivity to their presumed oppression.

The actions of both conservative and radical feminists came to national attention in 1966, when the Third National Conference of the State Commissions on Women met in Washington, D.C. According to Aileen Hernández, a former organizer for the ILGWU who was later to serve as president of the National Organization for Women (NOW), the mood among the hundreds of delegates was bitter and angry.[21] Most feminists felt that the government was not meeting its obligation to implement the recommendations of the various commissions on women or to enforce existing laws. Meanwhile, women who served on federal agencies concerned with women communicated this discontent to, among others, Betty Friedan, who was present at the meeting and whose book, *The Feminine Mystique*, had gained her national prominence as a feminist spokeswoman. The consensus was that there was need for an organization to pressure the government on behalf of women in the same way that the civil rights organizations functioned for blacks. These forces came to a head in Friedan's hotel room, where plans were formulated for the National Organization for Women. Events seemed to bear out Friedan's judgment that "the absolute necessity for a civil rights movement for women had reached such a point of subterranean explosive urgency by 1966 that it took only a few of us to get together to unite the spark—and it spread like a nuclear chain reaction."[22]

An advertisement sponsored by
the Legal Defense/Education
Fund of the National
Organization for Women
(NOW).

Kate Millett; best-selling feminist author; one of the first of many.

With the formation of NOW, the new feminism had its official, national birth. Other organizations soon followed. In 1968, academic and professional women formed the Women's Equity Action League (WEAL) for the purpose of ending sex discrimination in employment, education, and taxation. The Women's Political Caucus—a bipartisan group aimed at pressuring political parties to consider women's concerns and to elect women to office—was organized in 1971. By that time, job placement and counseling agencies for women, like Catalyst in New York City, had begun to appear. Courses in women's history, psychology, and sociology were introduced in colleges throughout the nation—in the spring of 1972, over 600 were being offered—and soon led to women's studies programs.

Meanwhile, during the late 1960s, the civil rights movement began to become factional, and blacks refused to allow any further white involvement in their movement. More and more, the antiwar protest focused on an antidraft movement, and the draft issue only secondarily affected women because they were not subject to conscription. With the outbreak of riots in the black ghettos, the increasing violence of the Vietnam War, and the official repression of radicalism, male

Germaine Greer, author of The
Female Eunuch *(1971).*

radicals began to resemble black militants in their adoption of violent
rhetoric and a style of male "machismo" that were inimical to women's
interests. Moreover, part of the radicalism of the 1960s had always
included the search for individual fulfillment—through sex, drugs,
communal living, and Eastern, mystical religions. By the late 1960s,
these strains began to influence radical politics: "Look to your own
oppression" became a common slogan. All of these developments led
to an increase in feminist commitment.

Women began to express their discontent and to translate it into
action. Feminist exposés poured from the presses. Kate Millett's *Sexual
Politics* (1969) became a national best-seller and was rapidly followed
by, among others, Shulamith Firestone's *The Dialectic of Sex* (1970),
Robin Morgan's *Sisterhood Is Powerful* (1970), and Germaine Greer's *The
Female Eunuch* (1971). Women formed feminist theater troupes and
rock groups; they made feminist movies. Throughout the nation, women
marched for the repeal of anti-abortion legislation, established day-
care centers, and, in New York and Atlantic City, picketed the *Ladies'
Home Journal* offices and the Miss America Pageant, respectively, for
perpetrating myths about women. In 1972, three scholarly journals

devoted to women's studies appeared. That same year marked the publication of *Ms.*, which became the first militant feminist magazine in the history of the nation to attract a sizable circulation.

THE FEMINIST POSITION IN THE 1960s

The spokeswomen of the new feminism made it their job to disprove the contentions of the moderates of the past—first, that women had, indeed, made substantial progress in achieving equality with men; and second, that women had special responsibilities to their families due to some biological predisposition.

Feminist scholars and polemicists scoured the available statistical evidence to demonstrate that women had made only superficial gains over the past decades. To their credit, they found impressive data to support their arguments. They turned to government reports, work-force studies, and census data, and they conducted their own studies. Much of this material had long been in the public domain. In effect, feminists forced Americans to pay attention to a deep strain of unattended discrimination against women.

They could demonstrate, for example, that between 1920 and 1970, only ten women had served in the U.S. Senate and only 65 women had served in the U.S. House of Representatives and that most of these women were widows of former senators and congressmen. Since 1920, two women had served in the cabinet: Frances Perkins, FDR's Secretary of Labor, and Oveta Culp Hobby, Eisenhower's Secretary of Health, Education and Welfare from 1953 to 1955. Neither Kennedy nor Lyndon Johnson appointed a woman to their cabinet. Between 1920 and 1970, three women had been governors; one woman had served as a state attorney general, and three women had served as lieutenant governors. Not until feminist researchers reached the level of local libraries and school boards did they find women represented in the political sphere in any significant numbers. In 1968, 3 percent of the nation's judges were women. Shirley Chisholm, black congresswoman from New York, stated that the greater discrimination against her in her political career had been because of her sex, not her race: "I was constantly bombarded by both men and women that I should return to teaching, a woman's vocation, and leave politics up to men."[23]

In the area of employment, feminists found similar evidence of inequality. In 1940, women held 45 percent of the professional positions in the nation (a statistic that included the large proportion of women professionals who were schoolteachers). In 1967, women held 37 percent of these positions. The percentage of workers in domestic service did decrease, creating a crisis for employed mothers, but it was clerical work into which these women moved. All indexes showed that women earned less than men and that the percentage difference was sharply rising. In 1959, women's earnings were 66 percent that of men; by 1968, this statistic had dropped to 58 percent. Statistics for 1970 showed that the average woman college graduate could expect a smaller annual income than the average white male who had graduated from elementary school.

As for their economic status, poverty among women was on the increase. In 1959, women constituted 26 percent of the total poor; in 1968, the figure stood at 41 percent. Black women in particular bore the brunt of poverty, but the situation was critical for white women as well. In 1965, the average income of black women was 70 percent that of white women, 50 percent that of black men, and 40 percent that of white men. In 1969, unemployment among black women seeking work stood at 6 percent. Among white women, the figure was 3.4 percent; among black men, 3.7 percent; and among white men, 1.9 percent. Experts estimated that among families headed by black women, 50 percent had an income below the poverty line, compared with 25 percent of families headed by white women, less than 25 percent of families headed by black men, and about 7 percent of families headed by white men. Finally, studies showed that most alimony payments were small and, in many cases, not paid, that the median payment for child support was $12 per week in 1970, that most banks would not lend money to women, and that women were discriminated against in pension plans, insurance policies, and Social Security payments.

In education, a corresponding pattern of inequity was apparent. The proportion of women to men in college dropped from 47 percent in 1920 to 35 percent in 1958. In 1930, two out of every five B.A.s and M.A.s and one out of every seven Ph.D.s were awarded to women. By 1962, these figures had dropped to one in three and one in ten, respectively. Textbooks in all fields customarily did not mention women; in children's stories and readers, women were unilaterally depicted in dependent roles, usually as wives or mothers. Powerful women were generally evil; in contrast, men were presented as adventuresome and strong, as professionals, explorers, and inventors. "Sex-stereotyping" was the term feminists coined to characterize this literature, and they contended that it was a powerful force in molding adults who adhered to rigid separations between gender roles and expectations.

In law, feminists found hundreds of state laws still on the books that variously forbade women to sit on juries, limited their rights to make contracts and to hold property, and held them in minor status longer than men. Prostitution, after a half-century of desultory attacks, was still thriving in many cities. Rape laws in many states made it nearly impossible for the rapist to be convicted.

So universal has men's domination over women been throughout the historical past as well as the present that some feminists argued it constituted a system of oppression called "patriarchy," especially galling in the area of men's sexual domination over women. Rape, prostitution, the double standard, pornography, Freudian counsels about women's sexual passivity, and gynecologists' presumed insensitivity to women's needs were not isolated occurrences, they argued, but rather a network of oppressive devices designed to keep women in their place. Women in the movement began to share their negative physical experiences; some women who had been in the civil rights and student movements were distressed over the sexual exploitation in these presumably egalitarian groups. Thus, the radical feminists of the 1960s concentrated on physical freedom for women by opening gynecological clinics, agitating for abortion rights, opposing the exploitation of women's bodies and their victimization in male pornography, and publicizing the new information on sexuality—particularly the primacy of the clitoral orgasm—developed in the pioneering investigations of William Masters and Virginia Johnson. "The personal is political," became the rallying cry, as women demanded not only economic and legal equality but also the right to control their own bodies.

Marriage and the Family

Feminists of all persuasions are in agreement on questions of politics, employment, education, law, and sexual oppression. When it comes to questions of marriage and the family, however, the moderate and radical wings of the movement divide. Radicals, like Kate Millett, argue that women can be free only when traditional patterns of marriage and family life are replaced by communal arrangements. Socialist feminists insist that liberation can be won only with the fall of the capitalist economy. Some radicals, like Shulamith Firestone, contend that woman's function as childbearer must be ended and the fetus brought to gestation, not in the woman's body, but in the uterus of a cow or in a laboratory setting. Others are particularly hostile to men and argue that as a result of their historic role as oppressors, men should be made subordinate to women. Some of these women espouse lesbianism as the most honest form of female behavior.

More moderate members of the movement share some, but not all, of these sentiments. The moderates are not especially antagonistic toward men. They are not opposed to marriage or to communal living arrangements; they advocate individual choice in these matters. They do, however, support abortion as well as the establishment of day-care centers. A distaste for domesticity, seen as confining, pervades their rhetoric, and the professional woman is their ideal. On the other hand, the most recent theme in feminist writing has focused on motherhood—both as a problem and an enriching experience. Much has been written about the difficulties of combining careers and motherhood (as in Betty Friedan's *The Second Stage*). Adrienne Rich in *Of Woman Born* presents motherhood as a revolutionary force; Nancy Chodorow, in *The Reproduction of Mothering*, and Dorothy Dinnerstein, in *The Mermaid and the Minotaur*, employ a Freudian perspective to argue that the early developmental years of intense involvement between mother and child create warped adult personalities and that both men and women must be intimately involved in raising children to maintain a healthy society.

To uphold their view that women are not necessarily bound to homemaking and childrearing, moderate and radical feminists point to recent scholarly studies. The consensus of the 1950s that only motherhood offered a woman real fulfillment and that the young child needed a mother at home no longer exists. Some childrearing experts believe that in many cases either the mother–child relationship develops into a neurotic dependency, or, pressured by economic want or other personal difficulties, the mother gives her offspring insufficient attention. Citing successful examples of communal childrearing in Israel and elsewhere, scholars in the fields of psychology and sociology argue that children are too valuable a natural resource to be entrusted solely to parents who have little expertise in the care and education of children. On the question of domesticity, other authorities argue that this interest is learned, not innate, and that working women are in fact much more content than housewives. In opposition to the postwar analysts, sociologist Jessie Bernard contends that the majority of the past and present studies of marital discontent decisively show that nonworking married women are much more prone to anxiety, depression, and mental breakdowns than married men, married working women, or single women.[24]

Although the feminist position has gained a strong foothold among experts and professionals, many psychiatrists and psychologists still regard the mother-child relationship during the first years of life as crucial to future development. Some medical experts contend that the different biological makeups of men and women yet may indicate a natural urge on the part of women toward domesticity and motherhood. Some recent studies, too, suggest that a pregnant woman's activities may influence the development of the fetus. Finally, one work indicates that Friedan, Bernard, and others may, in fact, be wrong about the discontent of the American housewife. In her study of 571 housewives in urban and suburban Chicago, sociologist Helen Lopata found that the majority were not unhappy with their lot. Those for whom the role seemed restrictive were the less well-to-do, generally of working-class background and limited education. These women often were passive and found it difficult to interact with others; they resented the domineering attitudes of their husbands, and lack of obedience from their children made them feel inadequate. Middle-class Chicago housewives, however, with adequate incomes and some education, had few of these problems. Absorbed in their family and home, they nonetheless found time to do volunteer work and to form extensive friendships. They were proud of their role and felt that they functioned creatively.

Thus, the debate continues. Feminists have brought to light undeniable evidence of widespread discrimination against women. Whether a restructuring of society is necessary to bring women social equality as well as personal satisfaction in their own lives, however, has yet to be resolved.

AN ASSESSMENT OF FEMINIST ACHIEVEMENTS AND POTENTIALS

By the late 1960s, the achievements of the women's movement began to be substantial. State and national equal-opportunity commissions pressed sex-discrimination suits filed by women; by 1971, the courts had awarded $30 million in back pay to women as a result of these suits. In 1970, the Women's Equity Action League brought class-action suits against 100 universities under an executive order that required federal contractors to file affirmative-action programs with federal investigators, committing themselves to schedules for ending sex discrimination. Faced with the cutoff of their federal funds, university administrators were quick to comply. The Education Act of 1972 specifically prohibited sex discrimination in colleges and universities. Under pressure from women's organizations, especially the National Abortion Rights Action League, many states repealed legislation prohibiting abortion. In 1973, the Supreme Court declared abortion to be a private decision between doctor and patient, thereby substantially liberalizing its availability to women (*Roe v. Wade*). Finally, in the spring of 1973, both the Senate and the House of Representatives passed the Equal Rights Amendment. In 1967, Alice Paul—still head of the Woman's Party and still dedicated to the ERA—had persuaded the National Organization for Women (NOW) to give the amendment special endorsement. This support, in addition to adroit political maneuvering by political supporters, especially Michigan Democratic Congresswoman Martha Griffiths, secured its passage 50 years after its introduction into Congress. By 1975, 32 of the required 38 states had also passed the amendment.

Evidences of women's advancements and of feminist successes continued to surface on a variety of fronts. Literary critics began to note the appearance of a host of gifted women writers who explored feminist themes. Some traced the beginnings of the trend to Erica Jong's *Fear of Flying* and Sylvia Plath's *The Bell Jar*, both published in 1973. Moreover, strong-willed female characters began to emerge in general literature, even in books written for mass consumption by male authors like Irving Wallace and Ken Follett. Women joggers ran the 26-mile Boston and New York City marathons and petitioned the Olympic Committee to rescind its stand that long-distance running was too

Sally Ride, the first woman
crew member of a space flight:
the women's movement provided
the impetus.

arduous for women and to open an Olympic women's event in mar-
athon running. Advertising firms designed consumption campaigns
directed toward working women. Women constituted almost 30 percent of all business travelers by the end of the 1970s, and many hotels
instructed their employees to stop calling women guests "honey" or
"dear" and to address them by their last rather than their first names.
In 1978, the astronaut program—bastion of the traditional male
endeavors of exploring frontier space, taming the new technology, and
defying nature by piloting flying machines—admitted its first group
of women. In 1983, astronaut Sally Ride became the first woman crew
member of a space flight. The holder of a Ph.D. in physics from Stanford, Ride credited the women's movement with providing a strong
impetus for her career.[25]

Passage of the ERA by Congress marked one milestone for women in the 1970s; another was the 1977 Houston National Woman's Conference. Composed of 1800 delegates elected by 56 states and territorial public meetings, it was funded by the government under an act mandating the final conference "to identify the barriers that prevent women from participating fully and freely in all aspects of national life." Throughout the selection process for conference delegates, attempts were made to include women of all races and walks of life, and observers at Houston were struck by the racial and ethnic mix of the conference. The National Plan of Action they adopted was fully feminist. It called for ratification of the ERA; free choice in abortion; extension of Social Security benefits to housewives; elimination of all discriminations against lesbians; federal- and state-funded programs for victims of child abuse and education in rape prevention; and state-supported shelters for wives physically abused by husbands.

With this record of attainment, why did the ERA fail to achieve ratification at the state level? Some analysts blame the women's movement itself, arguing that grass-roots organization at the state level was weak, that early successes made feminists complacent, and that once women did begin to organize voting drives and lobby legislatures, their political skills were virtually nonexistent. However, powerful forces were united in opposition to the amendment—as similar forces had opposed the earlier women's suffrage amendment. The traditionalist Catholic hierarchy and the Mormon Church, both dedicated to domesticity as women's primary role and opposed to birth control and abortion, were influential opponents. Feminists argue that the insurance industry, which profits from differential women's rates and is regulated by state legislatures, quietly lobbied behind the scenes against the amendment.

But more than anything else, the ERA campaign encountered head-on the resurgent fundamentalist conservatism of the 1970s and became its primary target for defeat. Led by Illinois lawyer Phyllis Schlafly and her National Committee of Endorsers Against ERA, right-wing groups contended that the ERA would enforce the military draft on women, invalidate all laws protecting the rights of women at home or in divorce, make separate toilets for men and women illegal, and ultimately undermine American morality and destroy the family. Drawing on the financial resources of powerful right-wing groups and on the fanaticism of their members, who perceived the nation's basic insti-

tutions to be under attack, members of Schlafly's coalition proved to be highly effective advocates for their cause and lobbyists before state legislatures, which were overwhelmingly dominated by males.

Yet it was not clear until the closing moments of the campaign that the amendment was lost. Whatever political naiveté feminists demonstrated in the early 1970s was rectified a decade later. The last several years of the ERA campaign witnessed the assemblage, under the auspices of NOW, of one of the most sophisticated fund-raising and public-awareness campaigns in recent memory. Between 1977 and 1982, NOW membership rose from 65,000 to 230,000; between January and June of 1982, NOW raised $6 million and brought in more money each month than the Democratic National Committee. In April 1982, pollster Louis Harris reported soaring national support for the ERA; 63 percent of all respondents to his poll indicated their support for the amendment—a 13 percent increase over the 50 percent of the previous year.

Such increased support for the ERA attests not only to the rapidly changing position of women in America but also to the changing nature of American feminism and of NOW, its major organizational expression. Once identified with the radicals and lesbians who formed a large part of its activist membership, NOW successfully changed both its image and its strategy during the late 1970s, particularly with the election to its presidency of Eleanor Smeal, who identified herself as a Pittsburgh housewife and seemed to be the epitome of respectability. NOW's overwhelming emphasis on passage of the ERA necessitated the attainment of political skills and the downplaying of inflammatory issues like abortion and lesbian rights. The media began to feature new types of women, often older and conservatively dressed, who were operating as NOW field representatives and lobbyists in the unratified states. Three former President's wives—Lady Bird Johnson, Betty Ford, and Rosalynn Carter—voiced strong support for the ERA, and Maureen Reagan, President Ronald Reagan's daughter, publicly disagreed with her father's politics toward women.

Supporters of the Equal Rights Amendment on Solidarity Day—an attempt to bring together Feminists, Unionists, and others behind a New Left coalition.

The point is that although the Equal Rights Amendment was not approved, NOW and the feminist movement became a major force in politics. They may have lost a battle, but they learned how to play the game—how to lobby, run candidates for office, hold news conferences, raise money, stage rallies, use the media effectively. It is telling that the ERA defeat did not plunge NOW leaders into gloom; instead, they immediately announced a campaign, first to resubmit the amendment to Congress and, more importantly, to defeat key antifeminist officials and to elect more women to office. These latter goals are not unreasonable. An analysis of recent election returns indicates the emergence of a separate women's vote on issues like social welfare, peace, and feminism—all of which women support in greater numbers than men. Support for conservative President Reagan is about 10 percentage points less among women than among men, and women are beginning to move into the Democratic Party in significant numbers. President Reagan recognized this factor when he appointed Sandra Day O'Connor—the first woman to serve on the U.S. Supreme Court—to office in the summer of 1981. A judicial conservative, O'Connor nonetheless had previously backed women's rights. Early in 1983, Reagan also appointed two women to his cabinet: Elizabeth Dole as Secretary of Transportation and Margaret Heckler as Secretary of Health and Human Services—and Heckler had been a strong ERA supporter. What had seemed to be firm evidence of a lack of women's consciousness and of male dominance in the area of voting behavior was now under serious question.

The Reagan administration has shown little interest in enforcing affirmative-action laws, and cutbacks in social-welfare programs predominantly have affected women. Supreme Court observers note an increasing willingness on the part of the high court to overlook sex discrimination. Indeed, in the famed Bakke decision, which cast a cloud on programs of special school admissions for blacks, Justice Lewis Powell explicitly stated that the constitutional guarantees of equal rights outlined in the Fifth and Fourteenth Amendments were much less clear for women than for blacks. At the time of this writing, anti-abortion forces have suffered major defeats in failing to maneuver any legislation through Congress, but their followers remain fanatically determined to gain their ends, precisely when fundamentalism seems to be winning increasing adherents in a time of economic downturn and social uncertainty.

Elizabeth Dole being sworn in   *with President Ronald Reagan,*
as Secretary of Transportation   *Senator Robert Dole, and Mrs.*
by Supreme Court Associate   *Dole's mother in attendance.*
Justice Sandra Day O'Connor,

Still, indications of increasing equality for women are strong within the nation. Growing numbers of women, for example, are moving into the professions. In 1970, 4.7 percent of all lawyers and 8.9 percent of all doctors were women. By 1979, these percentages had risen to 12.4 percent and 11 percent, respectively. By 1981, the percentage of women doctors had risen to 22 percent and 30.2 percent of the nation's law-school graduates for that year were women. The percentage of women being awarded engineering degrees increased from 0.8 percent in 1971 to 10.4 percent in 1981. More women, too, are winning political office. In 1969, there were 301 women state legislators nationwide; in 1981, there were 908. In 1975, 5,765 of the nation's elected officials were women; by 1981, the figure stood at 14,225. And advances are being made in breaking down many sex-segregated occupations; 47 percent of all bus drivers and bartenders are now women.

Moreover, issues of rape and wife beating have gained national attention; stronger laws against rapists have been passed in many

states, and federal money has been made available for the "battered wives" centers that have appeared in many areas. Within the labor movement, women have formed a Committee of Labor Union Women and begun to work toward the greater unionization of women and even of the vast group of nonunionized white-collar workers.

Striking gains also have been registered by black women, who have moved in impressive numbers into employment areas traditionally dominated by white women. These gains were one of the greatest successes of the civil rights movement. In 1965, 24 percent of all employed black women were white-collar workers, compared with 62 percent of all employed white women. By 1981, these figures were 46 percent for black women and 66 percent for white women. Most importantly, black women abandoned the category of domestic service, with which they had been identified for a century. In 1965, 30 percent of all employed black women were domestic workers; by 1977, the figure had dropped to 9 percent. In many instances, immigrants from Mexico and Latin America—part of the new migrant exodus to the United States in the 1970s and 1980s—came to replace them.

Yet major evidences of discrimination against women remain. The work force is still, for the most part, segregated by sex. In 1979, 70.8 percent of all noncollege teachers were women, 80.3 percent of all clerical workers were women, and 96.8 percent of all nurses were women. Such sex segregation still underlies wage discrimination; in 1982, women still made about 57 cents of every dollar men made. The majority of college undergraduates are women, but the vast majority of faculty members are male. More than one-third of all candidates for the M.B.A. degree are women, but only 5 percent of the executives in the top 50 American companies are women. Out of the 435 members of the House of Representatives, 19 are women; two of the 100 senators are women. Over the last decade, the greater incidence of poverty among women has increased precipitously. Bureaucrats and scholars now routinely discuss the "feminization of poverty"; 81 percent of all welfare recipients in the United States are women.

It cannot be denied, however, that the broad social changes affecting women's lives throughout America's modern age have recently fol-

The 1980s: *Growing numbers of women are moving into the professions.*

lowed a revolutionary direction, prompting some analysts to predict that the traditional ways in which Americans have lived will presently cease to exist. Census data consistently reveal that the birth rate is producing near-zero population growth, the age of first marriage is rising, more and more individuals are living alone, the divorce rate is rising, and women, especially married women and women with pre-school children, are increasingly moving into the work force. In 1965, about 39 percent of all American women were employed for remu-neration outside the home. In 1982, the rate stood at 52 percent, and it is expected to rise to 65 percent by 1995. Surveys revealed that only 19 percent of all Americans continue to live in the tradition of the legendary American family, in which the husband works and the wife stays at home with the children. As we move further and further into a post-industrial economy and technology changes our lives more radically than it has since the first industrial revolution, women may be eliminated from vast sectors of the work force, as clerical labor is taken over by sophisticated office machines that perform filing and typing chores with only a minimal need for operators. Or with the advent of computers and the decline in factory routinization, more and more work may be done at home, either thereby extending the privatization of the family or returning economic and social functions to a family setting.

Social indicators are never easy to interpret. The reported new inter-est on the part of young women in traditional marriages and the rise in sales of diamond engagement rings may indicate the resurgence of a new conservatism among the younger generation—or these trends may reflect a psychological need to adjust to new forces by reaffirming traditional rituals without a need for the substance behind them. The seeming decline in open sexuality may be a reaction against 1960s radicalism, but it may also be a response to the new, virulent strain of the herpes virus, which is transmitted sexually and for which there is no cure. The vast increase in sales of women's Gothic fiction, mystery stories, and Harlequin romances (in which rebellious women are mas-tered by older, powerful men)—to the point that 100 million Harle-quins were sold in the United States in 1977—may represent an anti-feminist reaction to the women's movement. Or does it indicate that some form of escapism is necessary for women to accept the new trends and their changing roles? Soap operas, which have come to

New social trends—threats to traditional definitions or an extension of equality to women?

dominate television programming in the evenings, as they always have in the afternoons, center around powerful families—not submissive women—and a number of the characters are career women. How do we interpret the increased incidence of rape in the last few years? Or the popularity of a sadomasochistic pornography centered around the victimization of women? Or a movie season in which two of the best-selling films offer us a romanticized treatment of army conduct extolling traditional sex roles *(An Officer and a Gentleman)* and Dustin Hoffman learning, through transvestitism, to integrate masculine and feminine traits into a new personality *(Tootsie)*?

On the one hand, Americans seem overwhelmed by the new social trends, by the incidence of divorce and the breakdown of the family, by the danger of nuclear war and the seeming inability of government administrators to solve the nation's economic difficulties, by women's new threat to traditional definitions of masculinity. On the other hand, many Americans seem willing to explore new sexual and social roles and increasingly to applaud the extension of equality to women. In 1980, polls showed overwhelming support for women's reproductive freedom and their right to political office. For the first time in the nation's history, a majority of Americans indicated that it made no difference to them if a man or a woman was the mayor of a town, a lawyer, a doctor—even "their own boss." A majority of the respondents to a survey on these issues conducted by the President's Advisory Committee for Women believed that husbands and wives should share financial decision making as well as household chores and care of the children. Such thinking represents a profound shift from the mid-1970s, when most Americans polled on this issue still defined housework exclusively as women's work. Responses to the 1980 survey indicated that most Americans still believed there were advantages to being a man, but their stance did not stem from sexist motives. Rather, they felt that women must still cope with a double standard that impeded their progress in most areas of their behavior.

What the future holds is difficult to predict. Once before in America's modern history, with the attainment of suffrage and the movement of women into the work force, equality for women seemed in sight, only to dissipate in the face of a depression and a war. But the feminist revolution of the last 20 years has so permeated the national consciousness that it is difficult to visualize its demise, holding out, as it does, a different and more humane way of life for men as well as women—for all Americans.

NOTES

[1] Harrison Smith, "Must Women Work?" *Independent Woman* (December 1947): 34.

[2] Alva Myrdal and Viola Klein, *Women's Two Roles: Home and Work* (London: Routledge & Kegan Paul, 1956), p. 134.

[3] Benjamin Spock, *Baby and Child Care* (1946; reprint ed., New York: Dell, 1957), p. 570.

[4] Mirra Komarovsky, *Women in the Modern World: Their Education and Their Dilemmas* (Boston: Little, Brown, 1953), pp. 297–98.

[5] Betty Friedan, *The Feminine Mystique* (1963; reprint ed., New York: Dell, 1970), pp. 29–63.

[6] Komarovsky, *Women in the Modern World*, p. 94.

[7] Friedan, *The Feminine Mystique*, p. 115.

8 Kate Hevner Mueller, "The Cultural Pressures on Women," in Opal P. David (ed.), *The Education of Women: Signs for the Future* (Washington, D.C.: American Council on Education, 1957), pp. 50–51.

9 Abraham Myerson, "Woman, the Authorities' Scapegoat," in Elizabeth Bragdon (ed.), *Women Today: Their Conflicts, Their Frustrations, and Their Fulfillments* (New York: Bobbs-Merrill, 1953), p. 305.

10 Michael Gordon and Penelope J. Shankweiler, "Different Equals Less: Female Sexuality in Recent Marriage Manuals," *Journal of Marriage and the Family*, XXIII, (August 1979): 459–66.

11 Komarovsky, *Woman in the Modern World*, p. viii.

12 Doris E. Fleischman, "Notes of a Retiring Feminist," *American Mercury*, LXVIII (February 1949): 161–68.

13 Helen Sherman and Marjorie Coe, *The Challenge of Being a Woman: Understanding Ourselves and Our Children* (New York: Harper & Row, 1955), p. 17.

14 Agnes Meyer, "Women Aren't Men," *The Atlantic Monthly*, CLXXXVI (August 1950): 33.

15 Margaret Bruton, "Present-Day Thinking on the Woman Question," *Annals of the American Academy of Political and Social Science*, CCLI (May 1947): 14.

16 Alice Rossi, "Equality Between the Sexes," in Robert Jay Lifton (ed.), *The Woman in America* (Boston: Houghton Mifflin, 1965), p. 99.

17 Cynthia Fuchs Epstein, *Woman's Place: Options and Limits in Professional Careers* (1970; reprint ed., Berkeley: University of California Press, 1971), p. 97.

18 David Reisman, "Two Generations," in Robert Jay Lifton (ed.), *The Woman in America* (Boston: Houghton Mifflin, 1965), pp. 72–97.

19 Judith Hole and Ellen Levine, *Rebirth of Feminism* (New York: Quadrangle, 1971), p 81.

20 Sara Evans, *Personal Politics: The Roots of Women's Liberation in the Civil Rights Movement and the New Left* (New York: Alfred A. Knopf, 1979), p. 51.

21 Kate Stimpson (ed.), *Women and the "Equal Rights" Amendment: Senate Subcommittee Hearings on the Constitutional Amendment, 91st Congress* (New York: R.R. Bowker, 1972), pp. 38–39.

22 Hole and Levine, *Rebirth of Feminism*, p. 81.

23 Kirsten Amundsen, *The Silenced Majority: Women and American Democracy* (Englewood Cliffs, NJ: Prentice-Hall, 1971), p. 86.

24 Jessie Bernard, *The Future of Marriage* (New York: World, 1972), pp. 26–27.

25 Sara Sanborn, "Sally Ride: The Making of an Astronaut," *Ms.*, XI (January 1983): 88.

BIBLIOGRAPHY

The best source for the history of women in the 1950s remains Betty Friedan, *The Feminine Mystique* (1963; reprint ed., New York: Dell, 1970). Although Friedan's feminist analysis may seem outdated, her historical sense is excellent. Eric Goldman, *The Crucial Decade—and After: America, 1945–1960* (New York: Alfred A. Knopf, 1960), and Douglas T. Miller and Marion Nowak, *The Fifties: The Way We Really Were* (Garden City, NY: Doubleday, 1977), provide a good sense of the troubled nature of the decade. The major statement of the Freudian position on women is Helene Deutsch, *The Psychology of Women: A Psychoanalytic Interpretation* (New York: Grune and Stratton, 1944–1945). For an interesting exploration of childrearing in the period, see Nancy P. Weiss, "Mother, the Invention of Necessity: Dr. Benjamin Spock's *Baby and Child Care*," *American Quarterly*, XXIX (Winter 1977): 519–46. Paul Robinson, *The Modernization of Sex* (New York: Harper & Row, 1977), provides an analysis of the changing ideas of sex experts in the twentieth century, and Vance Packard, *The Sexual Wilderness: The Contemporary Upheaval in Male–Female Relations* (New York: David McKay, 1968), explores the sexual revolution of the 1960s. In *Mirror, Mirror: Images of Women Reflected in Popular Culture* (Garden City, NY: Anchor Books, 1977), Kathryn Weibel provides a useful introduction to the subject of women and popular culture.

An insightful assessment of the feminism of the 1950s is Arnold W. Green and Eleanor Melnick, "What Has Happened to the Feminist Movement," in Alvin W. Gouldner (ed.), *Studies in Leadership: Leadership and Democratic Action* (New York: Russell & Russell, 1950), pp. 277–302. See also Leila J. Rupp, "The Survival of American Feminism: The Women's Movement in the Postwar Period," in Robert H. Bremner and Gary Reichard, *Reshaping America: Society and Institutions* (Columbus: Ohio State University Press, 1982), for an attempt to argue that feminism had some vigor in the 1950s. Some popular contemporary statements of various feminist positions can be found in Elizabeth Bragdon (ed.), *Women Today: Their Conflicts, Their Frustrations, and Their Fulfillments* (New York: Bobbs-Merrill, 1953); Beverly Cassara (ed.), *American Women: The Changing Image* (Boston: Beacon Press, 1962); Viola Klein, *The Feminine Character: History of an Ideology* (Urbana: University of Illinois Press, 1946); Helen Sherman and Marjorie Coe, *The Challenge of Being a Woman: Understanding Ourselves and Our Children* (New York: Harper & Row, 1955); and the May 1947 issue of *Annals of the American Academy of Political and Social Science*.

A large literature exists on the emergence of feminism in the 1960s. See especially Maren Lockwood Carden, *The New Feminist Movement* (New York: Russell Sage Foundation, 1974); Sara Evans, *Personal Politics: The Roots of Women's Liberation in the Civil Rights Movement & the New Left* (New York: Alfred A.

Knopf, 1979); Jo Freeman, *The Politics of Women's Liberation: A Case of an Emerging Social Movement and Its Relation to the Policy Process* (New York: David McKay, 1975); and Judith Hole and Ellen Levine, *Rebirth of Feminism* (New York: Quadrangle, 1971). In "A 'New Frontier' for Women: The Public Policy of the Kennedy Administration," *Journal of American History*, LXVII (December 1980): 630–46, Cynthia Harrison has surveyed the relevant government material. For understanding the position of women in the 1960s, contemporary documents and surveys are also useful. The 1963 report of the President's Commission on the Status of Women was published as Margaret Mead and Frances Bagley Kaplan (eds.), *American Women: Report of the President's Commission on the Status of Women and Other Publications of the Commission* (New York: Scribner's Book Companies, 1965). Another useful compilation is Kate Stimpson (ed.), *Women and the "Equal Rights" Amendment: Senate Subcommittee Hearings of the Constitutional Amendment, 91st Congress* (New York: R.R. Bowker, 1972). Also illuminating are Kirsten Amundsen, *The Silenced Majority: Women and American Democracy* (Englewood Cliffs, NJ: Prentice-Hall, 1971); Caroline Bird, *Born Female: The High Cost of Keeping Women Down* (New York: David McKay, 1968); and Cynthia Fuchs Epstein, *Woman's Place: Options and Limits in Professional Careers* (Berkeley: University of California Press, 1970).

On the new feminism, the outpouring of literature from the movement speaks for itself. In addition to Shulamith Firestone, *The Dialectic of Sex* (New York: William Morrow, 1974); Germaine Greer, *The Female Eunuch* (New York: McGraw-Hill Book Co., 1970); and Kate Millett, *Sexual Politics* (Garden City, NY: Doubleday, 1970), also consult with profit Susan Brownmiller, *Against Our Will: Men, Women, and Rape* (New York: Simon & Schuster, 1975); Vivian Gornick and Barbara K. Moran (eds.), *Women in Sexist Society: Studies in Power and Powerlessness* (New York: Basic Books, 1971); Robert Jay Lifton (ed.), *The Woman in America* (Boston: Houghton Mifflin, 1965); Juliet Mitchell, *Woman's Estate* (New York: Random House, 1971); and Robin Morgan, *Sisterhood is Powerful: An Anthology of Writings from the Women's Liberation Movement* (New York: Random House, 1970). Betty Friedan's more recent writings include *It Changed My Life: Writings on the Women's Movement* (New York: Random House, 1976), and *The Second Stage* (New York: Summit Books, 1981).

A large literature on women's participation in social institutions in the recent period continues to be produced. Among the most insightful studies are Cynthia Fuchs Epstein, *Women in Law* (New York: Basic Books, 1981); Rosabeth Kanter, *Men and Women of the Corporation* (New York: Basic Books, 1977); Helen Znaniecki Lopata, *Occupation Housewife* (New York: Oxford University Press, 1971); and Ruth Mandel, *In the Running: The New Woman Candidate* (Boston: Ticknor & Fields, 1981). On women and the family, see Mary Jo Bane, *Here to Stay: American Families in the 20th Century* (New York: Basic Books, 1976); Kenneth Keniston, *All Our Children: The American Family Under Pressure* (New York: Harcourt Brace Jovanovich, Inc., 1977); Christopher Lasch, *Haven in a Heartless World: The Family Besieged* (New York: Basic Books, 1977); and Sar A. Levitan and Richard S. Belous, *What's Happening to the American Family?* (Baltimore: Johns Hopkins University Press, 1981).

On working-class women, see Kathy Kahn, *Hillbilly Women* (Garden City, NY: Doubleday, 1973); Mirra Komarovsky, *Blue-Collar Marriage* (New York: Random House, 1964); Lee Rainwater, Richard P. Coleman, and Gerald Hendel, *Workingman's Wife: Her Personality, World, and Life Style* (New York: Institute of Social Research, 1959); Lillian Breslow Rubin, *Worlds of Pain: Life in the Working-Class Family* (New York: Basic Books, 1977); and Nancy Seifer, *Nobody Speaks for Me! Self-Portraits of American Working-Class Women* (New York: Simon & Schuster, 1976). An interesting exploration of the world of women service workers is contained in Louise Kapp Howe, *Pink Collar Workers: Inside the World of Women's Work* (New York: G.P. Putnam's Sons, 1977). On the attitudes of black women, see Toni Cade, *The Black Woman: An Anthology* (New York: New American Library, 1970), and Michele Wallace, *Black Macho and the Myth of the Superwoman* (New York: The Dial Press, 1979). For depiction of kin networks and survival strategies in a black urban ghetto, see Carol B. Stack, *All Our Kin: Strategies for Survival in a Black Community* (New York: Harper & Row, 1975). The film *Salt of the Earth* is a moving depiction of the participation of Mexican–American women in a New Mexico mining strike in the early 1950s. It is available from Films, Inc., 5625 Hollywood Blvd., Hollywood, CA 90028.

Scholars in the field of women's studies, since its inception nearly 15 years ago, have produced a sizable volume of theoretical works and scholarly studies. Among the most interesting are Elizabeth Abel (ed.), *Writing and Sexual Difference* (Chicago: University of Chicago Press, 1982); Jessie Bernard, *The Female World* (New York: The Free Press, 1981); Nancy Chodorow, *The Reproduction of Mothering: Psychoanalysis and the Sociology of Gender* (Berkeley: University of California Press, 1978); Mary Daly, *Beyond God the Father: Toward a Philosophy of Women's Liberation* (Boston: Beacon Press, 1973); Dorothy Dinnerstein, *The Mermaid and the Minatour: Sexual Arrangements and Human Malaise* (New York: Harper & Row, 1977); Nancy Henley, *Body Politics: Power, Sex, and Nonverbal Communication* (Englewood Cliffs, NJ: Prentice-Hall, 1977); Nannerl O. Keohane, Michelle Rosaldo, and Barbara Gelpi (eds.), *Feminist Theory: A Critique of Ideology* (Chicago: University of Chicago Press, 1982); Elizabeth Langland and Walter Gove (eds.), *A Feminist Perspective on the Academy: The Difference It Makes* (Chicago: University of Chicago Press, 1981); Rayna Reiter (ed.), *Toward an Anthropology of Women* (New York: Monthly Review Press, 1975); Adrienne Rich, *Of Woman Born: Motherhood as Institution and Experience* (New York: W.W. Norton, 1976); Michelle Rosaldo and Louise Lamphere (eds.),

Women, Culture, and Society (Stanford, CA: Stanford University Press, 1974); and Alice Rossi, "A Biosocial Perspective on Parenting," *Daedalus*, CVI (1977): 1–32.

Several women's studies journals regularly include articles of interest to historians of women. Among the most important of these journals are: *Feminist Studies* (associated with the University of Maryland); *Signs: Journal of Women in Culture and Society* (published through the University of Chicago Press and edited through Stanford University); and *Women's Studies* (associated with Queens College, City University of New York).

A number of biographies and autobiographies of interest have appeared. Among these are Carol Felsenthal, *The Sweetheart of the Silent Majority: The Biography of Phyllis Schlafly* (Garden City, NY: Doubleday, 1981), Kate Millet, *Flying* (New York: Alfred A. Knopf, 1974), and Sonia Johnson has documented her difficulties as a feminist in the Morman Church in *From Housewife to Heretic* (Garden City, NY: Doubleday, 1981). For the dramatic story of a woman's journey from a midwestern Jewish community through immigration to Israel to becoming head of the State of Israel, see Golda Meir, *My Life* (New York: Dell, 1975). Daisy Bates, *The Long Shadow of Little Rock: A Memoir* (New York: David McKay, 1962), and Anne Moody, *Coming of Age in Mississippi* (New York: The Dial Press, 1968), both detail the saga of black women in the civil rights struggle. For an interesting study of a woman's participation in the counter-culture of the 1960s, see George Plimpton (ed.), *Edie: An American Biography* (New York: Alfred A. Knopf, 1982).

Among the recent feminist novels of note are Marilyn French, *The Women's Room* (1980); Erica Jong, *Fear of Flying* (1973); Sylvia Plath, *The Bell Jar* (1973); Marge Piercy, *Small Changes* (1978); Alix Kates Shulman, *Memoirs of an Ex-Prom Queen* (1972); and Alice Walker, *The Color Purple* (1982).

APPENDIX

WOMEN IN THE LABOR FORCE

Women in Selected Professional Occupations, 1979

(Percentage of all workers)

Lawyers	12.8
Teachers (college and university)	31.6
Teachers (except college and university)	70.8
Clergy	4.6
Doctors	10.7
Engineers	2.9
Dentists	4.6
Biologists	36.4
Librarians	78.1
Nurses	93.2
Social workers	64.3
Clerical workers	80.3
Service workers	62.4
Manufacturing workers	39.9
Craftsmen	5.7

SOURCE   U.S. Department of Labor, Bureau of Labor Statistics, *Employment and Earnings* (1980).

Women in the Labor Force

	(Percentage of all workers)	(Percentage of all women)
1890	17	18
1900	18	20
1920	20	23
1930	22	24
1940	25	28
1945	36	37
1950	29	32
1955	31	34
1960	33	36
1970	40	44
1980	41.7	51

SOURCE Adapted from Esther Peterson, "Working Women," in Robert Jay Lifton, ed., *The Woman in America* (Boston: Houghton Mifflin, 1965), p. 145. Data for 1980 are from U.S. Department of Labor, Bureau of Labor Statistics, *Employment and Earnings* (1980), and *Handbook of Labor Statistics* (1980).

Women in Selected Professional Occupations

Occupation	(Percentage of all workers)						
	1900	1910	1920	1930	1940	1950	1960
Lawyers		1.0	1.4	2.1	2.4	3.5	3.5
College presidents, professors		19.0	30.0	32.0	27.0	23.0	19.0
Clergy	4.4	1.0	2.6	4.3	2.2	8.5	5.8
Doctors		6.0	5.0	4.0	4.6	6.1	6.8
Engineers					0.3	1.2	0.8
Dentists		3.1	3.2	1.8	1.5	2.7	2.1
Biologists						27.0	28.0
Mathematicians						38.0	26.4
Physicists						6.5	4.2
Librarians		79.0	88.0	91.0	89.0	89.0	85.0
Nurses	94.0	93.0	96.0	98.0	98.0	98.0	97.0
Social workers		52.0	62.0	68.0	67.0	66.0	57.0

SOURCE Cynthia Fuchs Epstein, *Woman's Place: Options and Limits in Professional Careers* (1970; reprint ed., Berkeley: University of California Press, 1971), p. 7.

Percentages of Women Employed in Professions and Occupations, 1910–1930

(Percentage of employed women)

	1910	1920	1930
Professionals	9.1	11.9	14.2
Clerical workers	7.3	16.6	18.5
Manufacturing workers	22.6	22.6	17.5
Trade (including saleswomen)	5.9	7.9	9.0
Transportation and communication	1.3	2.6	2.6
Domestic (including waitresses and beauticians)	31.3	25.6	29.6
Agriculture	22.4	12.7	8.5

SOURCE   Grace Hutchins, *Women Who Work* (New York: International Publishers, 1934), p. 24.

Percentages of Women Employed in Professions and Occupations, 1940–1962

	1940	1950	1962
Professionals	13	11	13
Managers, officials	5	5	5
Clerical workers	21	26	31
Manufacturing workers	18	19	15
(craftsmen, foremen)	1	1	1
Sales	7	9	7
Service workers (including waitresses)	11	13	15
Private household	18	10	10
Agriculture	6	5	3

SOURCE   Adapted from Esther Peterson, "Working Women," in Robert Jay Lifton (ed.), *The Woman in America* (Boston: Houghton Mifflin, 1965), p. 155.

Percentages of White and Black Women Employed in Professions and Occupations: 1972, 1979

	1972		1979	
	White Women	Black Women	White Women	Black Women
Professionals	14.9	11.2	16.4	14.2
Managers	4.8	2.3	6.8	3.4
Clerical workers	36.3	23.3	35.9	29.0
Manufacturing workers	12.5	12.3	10.2	14.7
(craftsmen)	1.3	.9	1.9	1.2
Sales	7.8	2.8	7.4	3.1
Service workers	16.2	26.8	16.1	24.6
Private household	3.0	15.2	2.0	6.8
Agriculture	1.9	4.4	1.3	.8

SOURCE   U.S. Department of Labor, Bureau of Labor Statistics, *Handbook of Labor Statistics* (December 1980).

PHOTO CREDITS

INDEX

Abbott, Grace, 107, 196
Abortion
Comstock Law and, 16
as demand of Houston National
Woman's Conference, 263
demonstrations for, 255
nineteenth-century attitudes toward,
16–17
and NOW, 265
right-wing opposition to, 266
state prohibitions on, 18
Supreme Court and, 261
Addams, Jane, 52, 105, 106, 107, 116,
125, 129, 130, 169, 183, 186, 189
Adkins v. Children's Hospital, 168
Advertising, and women, 150, 235, 262
Affirmative action, 250, 261, 266
Airline hostesses, 170–71
Allen, Florence, 141, 191
Allport, Floyd, 160
American Association of University
Women, 18, 147
American Federation of Labor, 71, 74–75,
76–77, 79, 202–204
American Home Economics Association,
117
American Legion, 152
American Medical Association, 152
American woman. *See* Women
Ames, Jessie Daniel, 185
Anderson, Margaret, 115, 184
Anderson, Marian, 190
Anderson, Mary, 76–77, 148
Anthony, Susan B., 2, 24, 26, 30, 34, 93,
96, 98
Anthropologists, women as, 40
Anti-abortion movement, 16–17, 266
Antifeminism
Freudian theory and, 232–33
in 1920s, 149–50
of postwar, 230–31, 246
Antilynching Crusaders, 185
Antioch College, 5
Antisuffrage movement, 94–96
Arden, Elizabeth, 163
Artists, women as, 164–65
Association of Collegiate Alumnae, 18,
99, 103
Association of Southern Women for the
Prevention of Lynching, 184–85
Association of Unemployed Single
Women, 199

Astronaut program, 262
Athletics, and women. *See* Sports
Austen, Alice, 28
Austin, Mary, 18, 40
Automobile strike, Flint, Michigan, 1937,
203

Baby and Child Care (Spock), 234
"Baby doll" look, 237
Back-to-the-home movement, 237–39
Bacon, Albion Fellows, 104
Baker, Ray Stannard, 66
Bakke decision, 266
Bara, Theda, 172, 173
Barnard College, 32, 111, 169, 237
Beauty contests, 169, 176, 255
Beauty parlors, appearance of, 84
Beauvoir, Simone de, 240
Bedford Hills (NY) Women's
Reformatory, 105
Beecher, Catharine, 30, 38
Behaviorism, 151, 232
Bellamy, Edward, 103
Bell Jar, The (Plath), 261
Bennett, Joan, 216
Bernard, Jessie, 260
Bethune, Mary McCleod, 193
Bicycling, 26–28
Bicycling for Ladies (Ward), 28
Bird, Caroline, 209
Birth control
Comstock law, and, 18
movement to attain, 115
in 1920s, 157
in 1930s, 208, 209
in 1960s, 243, 245
See also Abortion
Birth Control Review magazine, 109
Blackwell, Elizabeth, 34
Black women
as blues singers, 218
and civil rights movement, 251
family among, 66–67
on farms, 59, 61
job mobility for, 66
and lynching, 184–85
as "mammies" or temptresses, 66
in movies, 217–18
and New Deal, 189
poverty and, 65–67, 257
recent gains, 269
and the Second World War, 223

Black Women (*continued*)
  social welfare and, 257
  unemployment and, 257
  as workers and professionals, 30, 66,
    200
Blair, Emily Newell, 139
Blatch, Harriot Stanton, 97, 127
Blondie and Dagwood, 211
Bloomer dress, 24–25
Blue Angel, The, 214
Blues, and black women singers, 218
Bly, Nellie (Elizabeth Seaman), 36, 37
Boaz, Franz, 40
Boston marriages, 43
Boston Women's Municipal League, 101
Bow, Clara, 157
Boyce, Neith, 111
BPW. *See* National Federation of Business
    and Professional Women's Clubs
Brandeis, Louis, 116
Breckinridge, Sophonisba, 107
Brico, Antonia, 165
Bromley, Dorothy Dunbar, 150
Broun, Heywood, 146
Brown, H. Rap, 251
Bruton, Margaret, 242
Bryan, William Jennings, 190
Bryn Mawr College, 5, 39, 99
Buck, Pearl, 210
Bucks County Medical Association, 39
Business, women as executives and
    entrepreneurs, 163–64, 200, 269
Bustles, 26
Butler, Nicholas, 184

Cabinet members, women as, 256
Cagney, James, 214
California, University of, Berkeley, 210,
    251
Call-girl systems, 81
Carter, Rosalynn, 265
Catalyst, 254
Cather, Willa, 165
Catholic Church
  against ERA, 263
  as antisuffrage group, 95
  and immigrant women, 78–79
Catt, Carrie Chapman, 56, 127, 130, 132
Chafe, William, 223
Chase, Mary Ellen, 163
Chicago Civil Club, 101
Chicago Columbian Exposition (1893),
    20–21, 25, 41, 210

Chicago, University of, 107
Childbirth
  as "blinding glory," 56
  for middle-class mothers, 16
  in 1890s, 15–16
  in 1950s, 237–38
Child-care facilities, 167, 219, 249, 250
Child Labor Amendment, 139, 144, 147,
    153
Child-labor laws, 107, 139
Child-rearing
  of 1930s, 205
  of 1950s, 233–35, 239
  recent, 259–60
  Watson on, 151
Children's Bureau, 107, 147, 193, 196
Chinese immigrants, 64–65
Chisholm, Shirley, 256
Chodorow, Nancy, 259
Chrysler Corporation, 224
CIO. *See* Congress of Industrial
    Organizations
Circuit Court of Appeals, first woman
    judge on, 141
Civilian Conservation Corps, 193, 195
Civil Rights Act (1964), 250
Civil rights movement, 247, 251, 254
Civil Service, women in, 30, 195
Civil War, effect on women, 30, 33
Civil Works Administration, 193
Clark, Mae, 214
Clark, Thomas D., 34
Clarke, Edward H., 15
Clerical labor
  male dominance in, 12
  and 1930s, 198, 200–201
  rise in, 11, 30
  and Second World War, 223
  women in, 11–12, 80
Clothing styles. *See* Fashions in dress
Colbert, Claudette, 216
College education
  in 1920s, 157–58
  in recent period, 257, 269
  "rigors" of, unsuited to women, 15
  Western colleges, 33
  women's entry, 30–34
Columbia University, 32
Columbian College of Law, 36
Columbian Exposition. *See* Chicago
    Columbian Exposition
Commission on Interracial Cooperation,
    185

Commission on the Status of Women, 249–50
Committee for Industrial Organization, 202
Committee of Labor Union Women, 269
Committee to Defeat the Unequal Rights Amendment, 240
Communism
  feminists accused of, in 1920s, 204–205
  in 1930s, 204–205
  in 1950s, 239
  and unions in 1920s, 168
Community Chests
  and settlement houses, 144
Comstock, Anthony, 16
Comstock Law (1873), 16
Coney Island, 84
Congressional Union, 127, 128
Congress, women in, 256
Congress of Industrial Organizations, 202–204
Congress of Mothers, 18, 20
"Consciousness-raising" technique, 252
Consumerism, 160, 205, 235, 244, 262
Consumers' League, 76, 117, 144, 168, 187, 191, 193, 196, 241
Cooperative housing
  and women reformers, 103–104
Corsets, 22, 26, 211–12
Cosmetics industry, 150, 163
Cosmetics, use of, 173
Cotton factories, women in, 30, 32
Council for National Defense, 132
Crawford, Joan, 216–17
"Crib girls," 84
Crinolines, 26
Croly, Jane, 101
Croquet, clothing for, 26
Cummings, Edith Mae, 164

Daily Worker, 204
Daisy Chain, Vassar, 33
Dancing
  and dance halls, 84
  new styles of, 84–85
  in 1920s, 153
Dandridge, Dorothy, 218
Daughters of the American Revolution (DAR), 18, 103, 152, 190
Davis, Allen, 100
Davis, Bette, 213, 216
Davis, Katherine Bement, 104
Davis, Maxine, 213

Day-care centers, 167, 219, 221
Day, Doris, 236
Death of a Salesman (Miller), 52
Dentists, women as, 163
Democratic National Committee, 265
Democratic party, women in, 187, 189, 193, 249, 261, 266
Demographic factors
  of nineteenth century, 17
  of 1900s, 51
  of 1920s, 157
  of 1930s, 208
  of 1950s, 237
  of 1960s, 243–44
  recent, 270
Demographic transition, 17
Department stores, 84
Depression (1929–1940)
  family response to, 205–11
  marriage as security in, 205–11
  unemployment in, 198–202
Dewson, Mary, 192
Dialectic of Sex, The (Firestone), 255
Dickinson, Emily, 164
Dietrich, Marlene, 172, 175, 213, 214
Dinner at Eight, 212
Dinnerstein, Dorothy, 259
Dior, Christian, 237
Disillusionment, of 1920s, 148–51
Divorce rates, 51, 60, 78–79, 157, 205, 237
Doctors, women as, 11, 267
Dole, Elizabeth, 266, 267
Doll's House, A (Ibsen), 110, 111
"Domestic feminism," 39, 241–43
  See also Feminism
Domestic science movement, 3, 39, 54, 117
Domestic service
  and black women, 66
  and rural women, 59
  and women's discontent, 54, 67
  See also Servants
Donovan, Frances, 81, 85–86
Dorr, Rheta Childe, 15, 40, 99, 113, 121, 127
Draft, military, and women, 254–63
Dreiser, Theodore, 53
Dress reform, of 1890s, 24–27
Dress styles. See Fashions in dress
Duncan, Isadora, 26
Duniway, Abigail Scott, 95
Durant, Henry, 38

Earhart, Amelia, 169, 170
Eastman, Crystal, 147
Ederle, Gertrude, 149
Education
   arguments for, 3–6, 37–39
   college, in 1920s, 157–58
   of 1960s, 257
   self-confidence from, 5–6, 30–34
Education Act (1972), 261
Educational Opportunities, of 1890s, 3–6
   See also College education; Elementary
      schools; Women's colleges
Ehrenreich, Barbara, 56
Eisenhower, Dwight D., 249
Electric kitchens, changes in, 41, 149
Elementary schools
   admission of girls to, 5
   women teachers in, 10, 30
Eliot, George, 40
Employment
   of 1890s, 28–30, 6–14
   in First World War, 131–32
   of immigrant women, 60–63
   in 1920s, 161–67
   in 1930s, 198–202, 205
   in 1950s and 1960s, 243–44, 257
   in recent period, 269, 270
   in Second World War, 218–25
Engineers, women as, 267
Engle, Lavinia, 140
English, Dierdre, 56
Equal Pay Act (1963), 250
Equal Rights Amendment (ERA), 147,
      183, 184, 195, 241, 249, 261, 263, 265
Evansville (IL) Civil Improvement
      Society, 104
Eve, "curse of," 15
Eye makeup, 173

Factory forewomen, women as, 10
Factory work
   camaraderie among workers, 74
   exploitative conditions in, 67–69
   immigrants and, 61–65
   sexual harrassment in, 74
   transition to clerical, 80
Fair Labor Standards Act (1938), 194, 241
"Fallen women," prostitution and, 83
Family
   breakup of traditional, 270
   fundamentalist fears for, 263
   and middle-class women, 50–56,

   259–60
   in 1930s, 205–207
   in 1950s, 237–40
   and working-class women, 78–79
Farley, James, 189
Farmers' Alliances, 18
Farm life and work, 57–61
Farm Security Administration, 194, 207
Farnham, Marynia, 230, 232
Fashions in dress
   and dress reform, 24–28
   and the New Woman, 22
   of 1920s and 1930s, 211–12
   of 1950s, 237
   versus uniform clothing, 109
   Victorian modes, 26
Fauset, Jessie, 165
Fear of Flying (Jong), 261
Federal Art Project, 194
Federal Civil Service, women in, 30, 184
Federal Council on Negro Affairs, 193
Federal Emergency Relief
      Administration, 193
Federal Music Project, 193
Federal Theatre project, 189, 194
Federal Writers' Project, 194
Federation for Child Study, 55
Female Eunuch, The (Greer), 255
Feminine Mystique, The (Friedan), 236, 247
Feminism
   domestic, 39, 241–43
   growth of, 93–124
   husbands against, 40
   of 1920s, 151–52
   of 1950s, 241–43
   of 1960s, 246–66
   Progressivism and, 99–128
   radicalism and, 108–12
   and suffragist movement, 125–29
   See also Social feminists
Feminist achievements, assessment of,
      261–72
Feminist action groups, pre-First World
      War, 112–15
Feminist Alliance, 112–13, 147, 152
Feminist position, contemporary, 256–60
Feminist potentials, assessment of,
      261–72
Feminist scholars, 111–12, 256
Feminization, sociologists' definition of,
      12
Femme couverte, common-law doctrine of,
      1

Femme fatale, 171, 175
Femme sole, common-law doctrine of, 1
Ferber, Edna, 26
Ferguson, "Ma," 143
Fields, W.C., 214
Firestone, Shulamith, 255, 259
First World War, 129–32, 219, 222
Fitzgerald, Ella, 218
"Flaming youth" image, 153–61
Flappers, 153
  screen version of, 172, 173, 174
Fleischman, Doris, 210
Flexner, Eleanor, 129
Florodora girls, 172
Flynn, Elizabeth Gurley, 69, 113, 114,
  132, 204
Follett, Ken, 261
Food, Drug, and Cosmetic Act (1936),
  183
Fool There Was, A, 172
Foote, Edward Bliss, 15
Ford, Betty, 265
Fortune magazine, 209, 210
Freud, Sigmund, 150
Freudian theories
  in 1920s, 150–51
  in 1930s, 232
  in 1950s, 232–33, 239
  and recent feminism, 258, 259
  sex gratification and, 121
Friedan, Betty, 236, 237, 245, 247, 250,
  253, 259
Frontier, women's role on, 58
Functionalism, Freudian theory and,
  234–35

Gable, Clark, 216
Garbo, Greta, 172, 213
Gardener, Helen, 128
Garment industry
  Jewish women in, 61
  sex segregation in, 9
  sweatshops in, 67
Gaynor, Janet, 214
Gender gap, in voting, 266
General Federation of Women's Clubs,
  18, 96, 98, 125, 147, 183, 250
General Motors Corporation, 224
Generation of Vipers (Wylie), 230
Geneva Medical College, 34
"Gentlemen's Agreement" (restricting
  Japanese immigration), 65

George Washington University, 36
Gibson, Charles Dana, 22
Gibson girl, 22, 24
Gilman, Charlotte Perkins, 56, 104, 108,
  111, 112, 113, 114, 121, 123
Glaspell, Susan, 111
Goddess, The, 175
Goldman, Emma, 109, 114, 115, 123
Gone With the Wind, 211, 218
Gorman, Margaret, 176
Gothic fiction, 270
Grant, Cary, 214, 216
Grant, Jane, 146
Grapes of Wrath, The (Steinbeck), 207
Green, Arnold, 240
Greenwich Village, 112, 152
Greer, Germaine, 255
Griffiths, Martha, 261
Group, The (McCarthy), 208
Guest, Amy Phipps, 169
Gynecological surgery, increased
  knowledge in, 14

Hadassah, founding of, 102
Hale, Ruth, 146
Hamilton, Alice, 105, 163
Hamilton, Cicely, 110
Harlem Renaissance, 165
Harlequin Romances, 270
Harlow, Jean, 212, 213
Harper, Ida Husted, 1
Harriman, Florence Jaffray, 190–91
Harris, Louis, 265
Harris Poll, 265
Harvard Medical School, 34
Harvard University, 30, 32
Hecht, Ben, 111
Heckler, Margaret, 266
Held, John, 154
Hellman, Lillian, 153
Henrotin, Alice, 76
Henry Street Settlement, 105–106
Hepburn, Katharine, 216
Hernández, Aileen, 253
Heroines, of 1920s, 176
Heterodoxy, 113, 124, 145, 152
High schools, admission to, 5
Hindle Wakes, 111
Hobart College, 34
Hobby, Oveta Culp, 256
Hoffman, Dustin, 271

Home appliances
  advertising of, 150
  early, 41
Home-economics movement, 39, 117
  See also Domestic science movement
Homemaker image, of 1950s, 235
Homestead Act (1865), 61
Horne, Lena, 218
Horney, Karen, 233
Houghton, Katharine, 209
Housewives, current discontent of, 260
Hull House, 105, 106, 144
Hunt, Harriot, 34
Hurston, Zora Neale, 165
Hysterectomy, as surgery, 14

Ibsen, Henrik, 111
Ice skating, clothing for, 26
Illinois State Board of Charities, 107
Immigrants
  prostitutes and, 83
  as unskilled factory labor, 67–68
  work-force participation, nature of,
    61–63
  working class and, 69–80
Indiana, University of, 33
Industrial Workers of the World, 76
Insurance industry, opposes ERA, 253
International Association of Machinists,
    75
International Council of Women, 2
International Ladies' Garment Workers'
    Union (ILGWU), 71–72, 75, 168, 202,
    250, 252
International Woman Suffrage
    Association, 127
It Happened One Night, 216
Italian women
  as immigrants, 61
  overseen by fathers and brothers,
    62–63
  patterns of work, 62–63
  and prostitution, 83

Japanese immigrants, 64–65
Jazz, and black women singers, 218
Jewish women
  in garment industry, 61
  as immigrants, 61
  radicalism among, 76
  work-force patterns, 61, 63

Jewish women's organizations, 102
Johnson, Lady Bird, 265
Johnson, Lyndon, 256
Johnson, Virginia, 258
Jones, Mary "Mother," 69, 72
Jong, Erica, 261
Journalism, women in, 35–36
Judge magazine, 120

Kael, Pauline, 210
Kelley, Florence, 52, 107
Kennedy, John F., 249, 256
Key, Ellen, 110, 123, 124
Keyes, Frances Parkinson, 15, 16, 56
Keyes, Henry Wilder, 56
Kindergartens, 100–101, 108
Kitzinger, Sheila, 238
Klein, Viola, 234
Knights of Labor, 18, 74, 100
Komarovsky, Mirra, 234, 237, 240
Kraditor, Aileen, 99

Labor movement
  in 1900s, 69–78
  in 1920s, 167–68
  in 1930s, 202–204
  in recent period, 269
  and Second World War, 224
  See also Union activities
Labor-saving devices, advent of, 41
  See also Electric kitchens; Home
    appliances
Labor unions. See Labor movement;
    Union activities
Ladies' garment industry
  factory women in, 9, 67–68
  strikes in, 70–71
Ladies' Home Journal, 26, 55, 122, 255
Lady in the Dark, 216
Lady, The (Putnam), 111
Lafollette, Suzanne, 149
La Leche League, 237
La Maze natural childbirth method, 237
Lange, Dorothea, 194, 207
Langtry, Lily, 7
Lathrop, Julia, 107
Lawrence, Massachusetts, textile mills,
    63, 71, 76, 77, 114
Lawyers, women as, 11, 35–36, 163, 267
League of Women Voters, 139–43, 147,
    148, 183, 184, 187, 193, 241, 250, 251
Lease, Mary Elizabeth, 18

Legal codes, of 1890s, 1–3
Lemons, Stanley, 139
Lesbianism, 259, 263, 265
Lewis, John L., 196
Life magazine, 22, 156
Lindbergh, Anne Morrow, 156
Lindbergh, Charles A., 169
Lindsey, Ben, 155
Looking Backward, 103–104
Lopata, Helen, 260
Lowell Mills, 30
Luckinbill, M. Louise, 163
Lucy Stone League, 146, 241
Luhan, Mabel Dodge, 121
Lundberg, Ferdinand, 230, 232
Lynd, Helen, 41, 54, 205, 207, 208, 216
Lynd, Robert, 41, 54, 205, 207, 208, 216

Male and Female (Mead), 235
Man and Superman (Shaw), 111
Mansfield, Arabella, 36
Manufacturing, women in, 8–11, 30,
    61–78, 131, 165–68, 198–200, 203,
    221–24
Marriage
    "companionate," 53
    as main prospect for women, 51
    middle-class wife and, 50–57
    new freedoms and frustrations in,
        52–57
    in 1930s, 205
    in 1970s, 244–45, 259–60
    prenuptial ignorance in, 15
    and rural women, 57–61
    as "sex parasitism," 110
    and working-class women, 78–80
Marriage manuals, 15, 239
    sexual pleasure in, 150
Married women, employment of, 51,
    205, 224, 243
Martineau, Harriet, 7
Massachusetts Institute of Technology,
    117
Massachusetts Medical Society, 35
Massachusetts Vice Commission, 85
Masters, William, 258
Masturbation, early attitude toward, 15
McCarthy, Mary, 208
McDaniel, Hattie, 217
McDowall, Mary, 107
McKelvey, Blake, 105
McMurray, Fred, 216

Mead, Margaret, 235
Medicine
    female sexuality and, 14–17
    women in, 11, 34–35, 163
"Memorial Day Massacre" (1937), 203
Men
    as help and hindrance, 39–40
    sexual continence for, 121
Menstruation, early attitude toward,
    14–15
Mermaid and the Minotaur, The
    (Dinnerstein), 259
Methodist Board of Foreign Missions, 20
Methodist Women's Missionary Council,
    185
Mexican Americans, 166, 269
Meyer, Agnes, 242
Middle-class women, 52–56, 260
Middletown (Lynd and Lynd), 41,
    205–207, 216
Migrant families, during the depression,
    207
Mildred Pierce, 217
Milholland, Inez, 118, 119, 120, 121, 123
Militancy, in 1960s, 246–60
Milland, Ray, 216
Miller, Arthur, 52
Millett, Kate, 254, 255, 259
Minnesota, University of, 163
Minor v. Happersett, 2, 93
Miss America Pageant, 176, 255
Missionaries, women as, 40
Missionary movement, Protestant, and
    women, 20
Mitchell, Margaret, 211, 218
Modern Woman: The Lost Sex (Farnham
    and Lundberg), 230
Molnick, Eleanor, 240
Monroe, Marilyn, 214, 235, 236
Montagu, Ashley, 235
Morality, "single standard" of, 121
Morgan, Robin, 255
Mormon Church, in opposition to ERA,
    263
Morrison, Sarah Parke, 33–34
Motherhood
    glorification of, 55, 123
    of 1950s, 237–38
    penis envy and, 151
    romantic love and, 121–23
    war and, 145
Mother's Day, 55

Mother's pensions
   social feminist support for, 139, 144
Mount Holyoke Seminary, 5
Movie actresses
   flappers and, 172–75
   in 1920s, 171–76
   in 1930s, 213–17
   in 1950s, 236
   as sex symbols, 213–14
   as vamps, 213–14
Ms. magazine, 256
Muckraking journals, feminist exposés
   in, 100
Muller v. Oregon, 116
Music, as a career for women, 165
Myrdal, Alva, 234

Nancy Drew (fictional heroine), 210
Nathan, Maude, 41, 168
National Abortion Rights Action League,
   261
National American Woman Suffrage
   Association (NAWSA), 18, 56, 93,
   96, 125, 127, 129, 130, 139
National Association for the
   Advancement of Colored People
   (NAACP), 103, 185, 190
National Association of Colored Women,
   102, 185, 193
National Association Opposed to the
   Further Extension of Suffrage for
   Women, 94
National College Equal Suffrage League,
   99
National Committee, Democratic Party,
   139
National Committee of Endorsers
   Against ERA, 263
National Conference on the Cause and
   Cure of War, 144–45
National Congress of Parents and
   Teachers, 147
National Council of Jewish Women, 102,
   147
National Council of Negro Women, 193
National Council of Women, 18
National Federation of Business and
   Professional Women's Clubs, 139,
   146, 147, 197, 241, 250, 251
National Industrial Recovery Act,
   194–95, 202
National Labor Relations Board, 221

National Organization for Women
   (NOW), 112, 252, 254, 261, 265
National Parent–Teachers Association, 18
National Plan of Action, Houston
   National Woman's Conference, 263
National Recovery Administration,
   194–95, 196
National War Labor Board, 219, 224
National Women's Conference, Houston,
   263
National Youth Administration, 193
Natural childbirth, 237, 238
Natural Superiority of Women, The
   (Montagu), 235
Nazimova, 110
Neurosis, among women, 14
Nevelson, Louise, 194
New Deal, 185–98
New Harmony (Robert Owen), 103
"New look," 237
"New Woman" image, 21–22
Nineteenth Amendment, 129
Nobel Peace Prize, 183–84
NOW. *See* National Organization for
   Women
NRA. *See* National Recovery
   Administration
Nurses, women as, 11, 79, 105, 222, 249,
   269
Nye, Gerald, and Nye investigation, 184

Oberlin College, 5
Occupations, in 1890s, 6–14
   See also Employment; Factory work;
      Second World War; Working-class
      women
O'Connor, Sandra Day, 266, 267
Officer and a Gentleman, An, 271
Of Woman Born (Rich), 259
O'Keefe, Georgia, 165
Olsen, Tillie, 194
Olympic Games, 262
Owen, Ruth Bryan, 190

Pacifism, and women, 100, 144–46, 266
Pacifist organizations, 144–46
Parker, Dorothy, 165
Parks, Rosa, 246, 247
Patriarchal family, working class and, 78
Patriarchy, as feminist terminology, 258
Paul, Alice, 127, 128, 130, 139, 261
Peabody, Elizabeth, 16

Peace Corps, 107
Penny kitchens, 199
Perils of Pauline, 175
Perkins, Frances, 192, 196–97, 198, 256
Peterson, Esther, 249, 250
Pickford, Mary, 169, 170, 171, 172, 173
Pierce, Walter, 209
Pimps, prostitutes and, 81
"Pin-money" theory, 69
Plain Home Talk on Love, Marriage, and Parentage (Foote), 15
Plath, Sylvia, 261
Populist Party, 18
Pornography, 258
Poverty, feminization of, 269
Powell, Lewis, 266
President's Advisory Committee for Women, 272
Princeton University, 30
Professional associations, rise of, 143
Professional schools, admission to, 5, 34–36
Professions
  in 1890s, 7, 11
  in 1920s, 163–65
  in 1930s, 200–201
  in 1950s, 244
  in recent period, 257, 267
  women pioneers in, 35–39
Progressive movement, 99–108
  feminism and, 125, 130, 142–44, 183–98
Prostitution, 80–83, 108, 258
Protestant churches
  and women's organizations, nineteenth-century, 19
Pruette, Lorine, 160
Psychological Care of Infant and Child (Watson), 151
Public Enemy, The, 215
Public Schools
  restrictions on girls in, 5
  women teachers in, 10, 11, 30, 38–39, 201–202
Puerperal fever, 14
Pure Food and Drug Act (1906), 102
Putnam, Emily, 111
Putnam-Jacobi, Mary, 35, 39
Pygmalion (Shaw), 111

Radcliffe College, 32
Radicalism, of 1960s, 247, 251–56

Rainey, Ma, 218
Rankin, Jeannette, 142
Rape, 258, 263, 267, 271
Reagan, Maureen, 265
Reagan, Ronald, 265, 266
Red-light districts, 81
Red Scare (1919), 148
Reform, in 1960s, 246–56
Reisman, David, 245
Reproduction of Mothering (Chodorow), 259
Reynolds, Debbie, 236
Rich, Adrienne, 259
Richards, Ellen, 117
Ride, Sally, 262
Robins, Margaret Dreier, 76
Rockefeller Foundation, 105
Rodman, Henrietta, 112
Roe v. Wade, 261
Rogers, Ginger, 216
Roosevelt, Eleanor, 185–98, 242, 248, 249
Roosevelt, Franklin D., 185, 186, 187, 188, 189, 220
Roosevelt, Theodore, 17, 65, 124
"Rosie the Riveter," 219, 235
Rossi, Alice, 242
Round table, Algonquin Hotel, 165
Rubinstein, Helena, 163, 173
Rural women, 57–61
Russell, Lillian, 172
Russell, Rosalind, 216

Saint Joan (Shaw), 111
Saleswomen, in department stores, 67, 68, 168
Sanger, Margaret, 56, 108, 109, 121, 209
Sanger, William, 83
Schlafly, Phyllis, 263, 265
Scharf, Lois, 184
Schneiderman, Rose, 77, 196, 204
Schreiner, Olive, 110
Scott, Anne (Firor), 20
Scudder, Vida, 149
Seaman, Elizabeth (Nellie Bly), 36–37
Second Sex, The (de Beauvoir), 240
Second Stage, The (Friedan), 259
Second World War, and women, 218–24
Seelye, L. Clark, 38
Seldes, Gilbert, 215
Servants, women as, 54, 67, 80, 195, 257, 269

Settlement houses, 105–108, 143–144, 149, 169, 196
Seventh Heaven, 214
Seven-Year Itch, The, 235
Sewing machine, advent of, 41
Sex in Education (Clarke), 15
"Sex-parasitism," marriage as, 110
Sex roles, in home and school, 160
Sex-stereotyping, 258
Sex-story magazines, 151
Sexual intercourse, post-Victorian views on, 15–16
Sexual liberation, Second World War and after, 239, 270
Sexual Politics (Millett), 255
Sexual revolution, of 1920s, 150–61
Shaw, Anna Howard, 40, 96, 132, 139
Sheppard–Towner Act (1921), 148
Sheppard–Towner clinics, 148, 193
"Shirtwaist" blouses, 22, 26
Shirtwaist workers' strike, 70, 72
Single standard of morality, 121, 123, 151
Sister Carrie (Dreiser), 53
Sisterhood Is Powerful (Morgan), 255
Sit-down strikes, in 1930s, 203
Slavic women
    as immigrants, 61
    in work force, 63
Smeal, Eleanor, 265
Smith, Bessie, 218
Smith College, 5, 30, 38, 149, 156, 163
Soap operas, 270–71
Social activist coalition, breakup of, in 1920s, 139–48
Social feminist
    in 1920s, 147–48
    in 1930s, 185–98
    Progressive movement and, 99–108
    on reform and government activities, 115–24
    See also Feminism
Socialism, 76, 77, 100, 204
"Social purity" movement, 16–18, 81
Social Security Act, 183, 193, 195, 198, 257, 263
Social Security Administration, 140
Sorosis, 101
South, the (as region), 19–20, 59, 184–86
SPARS (Coast Guard), 219
Speakeasies, 149
Special legislation, for working women, 115–16, 123, 147, 240–41

Spock, Benjamin, 234, 239
Sports, and women
    and Gibson Girl, 22–29
    in 1920s, 149
    in recent period, 261
Stanton, Elizabeth Cady, 2, 24, 26, 93, 96, 97, 98
St. Denis, Ruth, 26
Steiglitz, Alfred, 165
Stein, Gertrude, 165
Steinbeck, John, 208
Stevenson, Adlai, 249
Stewardesses, 170, 171
Stone, Lucy, 34, 93, 96
Stowe, Harriet Beecher, 38, 164
Streetwalkers, 81
Strikes, 69–72
    and IWW, 76
    and Socialist women, 76
    in 1930s, 202–204
St. Vincent Millay, Edna, 165
Suburban housewife, role of, 239
Suffrage
    achievement of, 125–29
    aftermath of victory in, 129–33
    as cure-all, 117–20
    in 1920s, 139–42
    as symbol, 139
    united front for, 125–29
    on the wane, 93–99
Suffrage movement
    tactics and techniques in, 93–99, 125–29
Suffrage parades, 119, 126, 127
Suffragists, 93–99, 119–20, 129–33
Supreme Court, U.S., 2, 116, 168, 190, 261
Swanson, Gloria, 173
Sweatshops, 67

Take a Letter, Darling, 216
Teachers, women as
    entry into profession, 5, 11, 30, 39–40
    feminization in, 10
    in 1930s, 200–202
    in 1970s, 269
    in rural areas, 58–59
    in Second World War, 30
Technology, impact of on women, 40–43, 270
Television, feminine images in, 236
Temple, Shirley, 171

Terry, Ellen, 200
Textile worker's strike, Lawrence, MA
    (1912), 71, 77
Thelen, David, 100
Thomas, M. Carey, 39, 99
Thomas, Norman, 204
Tootsie, 271
Tracy, Spencer, 216
Triangle Shirtwaist Company, 69, 70, 72
    destruction of by fire, 69, 72, 74, 75
True Confessions magazine, 151
Truman, Harry S., 249
Two-car family, emergence of, 160

Unemployment, in 1930s, 198–200
Union activities
    in 1900s, 69–78
    in 1920s, 167–68
    in 1930s, 183, 202–204
    in recent period, 269
    and Second World War, 224
United Nations, 189, 190
United States Civil Service Commission,
    128
University of Minnesota, 163
Urban League, 103

Vacuum cleaner, early, 41
Vamps, 169, 172, 175, 213
Vassar College, 4, 5, 30, 39, 104, 118,
    149, 209
Venereal disease, 16, 81, 108, 121
Victorian culture, rebellion against, 153
Victorian dress, 26
Victorian era, prostitution in, 80–83
Victorian fashions, discarding of, 24–28
Victorian sex, satisfaction in, 14–16
Vietnam war, 247–54
Voluntary motherhood, 17

WACS (Women's Auxiliary Army Corps),
    216, 219
Waitresses
    sexuality among, 85–87
Wald, Lillian, 105, 107
Wallace, Irving, 261
Ward, Maria, 28
Ware, Susan, 192
War Manpower Commission, 219, 221
Washing machines, early, 41
Washington, Booker T., 103
Waters, Ethel, 218

Watson, John B., 151
WAVES, 219
WCTU. *See* Woman's Christian
    Temperance Union
WEAL. *See* Women's Equity Action
    League
Wedding Present, 216
Wellesley College, 5, 38, 147
Wells-Barnett, Ida, 103
West, Mae, 214
Wharton, Edith, 164
"White-collar" workers, as class, 52, 269
White House Conference on the
    Emergency Needs of Women, 193
White, Pearl, 175
"White-slave" traffic, 82, 85
Wife
    middle-class, 52–57
    rural, 57–61
    working-class, 78–80
    See also Marriage
Wife beating, 263, 267, 269
Willard, Frances, 27, 30, 43, 100
Wills, Helen, 149
Wilson, Woodrow, 128
Wisconsin, Progressivism in, 108
Woman's Advisory Committee (to War
    Manpower Commission), 221
Woman's Christian Temperance Union
    (WCTU), 16, 18, 43, 60, 97, 100, 121,
    132, 147
Woman's National Committee, Socialist
    Party, 125
Woman's Party, 128, 129, 130, 146–47,
    169, 240, 261
Women
    as cabinet members, 256
    and college education, 15, 157–58, 257,
        269
    in Congress, 256
    in First World War, 131–32
    in industry, 8–11, 61–78, 165–68,
        218–24
    and labor movement, 69–78, 165–68,
        218–24
    motherhood and, 55, 121–23, 151,
        237–38
    in professions, 7, 11, 35–39, 163–65,
        244, 257, 267
    and prostitution, 80–83
    screen image of, 170–75, 211–18, 236
    in Second World War, 218–24

Women (*continued*)
  in settlement houses, 105–108,
    143–44, 149, 169, 196
  special legislation for, 115–16, 123,
    147, 240–41
Women and Labor (Schreiner), 110
Women in the Modern World
    (Komarovsky), 234, 240
Women's and Professional Projects
    (Works Projects Administration), 193
Women's Bureau, Department of Labor,
    77, 139, 148, 162, 184, 193, 199–200,
    223, 241, 249, 250
Women's clubs
  in 1890s, 18
  and ERA, 240
  in 1900s, 101–102, 125
  in 1920s, 142–43
  in 1930s, 183
Women's colleges, founding of and
    mission of, 200
  See also Barnard College; Bryn Mawr
    College; Mount Holyoke Seminary,
    Radcliffe College; Smith College;
    Vassar College; Wellesley College;
    Women's Medical College,
    Philadelphia
Women's Committee, Council for
    National Defense, 132
Women's education, arguments for,
    38–39
  See also Education
Women's Equity Action League (WEAL),
    254, 261
Women's history, courses in, 254
Women's Hospital and Infirmary, New
    York City, 35
Women's International League for Peace
    and Freedom, 145–46, 183
Women's Joint Congressional
    Committee, 139, 147–48, 241
Women's Medical College, Philadelphia,
    39
Women's Municipal League, 101

Women's Network, New Deal, 192–98
Women's organizations
  in 1890s, 18–21, 76–78
  in 1920s, 139–49
  in 1930s, 183–98
  in 1950s, 240–41
  in Progressive era, 93–115, 125–132
  in recent period, 251–56
Women's Political Caucus, 254
Women's separate culture, 41, 43, 121,
    152, 189
Women's studies programs, 254, 265
Women's Trade Union League, 69,
    76–78, 108, 115, 144, 148, 149, 152,
    168, 187, 191, 193, 194, 196, 204, 241
Woodward, Ellen, 193
Working-class culture, mores of, 78–80
Working-class families, status of, 78–79
Working-class mothers, childbirth for, 78
Working-class women
  married life of, 78–80
  in 1920s, 165–68
  in 1960s, 260
  status hierarchy in, 67
  working conditions for, 67–68, 73–74
Working wives, hostility to, 202
Works Projects Administration, 189, 193,
    195
World Court, 147
World's Fair, New York (1937), 210
Writers, women as, 164–65, 261
Wylie, Philip, 230

Yale University, 30
Young, Roland, 110
Young Women's Christian Association
    (YWCA), 16, 18, 103, 104, 108, 146,
    185
Youth
  in 1920s, 153–61
  in 1930s, 209–10

Zionism, growth of, 102

C
D
E
F
G   9
H   0
I   1
J   2